SIGNS
of LIFE

D0391735

SIGNS *of* LIFE

DAVID JEREMIAH

W Publishing Group

An Imprint of Thomas Nelson

© 2007 David Jeremiah

All rights reserved. No portion of this book may be reproduced, stored in a retrieval system, or transmitted in any form or by any means—electronic, mechanical, photocopy, recording, scanning, or other—except for brief quotations in critical reviews or articles, without the prior written permission of the publisher.

Published in Nashville, Tennessee, by W Publishing Group, an imprint of Thomas Nelson.

Published in association with Yates & Yates, LLP, www.yates2.com.

Thomas Nelson titles may be purchased in bulk for educational, business, fund-raising, or sales promotional use. For information, please e-mail SpecialMarkets@ThomasNelson.com

Unless otherwise indicated, Scripture quotations are taken from the New King James Version®. © 1982 by Thomas Nelson, Inc. Used by permission. All rights reserved.

Scripture quotations marked AMPLIFIED BIBLE are taken from THE AMPLIFIED BIBLE: OLD TESTAMENT. © 1962, 1964 by Zondervan Publishing House (used by permission); and from THE AMPLIFIED BIBLE: NEW TESTAMENT. Copyright © 1958 by the Lockman Foundation (used by permission).

Scripture quotations marked MSG are taken from *The Message* by Eugene H. Peterson, © 1993, 1994, 1995, 1996, 2000. Used by permission of NavPress Publishing Group. All rights reserved.

Scripture quotations marked NIV are taken from the HOLY BIBLE: NEW INTER-NATIONAL VERSION®. © 1973, 1978, 1984 by International Bible Society. Used by permission of Zondervan. All rights reserved.

Scripture quotations marked NLT are taken from the Holy Bible, New Living Translation, © 1996, 2004. Used by permission of Tyndale House Publishers, Inc., Wheaton, Illinois 60189. All rights reserved.

Scripture quotations marked RSV are from the Revised Standard Version of the Bible, © 1952 [2nd edition, 1971] by the Division of Christian Education of the National Council of the Churches of Christ in the United States of America. Used by permission. All rights reserved.

ISBN 978-0-8499-4714-8 (trade paper)

Library of Congress Cataloging in Publication Data

Jeremiah, David.
        Signs of life / David Jeremiah.
            p. cm.
        Includes bibliographical references and index.
        ISBN 978-0-7852-2809-7 (hardcover: alk. paper)
        1. Devotional calendars. I. Title.
        BV4811.J493 2007
        242'.2—dc22

                                                                                                2007027597

Printed in the United States of America

15 16 17 18 19 RRD 11 10 9 8 7

Contents

Acknowledgments

The *Signs of Life* project began as an outline for a church-growth campaign and continues now in this format as a major trade book. Each chapter reflects a lesson we have learned as we have attempted to put into practice the message of the Great Commandment.

At the heart of this initiative is my longtime friend Paul Joiner. All of us who work with him at the Turning Point ministries are daily blessed by the creativity that overflows from his life into ours. I have said many times, "He is the most creative person I have ever met." Paul first saw the images of Signs of Life in his mind and translated them to paper so that the rest of us could see them as well. Thank you, Paul, for sharing the vision for this book.

While all the members of the Turning Point creative staff have played a part in the development of this project, I want to specifically thank Mary Cayot for her diligence.

Cathy Lord was the managing partner in putting together all the pieces of this puzzle. Thank you, Cathy, for the many hours you spent verifying all the quotations, interacting with the editorial department at Thomas Nelson, and making suggestions that have caused this to be a better book.

Some days the activity in my office complex is like the turbulence of a hurricane. But when I walk into my study and tell my administrative assistant, Diane Sutherland, that I need time to study and to write, she graciously protects me from all interruptions. Diane, you are God's greatest gatekeeper!

My relationship with Rob Morgan and William Kruidenier has now passed the five-year mark, and I could not have done this book without their considerable editorial contributions.

Sealy Yates has always been my go-to guy in the publishing world. He is my literary agent, my attorney, and, most of all, my friend. Joey Paul is my editor at Thomas Nelson. His commitment to excellence motivates all of us who work with him.

As I look over my shoulder at the last few years of the ministry of Turning Point, I am amazed at what the Lord has done to extend our influence throughout the world. Without the administrative leadership of my oldest son, David Michael, there would never have been any pockets of time to work on literary projects. David, you are a remarkable young man, and you make me proud!

I am especially thankful to my wife, Donna. She is my closest friend and advisor. Together we have shared the birth of four children, nine grandchildren, and twenty-seven books. Without her support, this book would never have seen the light of day, and I am happy to announce to the whole world that I did not work on this project during our vacation!

Finally, when I think of the privilege that I have been given to write words that bring honor and glory to God, I am filled with gratitude and joy. It is my earnest prayer that you will be drawn to Him as you read— and live—*Signs of Life!*

Introduction

It was October 27, 2003, when I sent this e-mail to our church family at
Shadow Mountain Community Church, the congregation I pastor in El
Cajon, California:

> This has surely been one of the most difficult times in our church's his-
> tory. Last night I stood on the campus and prayed that God would
> spare our facilities. During the next couple of hours, the wind shifted,
> and—at least for now—the campus is safe. We are still in the evacua-
> tion mode because the fire department has told us that if the winds
> were to shift, we could be back in jeopardy again.

Southern California's Cedar Fire was the state's largest wildfire in over a
century. It was a confluence of fifteen individual fires and the hot, dry
Santa Ana winds. More than 2,300 homes were destroyed; fifteen lives
were lost; and more than 280,000 acres were incinerated. Many precious
folks in our congregation lost their homes to the voracious flames. . . .

In the mountains just above our church campus is a small community called Crest. Almost every family in that community was severely
impacted by the firestorm. These people were our neighbors, and they
desperately needed our help.

So, for the next six weeks, we adopted the Crest community. We collected blankets, clothing, and toys. We took offerings for the needy in all
of our weekend services. We provided over 1,000 meals, delivered two
truckloads of water, gave out nearly $200,000, provided temporary
housing for many, and counseled and prayed with dozens of individuals
and families. The firestorm is now a part of San Diego history, but a

whiff of smoke in the air on a hot, dry day brings back a powerful rush of memories.

CROSS-COUNTRY COMPASSION

Now fast-forward to March 15, 2007. I was in Greensboro, North Carolina, where Turning Point, our radio and television ministry, was hosting a breakfast for pastors. I was teaching the series of messages that inspired this book, and we had combined efforts with the organization Feed the Children to provide 30,000 pounds of food for these pastors to distribute to needy families in their communities.

One pastor came from across the state line in Virginia. His community had been hit hard by plant closings, and over 10,000 jobs had been lost. As he left the breakfast that morning, he knew exactly where he was going to deliver one of the boxes of food. But the recipient of the other box was a mystery. When he stopped at his office, he found a form on his secretary's desk from a family seeking help to pay a utility bill. Mystery solved!

The address on the form led him to a mobile home located on a gravel road. The family of six was existing on the husband's small disability check plus a meager amount the wife earned working at a convenience store. The pastor's heart was filled with compassion when he saw the small children in this poverty-stricken home.

The next day a relative of this young mother called the pastor to express her gratitude for the kindness that had been shown to her extended family. She shared this comment from the mother who had received the box of food and essentials: "How did he know we needed those things, especially the soap and toilet paper?"

COMPASSION IS CONTAGIOUS

After I heard this story, I shared it with our congregation when I was teaching about living an open-handed life. Sitting in the auditorium that day was a woman visiting from New York. She slipped $25 in cash into one of our pew envelopes and wrote these words on the outside: "I am only visiting this church this one Sunday. I am from New York. If there is any way, please see that the family Pastor Jeremiah spoke of in his sermon this morning receives this."

We sent the $25 to the pastor in Virginia, who in turn described the incident for his congregation that following Sunday evening. He challenged the 98 people in attendance to have compassion for those around them who were in need. At the end of the service, a man came forward and added $20 to the initial cash gift. When the pastor arrived home, an envelope of cash was taped to his door, and another was waiting for him on the secretary's desk in the morning. On Monday afternoon the pastor gave that needy family a check for $250. Compassion is contagious!

THE CHURCH'S TREASURES

According to legend, Saint Lawrence, the third-century treasurer of the early church's resources, was brought before the authorities, who demanded that he hand over all the church's treasures to the emperor. Lawrence compliantly asked for three days to gather the church's treasures. He promised to then reveal to the Roman magistrate the extensive riches of the church. On the third day Lawrence appeared and brought with him orphans, the poor, the lame, and the widows in distress. Pointing to them, he said, "These are the treasures of the church." And for that reply he was sentenced to death.[1]

The Bible mentions the poor more than 150 times. If we add to that figure the number of times God's Word talks about caring for the widows, the fatherless, and the needy, we have more than 300 references reminding us of our responsibility to help people in need. These Scriptures have made such an impression on my own heart and life that I have included them at the end of this book.

THE GREATEST COMMANDMENT

One day a lawyer asked Jesus to identify the greatest commandment in the Law. Our Lord's answer to that question is one of the reasons why I wrote this book:

> Jesus said to him, "'You shall love the LORD your God with all your heart, with all your soul, and with all your mind.' This is the first and great commandment. And the second is like it: 'You shall love your neighbor as yourself.' On these two commandments hang all the Law and the Prophets." (Matthew 22:37-40)

We all know that we are to love God, but exactly how are we supposed to do that? Jesus answered the question like this: we love God by loving the people He created. Jesus taught that loving the least among His brothers was the same as loving Him (Matthew 25:40). In fact, He goes so far as to say that the entire Bible is summarized by these two commands . . . to love God and love our neighbors. No wonder God's Word has so much to say about caring for the poor and needy!

RESPONDING TO GOD'S COMMANDS

In this book you will find forty devotional readings designed to help you express your love for God by reaching out in compassion to others. The book is organized around the five signs of life: dusty shoes, worn-out knees, rolled-up sleeves, open hands, and outstretched arms. Each chapter ends with what we have labeled "Signs of Life." These practical suggestions will help you put the day's devotional thought into action.

At the back of the book, we have included some detailed suggestions for using *Signs of Life* as a call to action in your own life and in the life of your church. We have also developed a forty-day church campaign that will enable you to get everyone in your congregation involved in living out Jesus' Great Commandment.

ASCENDING TO HEAVEN

From Isaac Leib Peretz, a Jewish writer, comes this captivating tale:

> In a small Jewish town in Russia, there is a rabbi who disappears every Friday. His devoted disciples boast that during those hours, their rabbi goes up to heaven and talks to God.
>
> A stranger moves into town, and he's skeptical about all this, so he decides to check things out. He hides and watches. The rabbi gets up in the morning, says his prayers, and then dresses in peasant clothes. He grabs an axe, goes off into the woods, and cuts some firewood, which he then hauls to a shack on the outskirts of the village. There an old woman and her sick son live. He leaves them the wood, enough for a week, and then sneaks back home.
>
> Having observed the rabbi's actions, the newcomer stays on in the village and becomes his disciple. And whenever he hears one of the villagers say, "On Friday morning our rabbi ascends all the way to heaven," the newcomer quietly adds, "If not higher."[2]

As we start our Signs of Life journey together, our goal is to—like this rabbi—go up higher, to draw closer to God by serving His people—and not just on Friday, but on every day of the week.

DAVID JEREMIAH
San Diego, California
June 2007

Signs

of Life

Signs of Life

*This book is a mirror by which you
can see yourself as others see you.*

Bobbing on the sea like a pelican, the *Cruise Queen* was a floating mansion, as long as a gymnasium and dazzling white against the blue waters of the Aegean. But something was wrong: the yacht seemed strangely deserted. As silently as death, the detective boarded the ship, pistol in hand, looking for signs of life. . . .

How often have you watched a scene like that in a movie or on television?

One of the reasons whodunit shows are so popular is because there's a little detective in us all. We're all looking for signs of life, hints of our identity, and hidden secrets. Remember Sherlock Holmes? He could unravel a person's entire life by the mud on his shoes, the calluses on his hands, and the threads on his coat. Many of us have played Sherlock Holmes at airports or in waiting rooms, whiling away the time by people-watching, constructing a silent profile of their lives by their clothing, accessories, body language, facial appearance, and mannerisms.

The "hidden person of the heart" shows up in all kinds of ways. Your appearance and your home environment are extensions of your thoughts and values. Others can tell a great deal about us by the way we look, the car we drive, the language we use, the habits we keep, the friends we make, and the places we frequent. It's amazing how quickly we can size someone up—or how quickly someone can size us up!

As Christ's followers, we should exhibit certain signs of life that evidence our commitment to our Lord and His kingdom. Some of these are obvious to those who see us in our private moments when we're at prayer, reading our Bibles, writing our tithing checks, and resisting personal temptations.

Most people, however, don't have access to such personal moments. They see us from across the street, across the fence, across the hall, across the office, across the miles, or across the pews.

How do those people recognize that we are God's ambassadors?

It's by our smile . . . our joy . . . our compassion in the face of another's misfortune . . . our friendliness . . . our simple lifestyle . . . our willingness to commit random acts of kindness . . . our benevolence . . . our social ministries . . . our tears . . . our generosity . . . our public expressions of our private faith.

One man approached a cadet at the military academy at West Point a couple of years ago and said to him, "You must be a Christian." The surprised cadet said that he was indeed a follower of Christ. "But how did you know?" asked the young man.

"I saw you in the dining hall," replied the guest. "It was loud and chaotic there with bands playing, a pep rally going on, and a thousand cadets eating and laughing and shouting. But I saw you, in the middle of it all, quietly bow your head before eating your meal."

Does anyone ever come up to you and say, "You must be a Christian"? Do they ask a reason for the hope within you? Has anyone recently said, "There's something different about you; I can't figure it out, but I want what you have"?

Egged on by an entertainment industry and national media that often paint us in a negative light, our society tends to have an unfavorable view of Christians. At the same time, however, the very culture in which we live desperately needs genuine people who display signs of abundant living. This world is starved for love, joy, peace, patience, kindness, faithfulness, radiance, simplicity, honesty, and compassion.

Christians specialize in these things.

It's not enough just to talk about the Lord, as important as that is. It's not enough to serve Him in secret with our acts of private devotion. We have to display the lifestyle of the Nazarene in the midst of our corrupt culture. Jesus called it letting our light shine before men that they might see our good works and glorify our Father in heaven. The apostle Paul said, "Do all things . . . without complaining . . . that you may become blameless and harmless, children of God without fault in the midst of a crooked and perverse generation, among whom you shine as lights in the world" (Philippians 2:14–15).

Think of this book as a sort of mirror that can help you see yourself as others see you. It's also like a doctor's office where you can examine yourself for signs of life. And it's a pep rally where you can be encouraged to walk the talk.

All that—under one cover!

After all, we're not deserted yachts bobbing in paradise. We're fishing boats fitted for the Master's use.

May the Lord give us dusty shoes, worn-out knees, rolled-up sleeves . . . and other signs of life.

signs of Life

Life Sign: My words and actions evidence Christ's indwelling.

Life Verse: *Do all things without complaining and disputing, that you may become blameless and harmless, children of God without fault in the midst of a crooked and perverse generation, among whom you shine as lights in the world.*
—Philippians 2:14–15

Life in Action: What characteristics in my life offer solid evidence that I am a follower of Christ? What aspects in my life contradict the claim that I am a follower of Christ?

A Faith That Works

The world around us can't see our inner faith,
but it can see our good works that flow from our faith.

When the Ringling Brothers Circus went to New York City in April 2004, thousands of people jammed Madison Square Garden to see the greatest show on earth. What they saw instead was a terrifying accident. A performer named Ernando Rangel Amaya, a thirty-four-year-old Venezuelan high-wire daredevil, lost his balance and plummeted to the ground. The crowd gasped in horror as emergency workers rushed to his side. Rangel somehow survived the fall, but he taught us a valuable lesson: life is all about keeping your balance.[1]

Remember when you watched your toddler learning to walk? when you taught your child how to ride a bike? when you showed your teenagers how to balance their checkbooks? Many aspects of life are all about balance.

Well, we need a balanced theology too. The New Testament talks a great deal about the balance between faith and works. In Ephesians 2:8–9, we're told: "For by grace you have been saved through faith, and that not of yourselves; it is the gift of God, not of works, lest anyone should boast."

In other words, we might as well try to reach the stars on a pair of stilts as to try to qualify for heaven by living a good life, doing kind deeds, giving generous gifts, or sacrificing our bodies in the flames. We're sinners who can never redeem ourselves in God's sight by our own efforts. "Not by works of righteousness which we have done, but according to His mercy He saved us," Paul wrote in Titus 3:5.

But James, the half-brother of our Lord, apparently felt that some people were misunderstanding this fact, so his letter provides a counterbalance. Though we're saved by faith and not by works, said James, our faith must be the kind that works. We're not saved *by* good works, but *for* good works. Faith is the source of our salvation, but good works are the way we express the reality of our salvation.

"What does it profit, my brethren," asked James, "if someone says he has faith but does not have works? Can faith save him? . . . Faith by itself, if it does not have works, is dead" (James 2:14, 17).

In other words, if your faith doesn't express itself in compassion, love, kindness, generosity, helpfulness, mercy, and good deeds . . . well, it's not real faith at all. It might be intellectual assent or emotional release, but real faith trusts Christ alone for salvation—and then believes enough to be Christlike in daily practice.

I guess some people in James's day, like some people today, spoke the language of Christianity without reflecting the reality of its truths in their lives. That's why James wrote such a practical book. As you read through the book of James (you can read the whole epistle in less than ten minutes), you can't help seeing his emphasis on living out our faith. You'll also see that a faith that works . . .

- Enables us to have a positive attitude in troubled times (1:2).

- Inspires us to resist temptation (1:12).

- Makes us good listeners (1:19).

- Takes care of orphans and widows (1:27).

- Gives honor to the poor (2:5–6).

- Provides food and clothing for the needy (2:15–16).

- Controls and restrains the tongue (3:1–12).

- Doesn't speak evil of others (4:11).

- Doesn't grumble about others (5:9).

- Shows concern for the sick (5:14).

- Prays fervently (5:17).

Christians have changed the world by living out this kind of faith. In the third century, Tertullian wrote that the Christians of his day gave generously and without compulsion to a common fund that provided for the needs of widows, the physically disabled, orphans, the sick, those in prison, and even for the release of slaves.

History tells us of a pagan soldier in Constantine's army named Pachomius who was deeply moved when he saw Christians bringing food to fellow soldiers who were suffering from famine and disease. Curious to understand a doctrine that would inspire such generosity, Pachomius studied Christianity and was converted.[2]

Throughout the Middle Ages, the church sponsored orphanages, built schools, and fed the hungry. In the 1800s, believers such as A. H. Francke and George Müller provided homelike environments for unwanted children.

Also in the 1800s, a group of Christians in Great Britain worked tirelessly to reform child labor practices. The indefatigable Lord Shaftesbury devoted his life to making speeches and writing policy to improve the conditions of working children.

At roughly the same time, statesman William Wilberforce and his fellow Christians were fighting for the abolition of slavery in the British Empire.

It's been the influence of Christians in society that has built hospitals, halted infanticide, discouraged abortion, inspired relief societies, and enhanced the arts. The world around us can't see our inner faith, but it can see the good works that flow from our faith. That's why Jesus said plainly, "Let your light so shine before men, that they may see your good works and glorify your Father in heaven" (Matthew 5:16).

Some years ago, I read a satirical piece that brought this truth home to me:

> I was hungry, and you formed a humanities club and discussed my hunger. I was imprisoned, and you crept off quietly to your chapel in the cellar and prayed for my release. I was naked, and in your mind you debated the morality of my appearance. I was sick, and you knelt and thanked God for your health. I was homeless, and you preached to me the spiritual shelter of the love of God. I was lonely, and you left me alone to pray for me. You seem so holy, so close to God, but I'm still very hungry and lonely and cold.[3]

That's not biblical faith.

Consider what Bible teacher Manfred George Gutzke wrote:

> Faith is significant only when it promotes action. Faith without action is useless. This is the basic principle of everything everywhere, and it is true in every case. It would be true in the matter of farming. It would be true in the matter of insuring a home. It would be true in the matter of conducting a business. If we say that we have faith in anything and we do nothing about it, our faith does not amount to a thing.[4]

Now what about you and me?

Perhaps you don't know any orphans, but what child whom you do know needs some extra attention? Do you have a neighbor who needs her lawn mowed? Has a family in your community lost their home to fire? Does your local crisis pregnancy center need counselors? Perhaps your church is sponsoring a missions trip to provide medical assistance in an impoverished area. Perhaps a single person in your church would like an invitation to dinner.

🙰

Several years ago a pastor friend of mine was devoting a rare day off to his garden. Garbed in filthy cut-offs, he was lathered in sweat and dirt, fighting the weeds, and trying to get the last of his beans planted. Right then his sixteen-year-old daughter came running across the yard in a state of panic. "Dad," she yelled, "there's a man in the ditch a mile or so down the road. The cars are going by left and right, but no one has stopped to help. Come quick!"

Ron didn't want to "come quick." He was tired and dirty and involved in his gardening. He also knew that his daughter, a new driver, was easily excitable, and—truth be told—he thought she had probably misconstrued something. But at her insistence he finally pulled on a shirt, wiped away the sweat, found his keys, and went to see what had happened.

Sure enough, there was a man—elderly, dazed, half-asleep, and in the ditch. Ron and his daughter roused him and got him into their car. Revived by the air conditioning, he began mumbling incoherently. Finally, after repeated questioning, the old fellow muttered a street address several miles away. Ron drove him there.

As they walked up the sidewalk, an old woman came running out. "Praise God!" she exclaimed. "We didn't know where to find him. He's my older brother. He has Alzheimer's, and he wandered away this morning. I've been worried out of my head!"

Driving home, Ron had mixed feelings. He was thankful they'd done a good deed, but he also felt a nagging sense of guilt because he had done it reluctantly. His daughter had shown more compassion than he had despite his many years in ministry.

Lots of people are in the ditch. Real faith lends a helping hand gladly, freely, lovingly, and in the name of Christ. Real faith is a balanced faith: it is a faith that works.

So for Jesus' sake, do something for someone—and do it today.

SIGNS of Life

Life Sign: My faith is expressed through works.

Life Verse: *Thus also faith by itself, if it does not have works, is dead.*

—James 2:17

Life in Action: What am I doing for others that clearly reveals the presence of God in my life?

Turn On the Lights

*The human heart is dark without Christ,
but what a difference Jesus makes!*

Imagine a world without Christmas lights.

That would be the world before 1882. Oh, people built bonfires and attached candles to the limbs of their Christmas trees (sometimes burning down the town in the process), but it wasn't until Edward Johnson, Thomas Edison's associate, invented electric Christmas tree lights that American homes began to really sparkle and twinkle.

As Johnson's family decorated for the holidays that year, he poured his energy into producing a string of eighty small, brightly colored lights. As they sparkled through the front window, crowds of people lined up to gasp in wonder. It seemed magical, especially after Johnson developed a system for making them flash on and off. Wanting to see the lights more closely, people knocked on the front door. Newspapers sent reports all over the country, and reporters marched, one after another, into and out of the Johnson home.

Electric Christmas tree lights didn't immediately become a

commercial item, however, because no one except Thomas Edison, Edward Johnson, and a few others had electricity in their homes. Furthermore, it was rather expensive. Johnson's string of bulbs cost over $100 in materials—more money than some Americans made in a year.

Gradually, however, as more people got electricity, Christmas lights became more popular. In 1910, General Electric introduced a string of bulbs that could be produced and sold inexpensively, and Christmas lights have been household items ever since.[1] . . .

Nothing expresses the mission of Jesus Christ better than lights. In the Old Testament, the golden candlestick in the temple was a type of Christ signifying that the coming Messiah would be the light of Israel. And the prophet Isaiah predicted His coming by saying, "The people who walked in darkness have seen a great light; those who dwelt in the land of the shadow of death, upon them a light has shined. . . . For unto us a Child is born, unto us a Son is given" (Isaiah 9:2, 6).

In the Gospels, Jesus declared, "I am the light of the world" (John 8:12), and John opened his Gospel saying, "In Him was life, and the life was the light of men" (John 1:4).

Now, I'm not a physicist, but I know a few things about light.

First of all, light destroys darkness. In fact, some scholars claim there's no such thing as darkness at all. In their view, darkness is simply the absence of light!

What I have observed, though, is when light comes, darkness flees. The human heart is dark without Christ, but what a difference Jesus makes. Missionary E. Stanley Jones said, "When I met Christ, I felt that I had swallowed sunshine!"[2]

How sad, then, when people love darkness rather than light. Jesus predicted this in John 3:19, but it's still hard for us to understand. Maybe an old story about a desert nomad who awakened in the middle of the night can help. This man sat up, lit a candle, and began eating dates from a bowl beside his bed. He took a bite from one end and saw a worm in it, so he threw it out of the tent. He bit into the second date, found another worm, and threw it away also. Reasoning that he wouldn't have any dates left to eat if he continued in this way, he blew out the candle and quickly ate all the dates.

Many people love iniquity so much they'd rather swallow their sins and wallow in darkness than to turn on the light of Christ—and light truly does define Christianity. Ephesians 5:8 says, "For you were once darkness, but now you are light in the Lord. Walk as children of light." In Philippians 2:15, we're described as "children of God without fault in the midst of a crooked and perverse generation, among whom you shine as lights in the world."

We should picture ourselves like that! As you stroll up and down the aisles at the grocery store, remember that your smile, your attitude, your concern for others, and perhaps even your purchases should reflect the light of Jesus. As you work in your yard, remember that you're a mirror designed to reflect the light of Christ so that it shines into your neighbor's window. As you play a round of golf, remember that God may give you an opportunity to say a word for Him.

Now think of prison inmates. What a dark place they are in! Have you ever considered getting involved in a jailhouse ministry? Could you reflect Jesus' light by mentoring prisoners? distributing gifts at Christmas? regularly writing to someone behind bars?

We also need to shine a light into the streets of our inner cities. Does your church have a ministry to prostitutes? the addicted? alcoholics? the mentally ill? What about reaching out to the people in the nursing homes? Jesus said that when we do something for "the least of these," we do it unto Him (Matthew 25:40).

In His Sermon on the Mount, our Lord said, "You are the light of the world. A city that is set on a hill cannot be hidden. Nor do they light a lamp and put it under a basket, but on a lampstand, and it gives light to all who are in the house. Let your light so shine before men, that they may see your good works and glorify your Father in heaven" (Matthew 5:14–16).

As I was working on this chapter, newspapers reported that a massive blackout struck the whole country of Colombia. From the northern Caribbean coast to the southern Amazon jungle, the power suddenly went off. People in Bogotá were trapped in elevators. In cities and in the countryside, ten thousand traffic signals were darkened, mobile telephones went dead, the stock market suspended trading, and homes lost their lights and refrigeration. Authorities blamed the failure on a single electricity substation.

I think the same thing is happening to the United States, spiritually speaking. A massive spiritual blackout is spreading across America and Western Europe, and this is the darkest day we've ever had in our culture. Our society is more corrupt now than it has ever been.

But even in that harsh fact, I find a bit of encouragement. The darker the night, the more noticeable when our light shines brightly.

❧

A man I know recalls growing up in a little town in the mountains. There were few streetlights, and when bedtime came, the streets were dark. His bed was by the window, and every night the last thing he saw before closing his eyes was the tiny light of a neighbor's doorbell button— two blocks away. On a dark night, even a small light travels a long way.

So you may not be a famous humanitarian, a worldwide evangelist, or a well-known preacher. But when Jesus returned to heaven, He commissioned you and me to be His lights who must not hide our faith under a bushel. If we don't reflect the light of our Lord in our dark culture, it remains dark. God has graciously given His children the capacity to meet human need in the power of the Holy Spirit and, as we do so, to be His light in a dark world. And that's our very identity.

In the devotional book *Voices of the Faithful,* a missionary named Gerri told of working in an African town. One day exciting news reached her. The Lozi king was coming to attend church services and to eat at her house. As far as Gerri knew, the king usually didn't visit private homes, and word of his upcoming visit spread through the town like wildfire.

When the day finally arrived, the king entered Gerri's house. She explained in the Lozi language that she was a missionary and that, in Lozi, the name *Gerri* sounded like "Jelly" because the "r" sound is hard for the people to pronounce. She boldly asked the king for a Lozi name. Though she didn't know it at the time, such a request was against protocol, but the king just smiled and said, "I'll think about it."

Later as he prepared to leave, the king said, "My wife and I have decided upon a name for you. It will be Liseli [pronounced lee-SHE-lee]. It means 'light.' Just as the sun gives light and life to plants, animals, and people, I want God's Word to be life and light to the people of Western Province."

Gerri later wrote, "I was stunned and pleased to receive this blessing. After the king left the room, a lady seated nearby privately said, 'Ah, you are a very lucky woman to be given a name by the king.'"[3]

Well, the King of kings has given you a name—and it's LIGHT! Jesus said, "You are the light of the world."

So turn on the light for Him and then shine before men that people might see your good works and glorify your Father who is in heaven.

Signs of Life

Life Sign: I am a source of light in a dark world.

Life Verse: *Let your light so shine before men, that they may see your good works and glorify your Father in heaven.*
—Matthew 5:16

Life in Action: When people see me, do they see the light of Jesus shining through me? Here are four ways I can reflect the Light into others' lives today and every day:

Day 4

Living in the Moment

Live your spiritual life in the "always on"
position with God.

Who were the class clowns in your school? Or which co-worker keeps your office in stitches? We often say about this kind of person, "Man, that guy is always on!" When something happens, people like that don't have to get in the moment— they *live* in the moment.

Today, *always on* has a new, high-tech meaning that refers to the way we connect to the Internet on our home computers. If you were an early participant in the Internet revolution, you remember the cumbersome process of logging on. Your computer dialed a number, your modem squeaked and squawked for a few seconds, and—hopefully—you got connected. But, more likely than not in those early days, your connection would fail, and you'd have to go through the whole process of logging on again.

In those days you were either on or off the Internet. You dialed in, checked your e-mail, went to a Web site, and then logged off. Now, however, the days of logging on to the Internet are rapidly disappearing.

At the end of 2004, 37.9 million American users were accessing the Internet via broadband connections, and broadband access is now available to 99 percent of American homes.[1] By connecting through your television cable or digitally through your telephone line (DSL), you can maintain an always-on connection. As long as your computer is turned on (and many people never turn them off these days), you are connected; you are always there. In fact, the Web pages of many news sources automatically refresh themselves every couple of minutes, so a constant stream of current news and updated information appears on your computer screen. Again, you don't have to connect to communicate: with a broadband, always-on connection, you are "in the Internet moment" all the time.

BROADBAND SPIRITUALITY

I believe the dial-up mode of Internet access offers a helpful analogy for the kind of spirituality that relies on the daily quiet time (or church on Sunday or a weekly Bible study) to connect to God. Think back to the early days of the Internet when you logged on for a specific amount of time, did your business, and then logged off. There was still activity on the Internet while you were logged off—and you simply missed it. Well, I fear that too many of us live our spiritual lives in the dial-up mode instead of the broadband mode, so we miss a lot that God is doing in the world as well as a lot that He wants to do in our lives.

Too many Christians log on to God once a day when they have their quiet time or once a week when they go to church. They pray; they read their Bible; they've connected with God. And that's good . . . as far as it goes. The problem with that approach to the spiritual life is that there is no sense of being "always on"—no sense of living in the moment with God once you've finished your quiet time. You open your Bible, bow in prayer, conduct your business with God, and then log off for the day.

What we need is a revolution in spirituality like the Internet broadband revolution. We need Christians who are not logging on to God once a day or once a week. We need Christians who have an always-on connection with Him, Christians who are in constant communication with God because they are walking in the Spirit, Christians who live in the moment with God.

The danger with the dial-up mode of spirituality is that you're liable to miss something God wants you to see or hear or experience or learn from Him. It's as if He is sending you an important e-mail message, but you don't get it until the next day because you only log on to the Internet once a day.

Don't misunderstand me! I'm not suggesting that your daily quiet time is an outdated practice. The daily quiet time is essential to Christian maturity over the long run, and I hope every Christian reader practices that time-honored spiritual discipline. But your quiet time ought to be the equivalent of turning on your computer in the morning: you first connect with God in your morning quiet time—and you remain connected all day long until you go to sleep that night.

Begin to think about whether your spiritual life is more akin to the dial-up mode (log on, log off) or the broadband mode (always on, always in the moment). After all, should there ever be a time in our lives when we're not connected and communicating with God?

DANGERS OF DIAL-UP

If our spiritual awareness—if the time we're really conscious of God's presence—is limited to a half hour each morning or a couple of hours on Sunday, we're missing a lot. Every moment of every day is important to God, and if we're not living in every moment, we may miss what God is doing.

- *Divine Appointments*—How many people do you interact with face to face each day? How many of these interactions do you consider divine appointments (Proverbs 16:9)? If you're living in the dial-up mode instead of in the moment, you may miss something God wants you to give or receive in every encounter.

- *Divine Directions*—When we live in the dial-up mode, we're likely to be disconnected from God during a traffic jam or when our child makes us run late for an appointment—and we will react carnally. Or we might not consider that God is saving us from a calamity as He did Israel once by making them take the long way around (Exodus 13:17–18).

- *Divine Communications*—Thoughts pop in and out of our mind all day long. When we live in the dial-up mode and spend most of the day disconnected from God, we may never realize that some of those thoughts are from Him. God does speak to our hearts; but if we are not attentive to His voice, we may miss Him altogether (Matthew 13:15).

- *Divine Opportunities*—Often when we come to a crossroads in life, our intellectual due diligence doesn't leave room for God's input. It's possible that, logically speaking, Choice A seems best, but Choice B is really from God. The opportunity seems completely illogical, but actually it is right for us at that time. If you're logged off at that moment, you may miss the door God has opened for you.

THE BENEFITS OF BROADBAND

Now consider the number of benefits to living in the moment with God:

- *Attitude*—Just as we expect our home page to come up when we log on, we begin to expect to hear from God. We live with expectancy that God is going to be involved in our lives each and every moment (Mark 16:20).

- *Gratitude*—Living in constant communication with God enables us to see life as a gift from Him. We stop thinking in terms of "luck" and "coincidences" and start thinking in terms of His generous hand (James 1:17).

- *Beatitude*—When we live in the moment, we begin to experience blessings that we once overlooked. We also begin to dispense blessings since we live in the realm of divine appointments (1 Peter 3:9).

- *Latitude*—Our perspective on the range of God's activity broadens when we live in the moment. We better see the breadth of God's reach in the world, and we feel encouraged to get involved. We also more clearly recognize our value to Him as part of His grand plan for the world (Psalm 139:7–10).

- *Magnitude*—Living in the moment with God helps us get our eyes off ourselves and on to Him. Meditating moment by moment on God's awesomeness helps us keep our problems in perspective (Matthew 19:26).

- *Aptitude*—How much smarter and wiser would you be if you conversed with a certified genius all day long? How much wiser would you be if you conversed with God moment by moment? We will become like those with whom we constantly spend time and communicate (Psalm 119:99–100).

The way you access the Internet is up to you, but I strongly encourage you to live your spiritual life in the always-on position with God. Living in the moment with Him means living in a state of spiritual awareness that you'll never want to live without again.

siGNs of Life

Life Sign: Every moment of my life is a *living moment* with God.

Life Verse: *My sheep hear My voice, and I know them, and they follow Me.*

—John 10:27

Life in Action: Is my current relationship with God in a dial-up or broadband mode? What specific evidence from my life supports my answer? What can I do to keep my line of communication with God open at all times?

Pass the Salt

*There's a power in the presence of Christians
that permeates the society and sets into play the grace of God.*

The other day I heard about a baby camel that asked, "Mom, why do I have these huge three-toed feet?" The mother replied, "To help you stay on top of the soft sand while trekking across the desert."

"And why the long eyelashes?"

"To keep sand out of your eyes on our trips through the desert."

"Why the humps?"

"To store water for our long treks across the barren desert."

The baby camel considered that and then said, "That's great, Mom. We have huge feet to stop us from sinking, long eyelashes to keep sand out of our eyes, and humps to store water. But, Mom . . ."

"Yes, son?"

"Why are we in the zoo?"

That's a question for all of us to consider. If we've been given all the resources we need to carry our Lord's message far and wide, and if we're completely equipped to fulfill the Great Commission, why do we keep it within the four walls of our churches? The Gospel isn't something we come to church to hear; it's something we go from church to tell.

That point was on our Lord's mind when He preached His Sermon on the Mount and compared His church to a bowl of salt: "You are the salt of the earth; but if the salt loses its flavor, how shall it be seasoned? It is then good for nothing but to be thrown out and trampled underfoot by men" (Matthew 5:13).

In Christ's day, salt was more valuable than it is today, because it had many uses and it was hard to obtain. In fact, until modern times, salt was a major factor in the economies of entire nations. The Roman Empire valued salt as a form of currency, and workers were often paid with it. Our modern word *salary* comes from the Latin term *salarium,* meaning "salt." Jesus understood the value of salt, and His teachings on the subject have several relevant applications to us today.

Salt Prevents Decay

First of all, salt retards decay, and this was extremely important in biblical times when people had no ability to freeze or refrigerate food. The Middle Eastern sun caused meat to spoil rapidly; but with salt, food could be packed, preserved, and transported.

Without the salt of dedicated Christians, our society tends toward decay. Left to itself, a culture festers, rots, and putrefies. The bacteria of evil are everywhere; and without the presence of Christians, the decay would be unabated and final.

Our forefathers knew this, and that's why they established America on Judeo-Christian principles. In 1774, the very first Continental Congress invited Rev. Jacob Duché to begin each session in prayer. During the Constitutional Convention of 1787, Benjamin Franklin proposed that the Convention open each day in prayer.

Evidence of this spiritual heritage is engraved on our great monuments and public buildings in Washington, D.C. If you approach the chamber of the United States Senate from the east, for example, you'll see these words at the entrance: *Annuit Coeptis,* a Latin phrase meaning "God has favored our undertakings." The words "In God We Trust" are written above the southern entrance.

Calvin Coolidge, our thirtieth president, observed, "The foundation of our society and our government rest so much on the teachings of the Bible that it would be difficult to support them if faith in these teachings would cease to be practically universal in our country."[1]

I believe God has blessed our nation because of our legacy of faith, but every effort is now being made to expunge Christianity from the public arena. In the process, our national morals are decaying like an animal's carcass in the blazing sun.

But don't give up! America is filled with God-fearing Christians, and how much worse things would be without us! Our very presence retards decay and preserves godliness in our society. Our presence reduces crime, restrains ethical corruption, promotes honesty, elevates the moral atmosphere, and lifts up the hearts of our people.

You might be the only Christian in your office or in your classroom or on your sports team. What a challenge—and what an opportunity! Don't be afraid to be different. Remember that your influence may halt someone's descent into personal decay and despair.

SALT PROVIDES FLAVOR

Besides preserving food, salt also gives it a great flavor. The ancient patriarch Job asked, "Can flavorless food be eaten without salt?" (Job 6:6). When our Lord said, "You are the salt of the earth," that's what He had in mind, for He went on to warn of the danger of salt losing its flavor, its distinctive taste. It would then be good for nothing except casting into the dirt streets.

Again, salt is very useful because of its distinctive characteristic: it's salty and pungent. When it's in your food, you know it's there. If it loses that distinctive character of saltiness, it's no better than ordinary dirt.

As salt, we Christians also have a distinctive character. Specifically, whatever we do, we should do with excellence. We should write the best books, produce the best movies, record the best music, design the best buildings, and display the best manners. We should be the most generous people around, the hardest working employees, and the most dependable friends. And characterizing all we do should be the distinctive flavor of our faith.

Our character and ethics should reflect Jesus' values, and our personal interaction with others should be pleasant, personable, and evangelistic. In the rabbinic literature of biblical times, salt was a metaphor for wisdom, and perhaps that was what the apostle Paul had in mind when he wrote, "Let your speech always be with grace, seasoned with salt, that you may know how you ought to answer each one" (Colossians 4:6).

SALT PROMOTES THIRST

Salt preserves food, flavors food, and promotes thirst—as you know if you've ever eaten potato chips. Well, as Christians we should be making people thirsty for God. One woman, while giving her testimony, said that she began attending a church where the preacher was a zealous teacher of Scripture. He went verse by verse; and as she began understanding the Bible better, she grew excited. "That man made me want to know God better than I did," she said. "He made me hungry for the Word. I began to realize what the psalmist meant when he said, 'As the deer pants for the water brooks, so pants my soul for You, O God' (Psalm 42:1)."

Our commitment to Scripture, I believe, plus our cheerfulness and our enthusiasm for Christ can influence others in the same way. Journalist Henry Stanley said about missionary David Livingstone in central Africa, "If I had been with him any longer, I would have been compelled to be a Christian, and he never spoke to me about it at all."[2]

SALT PERMEATES FOOD

Finally, salt permeates food—and a little of it goes a long way. Its effectiveness isn't indicated by its size. Just a touch of salt can affect an entire dish. That's the way it is with Christians in this world. Sometimes people say, "But what can I do? I'm just one soul." Let me remind you that the apostle Paul and his two companions (Luke and Aristarchus) were apparently the only Christians among the 276 people aboard a ship bound for Rome in Acts 27. That's a ratio of nearly 100 to 1. At first they were disdained, but by the end of the voyage, their companions' attitude changed. In fact, the presence of these three Christians saved the lives of everyone else.

Even if we make up only one percent of our culture, there's a power in the presence of Christians that permeates society and sets into play the grace of God. And William Wilberforce, the statesman who almost single-handedly championed the abolition of slave trading in the British Empire, is living proof of this.

Dwarfed by disease, Wilberforce didn't appear to be a person who could accomplish much. But here's what biographer James Boswell wrote after listening to one of his speeches: "I saw a shrimp mount the table; but as I listened, he grew and grew until the shrimp became a whale."

It was said of Wilberforce, "Tiny, elfish, misshapen, he was salt to British society, not only bringing preservation but enticement to Christ by his beautiful life. A little salt makes its presence felt."[3]

Are you making your presence felt?

Jesus was talking to me and to you when He said, "You are the salt of the earth." Isn't it time we got out of the shaker? It's time to be salty.

signs of Life

Life Sign: I am conscious of influencing those around me.

Life Verse: *Salt is good, but if the salt loses its flavor, how will you season it? Have salt in yourselves, and have peace with one another.*

—Mark 9:50

Life in Action: As the salt of the earth, what am I doing that causes others to thirst for the living water?

Day 6

Witness Statements

*Our most effective witness comes when others see
hope and joy radiate from our lives.*

In the days before cameras were allowed in courtrooms, we depended
on artists like Walt Stewart to attend trials with their sketchpads in
hand. Their job was to capture electrifying moments for news organizations. Stewart's first assignment was the trial of Jack Ruby, the man
accused of shooting Lee Harvey Oswald. Stewart captured on his sketchpad the dramatic moment when the prosecutor, facing the jury, said
about Oswald, "Whatever he did, he was entitled to be tried before a
judge and jury." Then, whirling around to the defendant, he pointed a
finger at Ruby and said, "Just like you."[1]

Suppose you were on trial, accused of being a Christian. If the prosecuting attorney assembled a group of your friends to testify against you,
would there be any dramatic moments? Would they whirl and point
their finger at you?

God has always had a handful of people whose lives were so uniquely different that the world easily "convicted" them of being Christians. We're always on display, whether we realize it or not. Romans 14:7 says, "For none of us lives to himself."

〰

In his book *Ten Mistakes Parents Make with Teenagers,* Jay Kesler describes a conversation he had with a young lady at a Youth for Christ summer camp in Ohio. She told a sordid story of long-term abuse in a dysfunctional home. As they talked, Jay noticed that the girl's wrists were scarred, and he asked her about it. She admitted that she had tried to kill herself.

"Why didn't you do it?" Jay asked.

"Well, I got to thinking," said the girl. "We have a youth pastor at our church—"

At first Jay thought he was going to hear an ugly story about her getting involved with some youth pastor. But that wasn't it at all. She said, "He'd just gotten married before he came to our church, and I've been watching him. When he's standing in line in church behind his wife, he squeezes her right in church. They look at each other, and they hug each other right in our church. One day I was standing in the pastor's study, looking out the window, and the youth pastor walked his wife out into the parking lot. Now there was only one car in the parking lot; nobody was around; nobody was looking. And that guy walked all the way around the car and opened the door and let her in. Then he walked all the way around and got in himself. And there was nobody even looking."

Jay thought that was a nice story, but he couldn't make a connection between that, her problems at home, or her attempted suicide. So he asked why this was so significant.

She replied, "Well, I just got to thinking that all men must not be like my dad, huh?" Then she said, "Jay, do you suppose our youth pastor's a Christian?"

"Yes," Jay said, "I think he probably is."

"Well, that's why I came tonight," she said. "I want to be a Christian too." She wanted to be a Christian simply because she saw a man being respectful to his wife even when nobody was looking. That's the power of a consistent life.[2]

The poet Edgar Guest once wrote:

> I'd rather see a sermon than hear one any day.
> I'd rather one would walk with me than merely show the way.
> The eye's a better pupil and much sharper than the ear.
> Fine counsel can confuse me, but example's always clear.
> The lectures you deliver may be very wise and true,
> But I'd rather get my lesson by observing what you do.[3]

Many unbelievers don't attend church because of "all the hypocrites there." Perhaps we're all guilty of hypocrisy to some extent, for none of us is perfect. There aren't any perfect churches on the planet. We don't live as consistently and perfectly as our great example Jesus Christ did. But we should be trying. We should be maturing. We should be growing. And we should increasingly be learning to "walk the talk."

It's said that one day St. Francis of Assisi invited a young assistant at the monastery to go with him into town to preach. The novice was delighted to be singled out as Francis's companion. The two men passed through the main streets, turned down many of the byways and alleys, made their way into the suburbs, and at great length returned by a circuitous route to the monastery gate. As they approached it, the younger man reminded Francis of his original intention. "You have forgotten, Father, that we went to the town to preach!"

"My son," Francis replied, "we have preached. We were preaching while we were walking. We have been seen by many; our behavior has been closely watched; it was thus that we preached our morning sermon.

It is of no use, my son, to walk anywhere to preach unless we preach everywhere as we walk.'"[4]

This scene reminds me of an old poem:

> You are writing a gospel, a chapter each day,
> By the deeds that you do, by the words that you say;
> Men read what you write, whether faithless or true.
> Say—what is the gospel according to you?[5]

What can you do to improve the chances of your being "convicted" of being a follower of Jesus Christ?

Start each day by rededicating yourself to Him and asking Him to guide your thoughts, words, and actions during that day. Bishop Taylor Smith (1860–1937), British commanding army chaplain, once wrote: "As soon as I awake each morning I rise from bed at once. I dress promptly. I wash myself, shave and comb my hair. Then fully attired, wide-awake and properly groomed, I go quietly to my study. There, before God Almighty and Christ my King, I humbly present myself as a loyal subject to my Sovereign, ready and eager to be of service to Him for the day."[6]

Then enter each day with a joyful attitude. Our Christian faith should show up on our faces. Remember the exhortation of 1 Peter 3:15: "Sanctify the Lord God in your hearts, and always be ready to give a defense to everyone who asks you a reason for the hope that is in you." In other words, our most effective witness comes when others see hope and joy radiate from our lives.

Now imagine that a film crew were following you throughout the day with television cameras, waiting and watching for you, the Christian, to blow it. We need to guard against such moments. We can significantly damage our testimony by uttering that word, looking at that magazine, listening to that joke, or snapping at that employee.

> We are the only Bible a careless world will read;
> We are the sinner's gospel; we are the scoffer's creed;
> We are the Lord's last message, given in deed and word;
> What if the type is crooked; what if the print is blurred?[7]

When you do *fail as a Christian, be quick to admit it and apologize.* Recently a Christian father lost his temper with his children while trying to get them ready for church. He yelled at them, slamming his fist on the table and creating a frightening scene. As it happened that day, the sermon was about the importance of a father's influence in his family. Afterward, this man gathered his kids and said to them, "This morning I failed God and I failed you by losing my temper. I'm not a perfect man, but I try to live as I should each day. This morning I didn't do very well, and I'm sorry. I've confessed it to God and asked for His forgiveness, and I'd like to ask for your forgiveness, too." It was a moment his children will remember for a long time.

Finally, be growing each day as a Christian. The Lord wants to perfect anything that concerns you (Psalm 138:8). He desires you to be increasingly conformed into His image so that your testimony will grow increasingly effective. Your responsibility in this daily Christian growth is staying in the Bible, praying, trusting, and obeying.

Jesus said, "Let your light so shine before men, that they may see your good works and glorify your Father in heaven" (Matthew 5:16). That's His solemn command to you. Someone's eyes are on you, and you may be the only Gospel that person will ever see. If they keep watching for evidence of your Christianity, will there be enough evidence for them to convict you?

May we all be found guilty as charged!

SiGNs of Life

Life Sign: Those who witness my life see Jesus.

Life Verse: *And whatever you do, do it heartily, as to the Lord and not to men.*

—Colossians 3:23

Life in Action: What can I do to be a more effective representative of God?

The Mark You Leave Behind

*We don't stay on earth forever; but after we're
gone, our imprint remains.*

She thought she had gotten away with it. Francisca Rojas of Buenos
Aires, Argentina, had murdered two of her own sons. In an
attempt to deflect the blame, she had cut her own throat as well
and then blamed the attack on a nearby ranch worker named Velasquez.
Though the poor man proclaimed his innocence, he was arrested.

An Argentine police official named Juan Vucetich, however, had
been experimenting with a newfangled system of criminal identity that
relied on fingerprints. It was 1891, and fingerprints had never been used
in a criminal trial. Revisiting the scene of the attack, Vucetich studied
the bloody handprint on the doorframe of Francisca's house. It matched
the prints of Francisca's own fingers. As a result, Francisca became the
first person in history to be convicted of a crime based on fingerprint
identification.[1]

Today the FBI's Integrated Automated Fingerprint Identification
System (IAFIS) electronically stores millions of known fingerprints. In
this world of six billion people, each person's fingerprints are unique.

Each fingertip has a pattern of fine ridges on the skin that is slightly different from every other person's pattern, even from an identical twin. Therefore every person leaves his or her own unique mark.

❧

There's another sense in which we leave a mark. Every one of us leaves our spiritual fingerprints, metaphorically speaking, on the lives of other people and especially on our children. We don't stay on earth forever; but after we're gone, this spiritual imprint remains.

John Geddie, Canadian missionary to the New Hebrides, offers a vivid example of the imprint we can have on people. Arriving on the island of Aneityum, he found a wild tribe of cannibals who considered human flesh the most savory of foods. Violence, theft, and warfare were common. His journal for February 9, 1849, reads: "In the darkness, degradation, pollution, and misery that surrounds me, I look forward in faith to the time when some of these poor islanders will unite in the triumphant song of ransomed souls."

He lived to see it happen. Geddie died just before Christmas in 1872, and this tablet was afterward installed in his island church: "'In memory of John Geddie. . . . When he landed in 1848, there were no Christians here, and when he left in 1872, there were no heathen."[2]

You and I may not be responsible for converting an entire island, but we will leave our stamp on some people. The world will be better if we live a faithful life. What, then, can we do to leave our fingerprints—the fingerprints of Christ—behind us?

THE FINGERPRINT OF THE WORD

One of the simplest things we can do is to read the Word of God. Our children see us spending hours in front of the television watching football, following our favorite programs, and renting popular movies. But do they ever see us reading our Bible? When was the last time your child found you hunkered down at the kitchen table poring over God's Word?

Ruth Graham, wife of evangelist Billy Graham, once explained why she became a lifelong student of Scripture. Growing up in China, she saw her missionary parents study the Bible every day:

Each morning when I went downstairs to breakfast, my father—a busy missionary surgeon—would be sitting reading his Bible. At night, her work behind her, my mother would be doing the same. Anything that could so capture the interest and devotion of those I admired and loved the most, I reasoned, must be worth investigating. So at an early age I began reading my Bible.[3]

THE FINGERPRINT OF HONESTY

It's important that we live an honest life, because the people closest to us (especially our kids) are quick to pick up on our inconsistencies. Allen C. Emery, a successful businessman who served on the boards of many Christian organizations, was known for his integrity and common sense. In his book *A Turtle on a Fencepost*, Emery wrote this of his father:

Today I find myself still asking myself, "What would Daddy do?" when confronted with those decisions in business and in life that are so often not black and white, but gray. I am in debt to the memory-making efforts that my father made to imprint indelibly upon my mind the meaning of integrity. . . .

Once [my dad] lost a pair of fine German binoculars. He collected insurance only to find the binoculars a year later. Immediately he sent a check to the company and received a letter back stating that this seldom occurred and that they were encouraged. It was a small thing, but children never forget examples lived before them.[4]

Will our friends and family be able to tell similar stories about us after we're gone?

THE FINGERPRINT OF PRAYER

We must commit ourselves to leaving a legacy of prayer, as a wonderful old story about the great evangelist Dr. J. Wilbur Chapman illustrates. As a young man, he was elected pastor of Bethany Presbyterian Church in Philadelphia. An elderly man approached him after his sermon and said, "I am afraid you will not make it as pastor here." Allowing some time for that sober assessment to sink in, the man continued, "This is a large church with great responsibility falling upon its pastor. We need a man with equally large experience. But I have made up my mind to help you. I have resolved to pray for you every day . . . and I have made a covenant with two other men to do the same."

This prayer band grew from three to fifty to hundreds. So it's not surprising that, within three years, more than 1,100 people had professed Christ as their Savior. This one infirm, elderly man made up his mind to leave an imprint of prayer—and he did![5]

THE FINGERPRINT OF AN ENDURING TESTIMONY

We Christians must leave behind the imprint of an enduring testimony. As Paul told Timothy, "The things that you have heard from me among many witnesses, commit these to faithful men who will be able to teach others also" (2 Timothy 2:2).

Recently *Baptist Press* reported the story of Dr. Steve White, a New Mexico dentist. When White was a twenty-one-year-old college basketball player, his ailing mother called him to her bedside. "I just want you to know, Steven," she said, "that I have accepted Jesus Christ as my Lord and Savior."

Steve later said, "I walked out of that room and I thought, 'What is she talking about ?' As a family we never talked about that kind of stuff."

His mother died shortly afterward, but Steve went on to become a successful dentist, one who believed the material world was all that existed and that Christians were crazy to believe in God.

Twenty-four years later, while looking at a picture of his mom, her words came forcibly to mind. He suddenly realized that his mom had discovered the truth before she died. She had found the key to eternal life.

"Those two words kept going over and over in my mind: 'Jesus Christ.' For the first time in my life, I realized Jesus Christ is for real."

Under deep conviction, Steve took off in his truck. Switching on the radio, he heard a preacher explain the Gospel, and he instantly received Jesus Christ into his heart.[6]

With almost her last breath, a mother—herself a new Christian—left the legacy of an enduring testimony that bore fruit more than two decades later. Don't underestimate the power of sharing Christ. His Word does not return to Him void, and our work in the Lord is never in vain (Isaiah 55:11; 1 Corinthians 15:58). . . .

A blind man was once seen walking down the sidewalk at night with his flashlight shining. Someone asked him why, being blind, he carried a flashlight. "Because," he said, "I don't want anyone to stumble because of me."[7]

Do you have a habit or tendency in your life that might cause someone to stumble over you? Are you exercising excessive liberty in your personal habits? Or is your influence the kind that Christ can use to change the lives of others? What kind of imprint are you leaving?

As you consider your answers to these questions, read these lyrics:

After all our hopes and dreams have come and gone,
And our children sift through all we've left behind,
May the clues that they discover and the memories they uncover
Become the light that leads them to the road we each must find.

Oh may all who come behind us find us faithful;
May the fire of our devotion light their way.

May the footprints that we leave lead them to believe,
And the lives we live inspire them to obey.

Oh may all who come behind us find us faithful.[8]

SIGNS of Life

Life Sign: The imprint of my Christian life will remain for eternity.

Life Verse: . . . *It is required in stewards that one be found faithful.*

—1 Corinthians 4:2

Life in Action: In what specific ways am I leaving behind positive—or negative—fingerprints in the lives of my family, friends, co-workers, and community?

Dusty Shoes...
Living a
reLevant
Life

Day 8

Dusty Shoes

*Be willing to get your shoes dusty
on the streets of this world.*

See if you can guess what organization these prominent Christian leaders of a bygone era were speaking of:

- Josiah Strong: "Probably during no one-hundred years in the history of the world have there been saved so many thieves, gamblers, drunkards, and prostitutes as during the past quarter of a century through the heroic faith and labors of [this ministry]."[1]

- Charles H. Spurgeon: "If [this ministry] were wiped out of London, five thousand extra policemen could not fill its place in the repression of crime and disorder."[2]

- Booker T. Washington: "I have always had the greatest respect for the work of [this ministry] especially because I have noted that it draws no color line in religion."[3]

Those words would be considered high praise from anyone at any point in history. But they were spoken at a time when life in British and American cities was difficult for the downtrodden and marginal members of society. Few Christian ministries reached out to them; and when any did, they were rebuffed to such a degree that they often withdrew for lack of staying power.

But one man who would not be turned away from the inner cities of the world was William Booth (1829–1912) and, later, his wife, Catherine. The organization they founded—the organization being discussed above—became known as the Salvation Army, and it manifested the same traits that characterized Booth and his wife: compassion, courage, and caring. In 2005, the Salvation Army was serving in 111 countries around the world, continuing to reach out to the most needy among us with the gospel of Jesus Christ.[4]

But this ministry has never been easy. Historian E. H. McKinley wrote that William Booth conceived of the Salvation Army as being for "wife-beaters, cheats and bullies, prostitutes, boys who had stolen the family food money, unfaithful husbands, burglars, and teamsters who had been cruel to their horses."[5] Booth, his wife, and eventually their eight children took the Gospel of salvation into places that were neither clean nor comfortable. In fact, the bonnet worn by early Salvation Army women was designed by Catherine Booth to shield the women's heads from stones, dirt, rotten food, and other debris that were regularly thrown at them as they entered and ministered in high-risk areas of cities where the Gospel was needed but not welcomed. And the first Salvation Army brass band, so familiar today during the Christmas season, was formed by a father and his three sons who served as bodyguards to protect William Booth from attacks by hooligans.

In spite of these obstacles, William and Catherine Booth pressed on, refusing to be deterred. William's most well-known saying is "Go for souls and go for the worst!" In responding to that exhortation to himself, William Booth and his wife and children got their shoes covered by the dust of this world, but they counted it an honor and an obligation to do so. Daily they left the security of their own homes and ventured into the streets of the world's great cities to introduce people to the Christ who could meet their needs.[6]

❧

The question I have to ask myself is this: am I willing to get my own shoes dusty on the streets of this world in order to make the love of Jesus Christ available to those who do not know Him? If I am going to be like my Savior, the answer can only be yes.

Dust and Deity

In Jesus' day, people wore sandals and had dusty feet. You couldn't leave your home and walk more than a few steps on a dirt road, through a field, or on a mountainside or even on a paved street in Jerusalem without your feet becoming dusty. That's why it was a matter of common courtesy and hospitality for a host to provide a servant to wash the feet of guests as they entered a home (Luke 7:36–50; John 13:3–14).

Since most people don't wear sandals or walk on dusty streets today, that custom is no longer practiced, but it still serves as a worthy metaphor for us. In biblical times, the only people who got their feet and sandals dusty were those who left the cleanliness and safety of their homes. Whether they were going to the market or to minister, they had to leave home to do it. Likewise, if we are going to fulfill the Great Commission of Jesus Christ, we are going to have to leave home. It was Jesus who spoke these words in one of His parables: "Then the master said to the servant, 'Go out into the highways and hedges, and compel them to come in, that my house may be filled'" (Luke 14:23).

And the best example of Someone who left home and got His feet dusty—and His body broken—in the service of God's kingdom was Jesus Himself. In fact, He specifically said on one occasion that "foxes have holes and birds of the air have nests, but the Son of Man has nowhere to lay His head" (Matthew 8:20). Jesus lived and ministered in the highways and byways of this world among people with whom the religious elite of His day would have nothing to do. He was often criticized for eating with "tax collectors and sinners" (Matthew 9:11).

Jesus was even happy to socialize with those with whom He disagreed. When a woman with a sinful past washed Jesus' feet with her own tears and hair, He was eating a meal in the home of a Pharisee. Again and again Jesus made it clear that He came to help those who knew they needed help, not those who didn't (Mark 2:17). And in order to reach those people, Jesus lived His life where they were. He went to them; He didn't force them to come to Him.

John 20:21 summarizes what Jesus did *and* what He expects us to do: "As the Father has sent Me, I also send you." Jesus lived His life with dusty feet because He lived a life of obedience to His father. If our feet aren't equally dusty, it calls into question our obedience to His command to "Go therefore and make disciples . . ." (Matthew 28:19).

SOLES FOR SOULS

One mistake of the modern church seems to be that when someone is converted to Christ, all too often in the name of discipleship, we hurry that person out of his place in the world into the sanitized confines of the church. Instead, perhaps we need to challenge *ourselves* to leave the walls of the church and walk with that new believer back into the world to reach his friends for Christ.

Interestingly, this is often the very thing that the world expects of us. A reporter, an avowed atheist, wrote about the Salvation Army in the wake of Katrina, observing that aid was often administered without any hint of disapproval while meeting "needs that result from conduct regarded as intrinsically wicked." The writer suggested that it should be possible to live like a Christian without being one but acknowledged that only Christians are "likely to take the risks and make the sacrifices involved in helping others."[7]

These are examples of what it means to get dust on our shoes—to leave the "clean" environment of church and home and to go into our neighborhoods and communities and do what Jesus did: show people how much God loves them by meeting them where they are and providing what they need.

If you and I have dust on our shoes, it means we understand these four truths that I have paraphrased from Jesus' teachings:

1. **The Mission:** Jesus said, "Go into all the world."

2. **The Message:** Jesus said, "Go and find those who are needy and meet their needs."

3. **The Moment:** Jesus said, "Go and be ready for every encounter, every divine appointment."

4. **The Miracle:** Jesus said, "Unless one is born again, that person cannot see the kingdom of God."

Take a look at your shoes today. If most of what you see is lint from the carpet in your church and home, ask God to give you dusty shoes— shoes like those worn by William and Catherine Booth, shoes like those worn by our Savior.

If we are in the habit of polishing our shoes on Sunday morning, may it be because they are covered with a week's worth of dust from the streets of this world.

signs of Life

Life Sign: I am willing to get my feet dusty in the streets of my community.

Life Verse: *Then the master said to the servant, "Go out into the highways and hedges, and compel them to come in, that my house may be filled."*

—Luke 14:23

Life in Action: What opportunities can I actively pursue to be salt and light in my neighborhood? Which one will I pursue this week?

Walk Around the Clock

*The Christian walk should be filled with wonder
and the fear of the Lord.*

Her disguises didn't work. The Queen of France was young, energetic, and immature, and she longed to be with people her own age. Resenting the limitations of royal life, she attended dances, balls, and parties in disguise. But biographer Carolly Erickson said this about Marie Antoinette: "Her swift, purposeful gait was her trademark. It was said that she could never successfully disguise her identity at masked balls, for no matter how she dressed, she still walked like an Empress."[1]

Our walk always gives us away.

As Christians, we are called to walk worthy of our calling 24/7, morning, noon, and night. We have a manual—the Bible—that gives our marching orders. The Bible has 225 verses about walking, and the word *walk* occurs 406 times. Many of these verses refer to our daily behavior. For instance, Genesis 5:22 says, "Enoch walked with God." The Lord told Abraham, "Walk before Me and be blameless" (Genesis 17:1). He commanded the Israelites: "You shall . . . keep My ordinances, to walk in them" (Leviticus 18:4). The psalmist said, "No good thing will He withhold from those who walk uprightly" (Psalm 84:11). Paul told us to walk by faith, to walk in love, and to walk as children of light.

Open a concordance sometime, look up the word *walk,* and study some of the other verses. As you read the verses, look for the lessons they contain. For example . . .

WALK WITH THE WISE

The book of Proverbs warns us against walking with fools. Listen to these verses: "If sinners entice you, do not consent. . . . Do not walk in the way with them. Keep your foot from their path. . . . Do not enter the path of the wicked, and do not walk in the way of evil. . . . He who walks with wise men will be wise" (Proverbs 1:10, 15; 4:14; 13:20).

To use modern terminology, we're talking about peer pressure and the desire for approval from one's friends. Both are dead-end streets.

The influence of peer pressure on today's youth has increased as society has changed. The undermining of parental authority, more time spent with peers, and more freedom at younger ages can leave our young people increasingly susceptible to trying drugs, alcohol, and other harmful activities.

And not just young people struggle with peer pressure. Consider how easy it is to smile at an off-color joke, to go with the guys to an inappropriate movie, to gossip about someone with friends over lunch, or to begin skipping church to attend ball games with buddies. The apostle Paul wrote, "Brethren, join in following my example, and note those who so walk, as you have us for a pattern. For many walk, of whom I have told you often, and now tell you even weeping, that they are the enemies of the cross of Christ" (Philippians 3:17–18).

Perhaps the best question to ask yourself is "Who are my three wisest and most mature friends?" Once you decide who they are, make an effort to spend time with them. Watch them, listen to them, and let their seasoned knowledge and insight rub off on you.

Similarly, ask yourself "Which three friends pull me down the most?" Begin weaning yourself away from them. Or, better yet, tell them you'd love to be with them—in church!

WALK IN THE FEAR OF THE LORD

We're to walk with the wise, and we're also to walk in the fear of the Lord. Consider the first-century example Luke records for us: "the churches throughout all Judea, Galilee, and Samaria had peace. . . . And walking in the fear of the Lord and in the comfort of the Holy Spirit, they were multiplied" (Acts 9:31).

Walking in the fear of God, however, is an almost forgotten concept. Christians were once described as "God-fearing people," and pastors preached about the fear of the Lord. Nowadays, though, we're so eager to present the Gospel in an inoffensive way that we've gotten away from using—and practicing—the verb *fear*. Yet the phrase *the fear of God* appears repeatedly in Scripture. There are over 300 references to it in the Old Testament alone.

In his book *The Knowledge of the Holy*, A. W. Tozer wrote this:

> In olden days men of faith were said to walk in the fear of God. . . .
> However intimate their communion with God, however bold their
> prayers, at the base of their religious life was the conception of God
> as awesome and dreadful. This idea of God transcendent runs
> through the whole Bible and gives color and tone to the character of
> saints. . . .[2]

Such a fear of God isn't an unhealthy phobia, but a therapeutic sense of awe at His greatness. One way to cultivate this attitude is to visit a location that speaks of His grandeur. You might choose a classic cathedral where you can sit in silence awhile. Or you might find a mountain ledge or a thundering waterfall where the sheer, dangerous beauty of God's creation makes you dizzy. Perhaps a camping trip away from city lights will allow you to gaze into the black sky and see the splendor of the stars. Spending time like this is a way to cultivate a reverence for God Almighty, Omnipotent, Holy, and Eternal.

WALK IN NEWNESS OF LIFE

We walk with the wise, we walk in the fear of the Lord, and we are to walk in newness of life (Romans 6:4). This phrase describes the change of attitude and behavior that happens as we come to know Jesus Christ. Among other things, we find life more refreshing and uplifting, and we experience a sense of wonder in the day to day. As we sit in that lofty cathedral or gaze into the star-splashed sky, we not only develop a hearty fear of God, but we find ourselves full of wonder, the kind of wonder that leads to worship.

Evangelist D. L. Moody often talked about the sudden change of attitude and perspective he experienced as a newly converted teenager:

> I remember the morning on which I came out of my room after I had first trusted Christ. I thought the old sun shone a good deal brighter than it ever had before—I thought it was just smiling upon me; and as I walked out upon Boston Common and heard the birds singing in the trees, I thought they were all singing a song to me. Do you know, I fell in love with the birds? I had never cared for them before. It seemed to me that I was in love with all creation. I had not a bitter feeling against any man.[3]

Again, the Christian walk should be filled with wonder and characterized by the fear of the Lord. We should also walk in newness of life. And that leads us to walk in obedience.

WALK IN OBEDIENCE

The old apostle John wrote: "I rejoiced greatly that I have found some of your children walking in truth, as we received commandment from the Father. . . . This is love, that we walk according to His commandments. This is the commandment . . . walk in it" (2 John 4, 6).

In other words, we're to live an obedient life. Since the word *obedience* is abstract, we must attach specifics to it before being able to measure ourselves by it. Let's ask ourselves, for example, whether we've told any white lies recently (Ephesians 4:25). Have we said something in an angry tone or hurt someone else with our words (Ephesians 4:26, 29)? Have we contributed to an unhealthy argument (Proverbs 17:14)?

And the list goes on. Have we worried about our finances (Matthew 6:25)? Have we associated with a humble person today (Romans 12:16)? Have we given our tithes to the Lord this week (Malachi 3:10)? Have we spoken a word for Christ to someone recently (Psalm 107:2)? Have we talked with our children about God's Word today (Deuteronomy 6:7)?

The entire last half of Ephesians focuses on this theme: Walk worthy of your calling. Do not walk as the world does. Walk in love. Walk as children of light—and don't quit! We are to walk with the wise, in the fear of the Lord, in newness of life, and in obedience to God around the clock.

A recent report from Duke University touted the benefits of walking a half hour every day. "As little as thirty minutes of walking daily is enough to prevent weight gain for most sedentary people," said the report.[4]

The Christian walk, however, is a continuous walk. We're to walk around the clock. While we might have a great half hour of quiet time each, we are to walk in His presence 24 hours a day, 365 days a year.

If you're walking with the Lord, keep your eyes on Him and your head looking down on that straight and narrow path. If you aren't walking with the Lord, adjust your stride. Learn what one man called "the gait of Galilee."

Finally, hear how the prophet Jeremiah quaintly put it centuries ago:

> Stand in the ways and see,
> And ask for the old paths,
>   where the good way is,
> And walk in it;
> Then you will find rest for your souls.—Jeremiah 6:16

signs of Life

Life Sign: My walk supports my Christian talk.

Life Verse: *Stand in the ways and see,*
And ask for the old paths,
   where the good way is,
And walk in it;
Then you will find rest for your souls.

—Jeremiah 6:16

Life in Action: What can I do to stay focused on my walk with God around the clock? Here are four things I can do to implement a stronger walk throughout my day:

Day 10

The Keynote Speaker

*The world is a banquet, and you have
been invited to be the keynote speaker.*

Let's say your company is having the first of what is projected to be an annual Thursday-through-Saturday conference for its national sales team. At the concluding banquet on Saturday night, the company CEO wants to have a dynamic, nationally-known keynote speaker, someone who will send the sales force home with energy and excitement, someone who can use humor and personal stories to prove that obstacles can indeed be overcome, someone who has excelled and continues to excel in meeting personal goals.

As the CEO's assistant, you've been assigned the task of coming up with a short list of possible speakers for the event: who they are, what they would talk about, and how much they would charge. The boss tells you not to worry about the budget, to just do the research and then come back with some suggestions.

So you log on to the Internet, begin your research, and take notes. It doesn't take you long to discover that the CEO's ideal keynote speaker might exceed the dollars available. For instance, NASCAR racing legend and television commentator Darrell Waltrip is available for $50,000 plus fuel costs for his personal jet. Since the boss is a NASCAR fan, you dig a little deeper and do a little better: Jeff Hammond and Larry McReynolds, both veteran NASCAR crew chiefs and now TV commentators, are available for between $20,000 and $30,000—each—plus first-class air travel.

You switch to other sports. Officially, veteran NBA coach Pat Riley's lowball fee is $50,000 plus first-class travel. Meadowlark Lemon, legendary Harlem Globetrotter and the "Clown Prince of Basketball," is "only" $25,000. Jim Palmer, three-time Cy Young winner and baseball Hall-of-Famer, starts at $20,000. But a lot of the people you're really interested in—Johnny Bench, Julius Erving, Lance Armstrong, Bobby Bowden, Bob Costas, Magic Johnson, Mark Spitz—don't even advertise their fees. Uh-oh. This is a case of, "If you have to ask . . . ."

In light of what you discover about the cost of hiring a great keynote speaker, you hit on a brilliant plan: maybe you could offer the speaker stock in the company instead of a cash fee. After all, former president George H. W. Bush once accepted stock in a high-tech company in lieu of his $80,000 speaker's fee, stock that he ultimately sold for several million dollars shortly before the company went out of business.[1]

When you take your research to the CEO, he is amazed at what it will cost to get a keynote speaker for the closing banquet. And he poses a question that neither of you can answer: "How will we know we got our money's worth when the banquet is over?"

"LET'S WELCOME OUR KEYNOTE SPEAKER, [INSERT YOUR NAME]!"

During this week, we're talking about what it means to find your voice as a Christian, what it means to be so comfortable with who you are in Christ that you are prepared to speak, verbally and nonverbally, in a way that encourages others to consider how knowing Christ could change their life.

And we can take speech lessons from Jesus Christ Himself. After all, there's no better way to learn than to sit at the feet of the Master Speaker

Himself. But now we're talking about you being a keynote speaker at the banquet of life. That's right—*you're on!*

"Me, a keynote speaker? But I have to work just to get my spouse and kids to listen to me! Who in the world wants to hear what I have to say?"

I know exactly how you feel, my friend. As I step in front of groups of people several times a week, for most of the fifty-two weeks of every year, I pray, "Lord, please help me say something that will encourage these dear folks. They've come here seeking You, but You've given them me! Did you get the schedules mixed up, Lord? Isn't there somebody more eloquent, more powerful, and more entertaining that You could give these people?"

And God always speaks to my heart: "No, you're right on schedule. I haven't sent you to speak on your own. I have sent you to represent Me so that I can speak through you. Together, you and I will encourage these people. I am going to bring everything I have been doing in your life these past six decades to bear in this moment, in this place, for the benefit of these people. This is a divine appointment! I have arranged the banquet, I have prepared your voice, and I have paid the price to get you here. Now walk to the podium. *You're on!"*

I go through that thought process every time I speak. But I also have to go through it in all the same places you do: when I am talking with a neighbor, visiting a friend in the hospital, helping one of my children think through a problem, talking to a stranger on an airplane, or working with someone at the office. Every one of those situations is a mini-banquet, and you and I are the keynote speakers God has called to convey what is on His heart.

A QUALIFIED KEYNOTER

The simple reason why we are qualified to be keynote speakers for Christ is that without Him we can do nothing (John 15:4–5). The obvious implication of that truth is that with Him we can do whatever He asks us to do. When we choose to look at life as a series of divine appointments, then we are trusting that God would not set an appointment for us that we, with His help, cannot keep. And that includes being His voice in many, many different situations.

A number of passages of Scripture give us confidence when we consider our role as a keynote speaker for the Lord.

1. **Galatians 2:20**—Allow me to paraphrase Paul's very familiar words and apply them to the subject of being God's voice: "I have been crucified with Christ; it is no longer I who speak, but Christ speaks in and through me; and the life-message which I now live in the flesh I live by faith in the Son of God, who loved me and paid all the costs associated with my speaking for Him."

2. **Mark 16:20**—After giving the disciples the Great Commission, Christ ascended to heaven. Then the disciples "went out and preached everywhere, the Lord working with them." You are not called to speak for Christ by yourself. He is working with you in all He asks you to do.

3. **1 Corinthians 2:1–5; 1 Thessalonians 1:5**—Paul's voice for the Lord wasn't based on his "excellence of speech or of wisdom." In fact, he spoke "in weakness, in fear, and in much trembling." Sound familiar? It does to me! But Paul spoke anyway in order that his hearers' faith "should not be in the wisdom of men but in the power of God." God wants to show His power through you and me too.

4. **2 Corinthians 4:7–10**—Regardless of what you and I think about what we have to offer others, God calls our offering something very specific: a treasure. When we look at ourselves, we only see our "earthen vessels." But God sees the treasure He has deposited in us: the gospel of His grace, wisdom, love, and forgiveness. It is that treasure our voice conveys when we serve others.

5. **1 Corinthians 6:20; 7:23**—If you think the fees for some
   keynote speakers are amazing, consider the price God paid in
   order for you to share your voice: the cost was the life of His
   dear Son, Jesus Christ. God paid that price to redeem our
   voice and give us a message that the world is literally dying to
   hear. This payment means that we are free to speak whenever
   people ask us to share with them the "reason for the hope"
   that is in us (1 Peter 3:15).

THE WORLD IS YOUR BANQUET

Jesus has sent us into "all the world" (Mark 16:15) to speak for Him.
And "all the world" means that your voice is needed in your church,
your neighborhood, and your community. Wherever you go, God will
arrange an opportunity for your voice to be heard. The world is a banquet to which you have been invited to be the keynote speaker. And with
Jesus Christ as your agent and His Spirit your speechwriter, the content
of your message will be exactly what people need to hear.

Don't look now—but *you're on!*

Signs of Life

Life Sign: Opportunities to share Christ are divine
appointments.

Life Verse: *Sanctify the Lord God in your hearts, and always be
ready to give a defense to everyone who asks you a reason for the
hope that is in you, with meekness and fear.*

—1 Peter 3:15

Life in Action: How can I be more proactive about seizing
opportunities to share the Gospel with others?

Day 11

Tongue-Tied

The Lord can use a stammering tongue
better than a silent one.

D r. Wilbur Smith was a renowned professor, researcher, and author whose lectures and books trained a generation of Christian workers. Near the end of his life, Dr. Smith published his memoirs, entitled *Before I Forget,* and he began in the preface of his book by sharing a regret:

> I should, through the years, have been more faithful in witnessing for Christ to many of those whose friendship I have enjoyed. I am afraid there are booksellers and librarians, for example, with whom I have often conversed who are unbelievers, and to whom I have not borne witness of the Gospel. I was told that a few years ago, when a dinner was given in Tokyo in honor of Billy Graham, he found himself seated next to the crown prince of Japan. The first thing Mr. Graham said to him was, "What do you think of Jesus Christ?" I am afraid that for myself I have let many conversations continue without my asking that greatest of all questions.[1]

I'm afraid a lot of us harbor the same regret—and why is that? What's wrong with us? People are perishing every day. They're in danger of the fires of hell. So why are we tongue-tied? Have you ever had a golden opportunity to share a word for Christ with someone, but just couldn't or didn't speak up? Most of us can make conversation with others about the weather, sports, restaurants, and hobbies. Why does the cat get our tongue when it comes to speaking up for Jesus?

Second Kings 7:9 says: "We are not doing right. This day is a day of good news, and we remain silent." Well, I don't want to send you on a guilt trip over this, but I would like to suggest some ways for us to find our voices so we can always be ready to speak a word for the Savior.

ASK GOD SPECIFICALLY TO FILL YOU WITH HIS HOLY SPIRIT

Do you remember how tongue-tied Peter was on the night Jesus was betrayed? Despite multiple opportunities to speak up for Christ that evening, Peter found his voice failing him except for curses and denials. But in sharp contrast, on the Day of Pentecost, Peter was filled with the Holy Spirit, and he spoke the Word with boldness. Even when he was threatened with punishment, Peter said that he could not help but share the things he had seen and heard.

If you know Jesus Christ as your Lord and Savior, you already have the Holy Spirit living within you. Ask God to fill you to overflowing and to empower and control you by His Spirit. Ephesians 5:18–19 commands, "Be constantly controlled by the Spirit, speaking to one another in psalms and hymns and spiritual songs, singing and making melody in your hearts to the Lord."[2]

DEVELOP A BURDEN

Perhaps we would be bolder if we could imagine a label—For Whom Christ Died—across the forehead of those who cross our path daily. If we develop a burden for the lost by seeing them with that label, perhaps it will be easier for us to respond in love, and share with them about Christ.

What if we saw those words written across the foreheads of our loved ones, our work associates, our schoolmates, our bosses, our customers, and even the strangers we meet in the subway or while waiting in the doctor's office? Jesus hung on Calvary's cross for each and every human being, so shouldn't we care deeply about the people who are not yet aware of that truth? The world is facing the judgment of a holy God, and we are living on the edge of history, perhaps at the terminal point of time. How, then, can we go for days without sharing Christ with hell-bound, dying souls who cross our path every day?

Ask God to give you this kind of heart for the lost. Ask Him to help you see on the foreheads of those around you "For Whom Christ Died." Say with the apostle Paul, "For the love of Christ compels us" (2 Corinthians 5:14).

MEMORIZE SOME BIBLE VERSES

Another way to unloose your tongue is to memorize some Bible verses. A story Lorne Sanny, past president of the Navigators, tells illustrates the power of God's Word when we hide it in our hearts.

Some missionaries in India were unable to get the national Christians to share the Gospel. They tried everything, but these believers seemed completely tongue-tied. Then someone suggested, "Have you ever tried getting them to memorize Scripture?"

"No," they answered, "we haven't."

"Would you try?" suggested the visitor.

This they agreed to do; and a few weeks later, the Christians gathered for a testimony service. The young believers rose, one after another, quoting verses of Scripture they had recently committed to memory. They had also begun sharing these verses with people outside church. In fact, it seemed that just as they memorized a particular verse, occasions arose for sharing it with unsaved friends. By having Scripture written on the tablet of their hearts, these Indian Christians had something to say. They had lived out the truth of Psalm 119:42, the verse that says, "So shall I have an answer for him who reproaches me, for I trust in Your word."[3]

Start by memorizing John 3:16. Then tackle the "Romans Road" (Romans 3:23, 6:23, 5:8, and 10:9–10, 13). Next add Ephesians 2:8–9 and Acts 16:31 to your repertoire. These are verses that all great soul-winners have inscribed in their hearts and etched in their memories.

Another benefit to memorizing Bible verses is the cleansing effect they will have on your heart. I know that some Christians don't share their faith because they're ashamed of their lives; they don't want others to know they are Christians because those people will see how hypocritical they are. These believers are right: an impure life doesn't have any evangelistic power. Scripture meditation, however, is a way of washing your mind with the Word of God, and as you do so, you'll notice a greater desire to walk more closely with Christ and to share more freely the truth about Him. . . .

I recently read about a Christian in Norway who felt he should travel to Ingøy, a small island sixty kilometers west of North Cape, the northernmost mainland port in the world. This man felt God calling him to give copies of the New Testament to schoolchildren there. Upon investigating, he learned that only three children attended school on this remote island and that the trip would be rigorous.

The sense of God's call persisted, however, so this man drove several hours over the mountains and then boarded a launch to the island. He gave little red New Testaments to the children and was invited to have coffee and sandwiches with their teacher. Suddenly there was a knock on the door, and one of the schoolboys ran in with tears.

"I just want to say thank you for coming," said the boy. "I have been thinking about Jesus the past few days, and when I saw you coming all this way just to give the three of us a New Testament, I thought, 'Jesus, You sent him here.'"

The man was able to share the Gospel, and both the boy and the teacher confessed Christ as their Savior. Going home in the open boat with the rain and wind pouring in, the man rejoiced that two souls had been saved.[4]

❧

If you've been a tongue-tied saint, ask God to loosen your tongue and give you boldness to share Christ. Don't be afraid of messing up. The Lord can use a stammering tongue better than a silent one. So speak up whenever the Spirit nudges and share the Word in season, out of season, every season. The Lord will surely bless your witness with life-changing results.

This is the day of Good Tidings! How can we be tongue-tied?

SIGNS of Life

Life Sign: The most important thing I can say is "Jesus loves you."

Life Verse: *Have I not commanded you? Be strong and of good courage; do not be afraid, nor be dismayed, for the LORD your God is with you wherever you go.*

—Joshua 1:9

Life in Action: What keeps me from witnessing to others? What practical steps can I take to overcome these obstacles?

The "Other" Mentality

*Changing your focus will soon result
in a change in you.*

Being in the dark one night, you open the drawer and pull out your little two-cell flashlight. Besides the click of the switch interrupting the midnight silence, nothing changes. Being astute, you quickly discern that the batteries are dead. Being prepared and having fresh batteries, you screw off the cap and try to shake out the old ones. Being observant, you notice nothing in your hand except some crusty brown chips of . . . something. Being irritated, you whack the flashlight on the counter a few times until a crusty, acidic two-battery mess falls out. Being forgetful, you realize that you haven't used this flashlight in a year or more; the batteries have died and started corroding through lack of use.

Has that ever happened to you? Batteries work better when they are regularly used, fully exhausted, and then completely recharged. Consider cordless phones. Some manufacturers say it's best to take the phone off the charger in the morning, allow it to use up its battery power during the day, and then recharge it at night. The battery life is extended through this kind of consistent, exhaustive use followed by regular recharging. In fact, a sure way to allow a battery to deteriorate is to never use it at all.

Too many Christians are like batteries that never get used. These believers stay fully charged all the time: they're in church and Bible studies several times a week, they listen to Christian music, they read the latest Christian bestsellers. The problem is, their batteries never get drained in service to others. They never dispense any of that power they're storing up.

I have witnessed many such Christians over the years who have grown lethargic, apathetic, demoralized, or powerless. They remind me of high-tech batteries that were charged up, put in a drawer, and never used. Without knowing it, these Christians have conformed to the world's standard of focusing primarily on self instead of others; these Christians need the "other" mentality.

As usual, this biblical message to love others is poles apart from what the world preaches. Instead of focusing on self, we are to focus on serving others. Let me say emphatically at the outset, though, that the call to serve *doesn't mean we don't set aside resources and time to take care of our own needs.* Just as Jesus periodically withdrew from serving the crowds to rest and recuperate, so we need our own times of R&R as well. Just as a battery that never serves will soon wear out, so will one that is never recharged.

The standard of service we are to look to is the Lord Jesus Christ Himself. He even defined His purpose in coming to earth in terms of service: "The Son of Man did not come to be served, but to serve, and to give His life a ransom for many" (Matthew 20:28). We learn about service to others when we read the "one another" passages in the New Testament epistles (for instance, Romans 12:10, 16; Galatians 5:13; Ephesians 4:32). These verses describe how we are to spend ourselves in service to one another. The immediate concern that some individual Christians have about investing themselves in the lives of others is relieved when we remember this: if all Christians are serving one another, then every Christian's needs will be met. Servants in the body of Christ will be served by others even as they serve.

And as we serve—as we demonstrate the "other" mentality—two things happen to us.

OUR FOCUS CHANGES

Let's face it. We have to make a conscious choice to focus on serving others. Our sinful human nature, utterly self-centered in its orientation, naturally puts self first. Our culture, which is a corporate expression of natural (fallen) human nature (except where that expression is mediated by the presence of the Holy Spirit through the church body), further encourages us to think of ourselves. To the degree that we, as Christians, focus on ourselves, we cooperate more with the culture than with Christ, thereby denying the Holy Spirit the opportunity to manifest Christ in the world.

A change in this natural focus requires choice. If we are to be obedient to the Scriptures and serve one another, we have to buck the trend, go against the grain, and battle uphill to change our focus. How do you think Jesus Himself arrived on Planet Earth? It was certainly no act of happenstance. Philippians 2 tells us how it happened—and note the key verbs:

> Christ Jesus, who, being in the form of God, *did not consider it robbery* to be equal with God, but *made Himself* of no reputation, *taking the form* of a bondservant, and *coming* in the likeness of men. And being found in appearance as a man, He *humbled Himself* and *became obedient* to the point of death, even the death of the cross (Philippians 2:5–8, emphasis added).

Jesus considered, made, took, came, humbled Himself, and obeyed. Now if those aren't verbs reflecting conscious choice, I don't know what would be! Jesus chose to change His focus from heaven to earth in order to serve us.

In light of that truth, the most important part of this passage for us is the call to "let this mind be in you which was also in Christ Jesus" (Philippians 2:5). That is, we are to change our focus just as Christ Himself did. We are to consider, make, take, go, humble ourselves, and obey. We are to change our focus from self to others.

CHANGING OUR FOCUS CHANGES US

As with many issues pertaining to the kingdom of God, serving others introduces something of a paradox. You see, the strength, attitude, desire, and skills we think we lack and think we need before we will be able to serve are often only acquired in the act of serving! This paradox is also found in the principle of sowing and reaping (Galatians 6:7). Do we eat our last handful of grain because it's all we have, or do we sow it into the field in order to reap a bountiful harvest in the future? In God's kingdom, we get what we need by giving away what we think we need to hold on to. Just as one kernel of corn can produce a corn stalk with hundreds of new kernels on multiple ears, so one single act of service to another person can pay back bountiful blessings in the life of the one who serves.

Let me make this point more personal now. Have you ever said to yourself, "I'm not qualified to teach Sunday school," "I'm too discouraged to attend my small-group meeting," "I'm too stressed to prepare a meal for my sick neighbor," or "I'm tired of always giving and never getting anything in return"? If those thoughts echo in your own mind, don't worry. My intent is not to make you feel guilty. Similar thoughts have found their way into my thinking at times too. But I have learned over the years that the way to acquire skills, experience lifted spirits, find renewed energy, and ultimately be built up by others is . . . to serve.

Times of reluctant service have taught me that when we do things we are not naturally inclined to do, we come away changed by the experience—and that is never truer than when we serve. Why? Because God has established a timeless, unchanging relationship between being a blessing and receiving a blessing: "All of you should be of one mind. Sympathize each other. Love each other as brothers and sisters. Be tenderhearted, and keep a humble attitude. Don't repay evil for evil. Don't retaliate with insults when people insult you. Instead, *pay them back with a blessing. That is what God has called you to do, and he will bless you for it*" (1 Peter 3:8–9, NLT, emphasis added).

Are you in need of a blessing from God? The surest way to receive it is to be a blessing to others. And the most direct way to be a blessing to others is in the same way Jesus Christ was—and is—a blessing to us: through service. There are countless ways to serve—and don't overlook the little ways. Give a hug, send a card, take a meal for a friend or someone in need of a friend. Step out in a challenging new role of service to the body of Christ. Or take Christ into the public square through service in your community.

Since the "other" mentality can't help but create an "other" attitude in you, changing your focus will soon result in a change in you. Be a blessing and be blessed—what could be simpler?

signs of Life

Life Sign: The needs of others are as important as my own.

Life Verse: *Let each of you look out not only for his own interests, but also for the interests of others.*
—Philippians 2:4

Life in Action: What steps can I take to change my focus from self to others? Who around me needs a blessing from my hands?

Day 13

Attention to Decals

If you were a walking advertisement for the Lord,
what would people learn about Him?

When Sam Bass was seven years old, he'd take his shiny new Hot Wheels from their boxes, tear off their wheels, and repaint the bodies. When his mom complained and asked him why he was doing it, he'd say, "Mom, I want them to look the way I want them to look."

Sam still feels that way. As NASCAR's preeminent artist, he has designed over 350 paint schemes for drivers like Bobby Allison, Dale Earnhardt, and Jeff Gordon. He views his job as that of an artist. "These cars are really 200-mph paintings," he says.[1]

Others have called the cars 200-mph billboards. When a company sponsors a NASCAR vehicle, it's investing between $15 and $20 million; and in return, it expects the race car to effectively advertise its brand. Marketers know that a TV camera will only stay on their car for a few seconds, so the color of the paint, the clarity of the logo, and the placement of the words or image—all this is determined with scientific care to insure the sponsor's name can be quickly and clearly seen.

These main sponsors, however, are facing some competition for advertising space because smaller sponsors are crowding into the picture, and cars are being plastered with a bumper-to-bumper assortment of smaller decals, each representing a sponsoring company's investment. And the financial investment is sizable—hood and rear quarter placement is running in the neighborhood of twenty million dollars. Decal placement on the smaller, lower rear quarter panel can run upwards of half a million dollars. It's arguably the most expensive advertising space in the world.[2]

Now, let's imagine something. If God's blessings on your life were emblazoned on you like decals, what would people see? What would they read? Since you are a walking advertisement for the Lord, here are some suggestions for how to decal your life.

DECAL #1: "DESIGNED BY GOD"

Your life—your body and your spirit—were personally designed by the ultimate Craftsman/Creator, the God of the universe. He has made you perfectly fitted for what He intends you to be and to do. He made you by His power, and He redeemed you by His blood. He gave you the skills, abilities, characteristics, and traits that you need to fulfill His plan for your life.

Keep that truth in mind as I ask you a question. What would you call a car that didn't have doors or windows, a backseat or a passenger seat, brake lights or headlights, a stereo or speakers, air conditioning or heating, automatic transmission or anti-lock brakes, cruise control, air bags, door locks, a glove compartment, or a horn? You'd call it a race car. As you may already know, NASCAR vehicles have none of those things. (In fact, they don't even have a key ignition. Drivers just flip a switch to get the car going.) These vehicles are stripped down for racing; they're uniquely designed for the role for which they're intended.

Now you may long for certain qualities you don't have. Perhaps you'd love to have a great singing voice, an extroverted personality, or a

71

more beautiful face. Perhaps you'd like to be a dynamic evangelist who could preach to millions. But the Bible says we are fearfully and wonderfully made and that each of us has the qualities of body and soul that best correspond with God's purpose (Psalm 139:14–16). Jesus Himself said, "A body You have prepared for Me" (Hebrews 10:5). . . .

❧

When she was a little girl, Amy Carmichael earnestly prayed that God would turn her brown eyes into blue ones, for she longed for blue eyes. Later in life, she came to understand why brown eyes were important for her. In rescuing girls from Hindu slavery, Amy often had to cover herself with a scarf that revealed only her eyes. Blue eyes would have betrayed her identity in brown-eyed India.[3]

So learn to thank God for the body and personality He has given you, for no one else is exactly like you—and for God's good reasons!

DECAL #2: "FUELED BY LOVE"

The Lord wants to use you as His unique creation to change the world, but that assignment requires a special high-performance fuel called love. Paul warned that we should preach Christ not out of selfish ambition, but out of love, speaking the truth with the spiritual love that the Holy Spirit pours into our hearts (Philippians 2:3; Ephesians 4:15; Romans 5:5). He said, "The love of Christ compels us" (2 Corinthians 5:14). Read about how this love became real to one child of God . . .

In his autobiography *Servant on the Edge of History,* missionary Sam James writes of a time when he was living in Thu Duc, a village about twelve kilometers north of Saigon. One morning he awakened to find his home had been robbed during the night. Shortly afterward, his workplace was also robbed. He reported it to the police, but he soon realized they were in on the robberies—and he was warned to keep quiet for his family's safety. Sam became so furious that he felt nothing but utter rage toward the very people whom he was seeking to win to Christ.

One day a taxi driver asked him, "You have been in Vietnam a long time, haven't you?" Sam had been in the country for about ten years. "Then," said the driver, "you must like the Vietnamese people."

"Oh yes," said Sam hypocritically, "I love the Vietnamese people!"

That evening, he went to bed, but he couldn't sleep. In the wee hours, he got out of bed, knelt by the sofa, and poured out his heart to God through the rest of the night. The Lord seemed to say to him, "My son, you are not in Vietnam because you love the Vietnamese people. You are here because I love them. I want to love them through you."

Sam later said that was the night he really became a missionary.[4]

Like Sam, you and I can't manufacture our own fuel within us. We have to learn to let the Lord fill our tanks with His own, blood-red, high-octane formula of love. He wants to love others through us. Through you.

Decal #3: "DGS—Divine Guidance System"

Can you proudly wear a decal advertising God's DGS, His Divine Guidance System? Now NASCAR vehicles don't have navigational systems because they only go around in short circles where there's little chance of getting lost. After all, Darlington is shaped like an egg and only 1.366 miles long. Daytona is a triangularly shaped oval of 2.5 miles. Watkins Glen is a little more complicated with eleven turns, but the distance is only 2.45 miles—and the traffic all travels one way![5]

Many passenger cars today, however, are outfitted with Global Positioning Systems (GPS) that use satellites to help drivers navigate their trips. Sometimes as Christians we feel like we're going around in circles, but we need to remind ourselves that we're actually moving along an appointed way and that we have a constantly available DGS—a Divine Guidance System—to help navigate every inch of the trip.

The owner's manual for this tool says simply, "Trust in the LORD with all your heart, and lean not on your own understanding; in all your ways acknowledge Him, and He shall direct your paths" (Proverbs 3:5–6).

Through all my years of ministry, I've never known God's DGS to fail. There have been times when *I* was the one who failed—who failed to trust Him with all my heart, who failed to lean not on my own understanding, who failed to acknowledge Him in all my ways. But when I've faithfully fulfilled those conditions, the Lord has always been faithful to honor His promise.

I can easily echo Dr. A. T. Pierson, who once said, "To go *as* I am led, to go *when* I am led, to go *where* I am led—that has been for twenty years the one prayer of my life."[6] That's a good prayer for me to recommend to you.

DECAL #4: "FAITH-INSTALLED SHOCK ABSORBERS"

Even with God's guidance, we'll encounter rough spots on the road. Every character in the Bible, even the holiest, had a bumpy trip. Read Hebrews 11 and see how some of God's greatest heroes encountered brutal, potholed terrain. But the key phrase in the chapter is "by faith . . . by faith . . . by faith . . . by faith . . . ."

As you drive the custom-designed vehicle God has made for you, as you're fueled by His love and guided by His wisdom, you'll nevertheless encounter bends and bumps and potholes. It won't be an easy trip. But remember—your shock absorbers are installed by faith. Your ability to trust God with life's disappointments and disasters is the tool that absorbs and dissipates life's hardest blows, leaving you with a joy in your heart and with steadiness in your step that the world can't give—or take away.

Body by Design
High-Performance Love
Divine Navigation
Faith-Installed Shock Absorbers

Are these decals evident in your life? Are you paying attention to what your decals advertise about whose you are and how you are to live your life?

siGNs of Life

Life Sign: I am a walking, living advertisement for the Lord.

Life Verse: *I have been crucified with Christ; it is no longer I who live, but Christ lives in me; and the life which I now live in the flesh I live by faith in the Son of God, who loved me and gave Himself for me.*

—Galatians 2:20

Life in Action: What fuels me? What can I do to ensure that my power comes from God and not from another source?

Day 14

Physical Evidence

*Evidence always trumps personal impressions when
it comes to establishing a solid verdict.*

In the last few years, the debate over capital punishment has taken a
new twist. Many people who support capital punishment are calling
for a moratorium on carrying out death sentences. The reason is the
use of a new type of physical evidence, the use of DNA.

Using DNA—an individual's genetic "cell-print"—to acquit or convict the accused is history's biggest breakthrough in forensic science. All
over the world, many criminals assigned the death penalty have been
found innocent on the basis of DNA analysis that wasn't available at the
time of their conviction. Searching back through evidence decades old,
investigators find a hair, a saliva sample, or a bit of skin tissue, slivers of
evidence but enough from which to extract some DNA. In some cases,
convictions are being upheld. But, in unsettling numbers, convictions
are being overturned and prisoners set free.

DNA is perhaps the most powerful form of physical evidence available to crime-scene investigators. Why? Because of its permanence.
DNA is not a memory or an opinion, an odor or a color. It is hard,

physical evidence that does not change over time. DNA identified the body of Nazi executioner Josef Mengele; the Child Recovery and Identification System uses DNA records to unite parents with missing children; and probate courts are using DNA evidence to settle conflicting claims regarding inheritances. DNA evidence—and, as a rule, physical evidence of any kind—is almost impossible to refute.[1]

What is physical evidence? In his standard text on the subject, *Criminalistics* author Richard Saferstein defines physical evidence as "any and all objects that can establish that a crime has been committed or can provide a link between a crime and its victim or a crime and its perpetrator."[2] In short, physical evidence is anything and everything that tells investigators about a crime. The goal of the crime-scene investigator is to build a bridge from the crime to the criminal, to connect a person with an act. And physical evidence provides the foundation stones for the bridge. Forensic scientist Paul L. Kirk has said, "[Physical evidence] does not forget. It is not confused by the excitement of the moment. It is not absent [when] human witnesses are; it is factual evidence. Physical evidence cannot be wrong, it cannot perjure itself . . . only its interpretation can err."[3]

Despite such endorsements of DNA evidence, prosecutors and attorneys face an interesting problem when trying to prove a crime: even though physical evidence is best, juries almost always value eyewitness testimony. Because jurists value their own memories, they feel an eyewitness couldn't possibly be wrong. But memories are ever-changing because they can be influenced by many things: feelings, opinions, experiences, moods, and prejudices, to name a few. But—as I mentioned earlier—physical evidence does not lie or change.

As Christians, we can be guilty of letting personal mental impressions of our spiritual life take precedence over physical evidence. We may, for instance, too often think more highly of ourselves than we ought to think, but physical evidence will help us think soberly about how we are truly doing in our Christian walk (Romans 12:3). For instance, if we spend two minutes in prayer, later in the day we are convinced it was ten. If we read a few verses of Scripture, we describe it as having studied a chapter. When we say we attend church every Sunday, over the course of a year it may be three weeks out of four. And instead of being 10 percent, our giving may average 3 or 4 percent over time.

Are these statements of ours blatant lies and exaggerations? They could be, but more often they are just subtle tricks our memory plays on us. We are eyewitnesses to our own spiritual life, yet we often fail to perceive it as it really is. What we need is some hard, physical evidence—the kind that consistently tells the truth—in order to get an accurate picture of our spiritual life.

Now physical evidence at a crime scene consists of things like firearms and gunshot residues, footprints, fingerprints, hair and fibers, tool marks and other impressions, chemical traces, blood, and body tissues or fluids. But what physical evidence marks us as guilty of being a Christian? I want to discuss four kinds of physical evidence that can easily be observed by anyone—including, hopefully, ourselves. The categories are who you are, what you do, where you go, and whom you associate with. We Christians should leave behind us evidence of these four types, evidence that ultimately identifies us as followers of Christ.

1. WHO YOU ARE

By "who you are" I mean the overall picture of yourself that you present to the world. When people first meet you, what do they think?

By reading the four Gospel accounts in the New Testament, we come away with the impression that Jesus was a very remarkable Person. Crowds followed Him everywhere. People listened attentively to His every word. Scholars were either amazed or silenced by the wisdom of His teaching. Jesus wasn't physically different from us—He didn't look like a king (Isaiah 53:2)—but He was different spiritually. People may not stand amazed at us when we pass them on the street, but when they get to know us, what do they think?

Through the centuries many people have been won to Christ because they came in contact with a person about whom they said, "There's something different about that person, and I want in my own life whatever he has."

2. WHAT YOU DO

One of the most compelling teachings of Jesus Christ is that people are known by the fruits of their life (Matthew 7:16–20; 12:33). Good trees bear good fruit, and bad trees bear bad fruit. Similarly, fruit trees bear fruit, but thornbushes do not.

If the apostle Paul were to examine our life expecting to find the fruit of the Holy Spirit (Galatians 5:22–23), but instead found only the works of the flesh (Galatians 5:19–21), he would go with the physical evidence. We can say all we want that we are a Christian, but if no fruit of the Spirit—no tangible evidence—is present, then we stand condemned. Our behavior, words, attitudes, habits, and practices constitute a train of evidence about our spiritual life.

3. WHERE YOU GO

The sons of Korah, who made up the temple choir in Israel, are credited with these telling words: "For a day in Your courts is better than a thousand. I would rather be a doorkeeper in the house of my God than dwell in the tents of wickedness" (Psalm 84:10). When I meet Christians who consider going to church or gathering with other believers for Bible study and fellowship not as exciting as recreational activities with non-Christians, I wonder what that evidence reveals about their soul.

Because our culture has made entertainment an idol, Christians justify their absence from the house of God by saying they're bored. Not only does that evidence reveal what our soul is most nourished by (entertainment instead of worship), it also reveals a profound misunderstanding of the purpose of the body of Christ and each believer's place in it. When the church of Jesus Christ gathers, not to be in attendance is to leave suspicious physical evidence about our faith—or lack thereof (Hebrews 10:24–25).

4. WHOM YOU ASSOCIATE WITH

Darkness and light cannot coexist since darkness, by definition, is the absence of light. Jesus and the apostle John talked about the incompatibility of spiritual darkness and spiritual light (John 3:19; 8:12 and 1 John 1:5; 2:9, respectively), and Paul expanded on the differences between believers and unbelievers (2 Corinthians 6:14–18). So when professing Christians never seem to find themselves hanging out with other Christians—for recreation, service, fellowship, study, or worship—they are creating telling evidence of their preferences. We wonder why they are choosing darkness over light.

Detective Tom Hill, a thirty-year veteran of the Fort Lauderdale Police Department, summarizes the point of this chapter: "You just can't argue with physical evidence—you can't."[4] That's a tough statement. It is equally tough in the world of CSI—Christian Scene Investigation: the evidence tells the truth.

So who are you? What do you do? Where do you go? And who are your friends? Take a fresh look at the physical evidence of your spiritual life. Remember, evidence always trumps personal impressions when it comes to establishing a solid verdict.

SIGNS of Life

Life Sign: Every day I create incriminating evidence to prove that I am a follower of Christ.

Life Verse: *The good works of some are clearly evident, and those that are otherwise cannot be hidden.*
—1 Timothy 5:25

Life in Action: What can I do to improve my chances of being convicted of being a Christian?

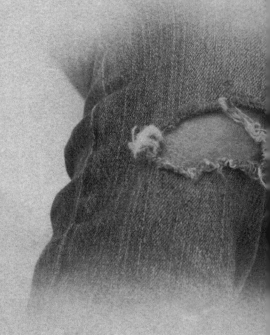

Worn-Out Knees
Living a
yielded
Life

Worn-Out Knees

*One of the reasons we're so worn out from life
is that our knees aren't!*

On February 26, 1829, a Jewish boy named Loeb Strauss was born in a cottage in the Bavarian village of Buttenheim. As a young man, Loeb changed his name to Levi and wound up in California where he opened a textile company in San Francisco. One day a gold miner walked into Levi's shop and assailed the young merchant.

"Look at these," said the miner, pointing to his pants. "I bought 'em six months ago, and now they're full of holes!"

When Levi asked why, the miner explained, "We work on our knees most of the time."

"What you need is some really strong material," replied Levi. "We have some canvas. It's used to make tents. If we make your trousers out of canvas, I'm sure they won't get holes."

A tailor was called, and presently the miner had a set of trousers— and the rest is history. Soon miners across the West were wearing Levi Strauss's jeans.[1]

Well, it seems to me that we Christians should have the same problem that plagued that miner—pants with worn-out knees—for we ought to do most of our kingdom work on our knees. As British hymnist William Cowper wrote, "Satan trembles when he sees the weakest saint upon his knees."[2]

WORN KNEES MEAN REVERENCE

Of course we don't *have* to kneel to pray. The Bible describes many postures of prayer. Jesus, for instance, stood and prayed with His eyes lifted to heaven. In Gethsemane He fell prostrate. In 1 Chronicles 17:16, David sat before the Lord in prayer. Sometimes Bible heroes prayed while lying on their beds or, as the disciples did with Jesus, while walking along the road.

No specific posture is required for effective prayer, but each possible posture conveys a different prayer attitude. Standing implies a certain boldness. Walking conveys a sense of fellowship. Sitting before the Lord implies a down-to-earth businesslike approach. And kneeling represents submission, earnestness, and yieldedness.

In her book *Adventures in Prayer,* Catherine Marshall wrote that, as a teenager, she dreamed of going to college, but the mountain church where her father served was struggling during the Great Depression. Catherine applied to Agnes Scott College in Georgia, but was short of the needed funds.

> One evening Mother found me lying across my bed, face down, sobbing. She sat down beside me. "You and I are going to pray about this," she said quietly. We went into the guest room and knelt beside the old-fashioned, golden oak bed, the one that Mother and Father had bought for their first home. "I know it's right for you to go to college," Mother said. "I believe God planted this dream in you; let's ask Him to tell us how to bring it to reality."[3]

There, side by side, the two knelt in the presence of the Lord. Even decades later Catherine could still recall the quiet confidence and fresh determination that flowed into her as she and her mother prayed. A short time later, her mother received an offer from the government to write a history of their county, and payment was enough to provide the necessary funds for college.

Yes, our victories in life are gained on our knees. When we bow before Almighty God, we acknowledge Him as our "Maker, Defender, Redeemer, and Friend." As we yield ourselves, our plans, and our problems to Him, He intervenes for His glory and our good.

WORN KNEES MEAN OBEDIENCE

Worn knees also imply obedience. . . .

One of the strangest incidents in the life of King David involved moving the ark of the covenant from the village of Kirjath Jearim to its new home in Jerusalem. According to 1 Chronicles 13, David anticipated the day with excitement, for "the thing was right in the eyes of all the people" (verse 4). The nation gathered with jubilation. Having placed the ark in a new cart, the drivers started off, while David and all Israel played music before God "with all their might, with singing, on harps, on stringed instruments, on tambourines, on cymbals, and with trumpets" (verse 8).

The music stopped abruptly, however, when the oxen stumbled, the cart tottered, and a man named Uzza reached out his hand to steady the ark. God instantly struck him dead, "and he died there before God" (verse 10). The ark of the covenant was shuttled to a nearby house and there it stayed, for now everyone was afraid to move it.

It wasn't until afterward that David realized what had gone wrong. First, David had failed to arrange for the ark to be transported as prescribed by Mosaic Law. It should not have been carried in a wagon, but on poles borne by Levitical priests. Second, David had failed to pray and inquire of the Lord about how to go about it. "We did not consult Him," David confessed in 1 Chronicles 15:13.

Sometimes we make the same mistake. We should be on our knees before accepting a job offer, making a purchase, choosing a new church, or making a decision of any consequence. People are quietly watching, and they know when we're living in prayerful obedience or when, on the other hand, we act without consulting Almighty God, our heavenly Father.

WORN KNEES MEAN DEPENDENCE

It's also obvious to others when our bent knees draw down blessings from above. Case in point.

Elmer Towns shared that he and his wife made it through college by faith, praying together and trusting God to meet their needs. Elmer earned a dollar an hour driving a school bus, but his income barely met their needs.

"One evening," he wrote, "the only thing in the kitchen cabinet was a can of tuna, so my wife served a tuna casserole. As we clasped hands to thank God for the food, I prayed, 'God, You know we are broke. You know it's two days until payday. You know we are willing to fast until we get money, but we ask You to please take care of our needs.'"

Just as they finished, the laundryman came to the door. Ruth greeted him, telling him they had nothing to send to the laundry, for they couldn't afford to have anything cleaned.

The man quickly explained that he hadn't come to pick up but to deliver. "A few months ago," he said, "your landlord asked me to pass along twenty dollars to you to pay for thawing the pipes for him. I had forgotten about it until today."

The timing was no coincidence. Elmer and Ruth earnestly believed that their prayer had reminded the laundryman that he had money for them.[4] . . .

❧

If you want to pull down blessings from above and impact the world around you, you have to be surrendered to God's will, approaching life on your knees, bowing in humble reverence, obedience, and dependence on Him. Again, one of the reasons we're so worn out from life is that our knees aren't!

- Hudson Taylor challenged, "You must move forward on your knees," as Jonathan and Rosalind Goforth began their pioneer ministry in China—the hallmark of their careers.[5]

- Dr. Martyn Lloyd-Jones wrote in his studies on the Sermon on the Mount: "Prayer is beyond any question the highest activity of the human soul. Man is at his greatest and highest when, upon his knees, he comes face to face with God."[6]

- Charles Haddon Spurgeon wrote, "If I cannot rise upon the knees of my body because I am so weak, my prayers from my bed shall be on *their* knees, my heart shall be on its knees, and pray as acceptably as aforetime."[7]

- The late Gypsy Smith told of the conversion of his Uncle Rodney. Among gypsies, it was not considered proper for children to address their elders unless spoken to, so young Gypsy prayed and waited for an opportunity. One day the boy's uncle took note of Gypsy's worn trousers.

  "Laddie," said Uncle Rodney, "how do you account for the fact that the knees of your trousers have worn nearly through, while the rest of the suit is almost like new?"

  The boy answered, "I have worn the knees through praying for you, Uncle Rodney." Then he added with tears, "I want so much to have God make you a Christian!"

  Uncle Rodney put his arm around Gypsy in a fatherly embrace, and a few moments later, he fell on his knees, confessing Christ as his Savior.[8]

❧

It's great to have good habits, high hopes, bold strategies, deep pockets, and passionate zeal. But nothing can replace humble hearts, bent knees, and worn-out pants.

Do your knees show signs of life? Like a California miner, let's each declare, "I do most of my work on my knees."

SIGNS of Life

Life Sign: Hearing the Lord's direction begins with prayer.

Life Verse: *Praying always with all prayer and supplication in the Spirit, being watchful to this end with all perseverance and supplication for all the saints.*

—Ephesians 6:18

Life in Action: What evidence of a yielded life, if any, do my knees bear? What can I do to guard my time of prayer each day?

Day 16

The Heavenly Frequency

Genuine prayer—offered with open hands—is saying,
"Your will be done."

John MacVane was a reporter for the National Broadcasting Company during World War II, and his broadcasts from the battle-front kept Americans riveted to their radios.

One day in November 1942, while he was in North Africa, he was told to prepare the *Army Hour* broadcast from Algiers for the following Sunday. It was a tremendous undertaking. MacVane had to interview leaders, obtain messages from chief commanders, write scripts, and then have them approved by war censors. Then there was the music. MacVane found some American GIs who could play jazz, and he started them practicing.

Finally the night of the broadcast came, and a cast of fifty assembled in a makeshift studio, all of them excited about beaming a wartime broadcast to the people of America. Precisely at 8:30 PM, the orchestra began playing. MacVane leaned into the microphone and said in his most sober voice, "This is Algiers, the heart of North Africa."

During interviews with MacVane, soldiers and pilots for the RAF and the US Air Force told their dramatic stories. The show ended with the band playing America's national anthem. It was a great program, and afterward all the participants were ecstatic. They had just given a riveting account from the warfront—and it had been heard live by forty million people back home.

Several days later, however, MacVane received a telegram asking what had happened to the expected broadcast. Nobody had heard it. Apparently it had gone out on the wrong frequency and was never picked up by engineers in New York. Nobody at home heard so much as a single word. MacVane's program had disappeared into thin air.[1]

Let me ask you a question: Can the same thing happen to prayer?

Prayer is the most powerful kind of broadcast the world has ever known. It wings its way from our lips and hearts through the heavens to the very Throne Room of God. The Lord promises to move heaven and earth to answer our prayers. But is it possible to send prayer out on the wrong frequency?

Not if we pray as Jesus did and in His Name. He's the Bible's great Model when it comes to prayer; and as the disciples watched Him pray, they asked Him to teach them how to do it as He did. Being good Jews, they had prayed thousands of times, had heard many lessons about prayer in the synagogue, and had joined in the public prayers at the temple. But when they heard Jesus praying, they saw prayer on a higher frequency; and one said, "Lord, teach us to pray" (Luke 11:1).

Thankfully, the Gospels include many stories and lessons from the prayer life of Jesus, so we ourselves can learn from the Master. In fact, I'd encourage you to read through the Gospels and highlight every reference to prayer. We don't have time for that in this chapter, but let me show you some of the highlights you'll find.

Pray As Jesus Did: To the Heavenly Father

First, we should pray—as Jesus did—to the heavenly Father. Jesus prayed very personally, addressing God as His Father, and He taught us to do the same.

This approach to prayer, though, was radical to the Jewish people of our Lord's day. If you study the prayers of the Old Testament, you'll virtually never find people addressing God as their heavenly Father. He was *Sovereign Lord* or *God* or *Jehovah/Yahweh* or *Lord of Hosts.* On those rare times in the Old Testament when God *is* referred to in fatherhood terms, it's almost always with respect to His authority or discipline. The saints and sages of the Old Testament weren't comfortable calling God their Father: doing so seemed too familiar, presumptuous, and disrespectful.

Then Jesus came, calling God His Father without hesitation or restraint. In His opening message, the Sermon on the Mount, Jesus referred to God in His role of Father more times than we find in all the Old Testament books combined. In John's Gospel alone, Jesus referred to God as His Father 110 times.

What a difference it makes when we pray like this. Yes, we should approach God with reverence, and it's good to address Him as our Lord, God, King, and Master. But Jesus also taught us to pray, "Our Father in heaven." In Luke 11:11–13, He told us that if we, being evil, know how to give good things to our children, how much more will our heavenly Father give blessings to those of us who ask Him.

So when you pray, talk to God as personally as if you were talking to a family member whose authority and wisdom you revere.

Pray As Jesus Did: In Secret

To pray effectively, pray as Jesus did: in secret. He knew the value of being alone with His Father, and He frequently slipped away to deserted places to be alone with God. Mark, for example, gives us a glimpse of how Jesus did it: "Now in the morning, having risen a long while before daylight, He went out and departed to a solitary place; and there He prayed. And Simon and those who were with Him searched for Him. When they found Him, they said to Him, 'Everyone is looking for You'" (Mark 1:35–37).

I don't want you to alarm your family or be reported to the police as a missing person, but when was the last time you dropped out of sight so you could spend time in prayer? Theologian James Stalker suggested that "when Jesus reached a new town, His first thought was which was the shortest road to the mountain just as ordinary travelers inquire where are the most noted sights."[2]

PRAY AS JESUS DID: ALL THE TIME

Jesus spent extended time alone with God in prayer, but He also "pray[ed] without ceasing," as Paul later put it in 1 Thessalonians 5:17. Luke records nine occasions when Jesus prayed: at His baptism, after a day of miracles, before choosing His disciples, before He told His disciples about His coming death, on the Mount of Transfiguration, before teaching the disciples to pray, when the seventy returned, in Gethsemane, and on the cross.

Oswald Sanders made this observation:

> Jesus prayed in the morning at the gateway of the day, and in the evening when the day's work was over. Great crises were preceded by prayer. Great achievements were preceded by prayer. Great achievements were followed by prayer. Great pressure of work was a call to extra prayer. Great sorrows were met by prayer. He died praying.[3]

Missionary Frank Laubach became well known because of his personal efforts to "practice the presence of God." He trained himself to remember how near at hand his God was. He taught himself to consciously pause throughout each hour of the day to remind himself the Lord was with him. He suggested that we, too, during our little pauses throughout the day, learn to go to God for advice on what to do next and to remind ourselves that He is standing there beside us, near at hand, present always, and available to help us.[4]

That's praying without ceasing. It's both a habit to cultivate and a presence to enjoy—just as Jesus Himself did.

PRAY AS JESUS DID: SUBMISSIVELY

Finally, we learn to pray like Jesus when we learn to echo His deepest and most poignant prayer, offered in the Garden of Gethsemane: "Nevertheless, not as I will, but as You will. . . . Your will be done" (Matthew 26:39, 42).

Prayer isn't our way of getting God to go along with our wants and wishes; it's God's way of making our hearts willing to go along with His designs for us. Genuine prayer is offered with open hands, saying, "Father, here is what I want and here is what I think I need; but I defer to Your will, for You know what is best for me. Your will be done."

Some of our greatest blessings come when God says no to our earnest prayers. Remember the time when Abraham prayed that God would make Ishmael his heir and the son of the covenant (Genesis 17:18). The next verse says plainly: "Then God said: 'No. . . .'" Later the Lord gave him Isaac.

Remember, too, that Paul prayed in 2 Corinthians 12 that God would heal his thorn in the flesh? The Lord said no, but He added, "My grace is sufficient for you" (verse 9). We don't always know what's best for us. In effective prayer, though, we defer to the Father's will—submissively, trustingly, and willingly.

❧

So when you pray, get on the heavenly frequency and pray as Jesus did— to the Father, privately, frequently, and submissively. Discover, as Jesus did, the wonder of that . . .

Sweet hour of prayer! sweet hour of prayer!
That calls [you] from a world of care,
And bids [you] at [your] Father's throne
Make all [your] wants and wishes known.[5]

The prayers of a righteous person are powerful and effective.

signs of Life

Life Sign: I am open and listening for God's direction.

Life Verse: *Pray without ceasing.*

—1 Thessalonians 5:17

Life in Action: Write out a prayer of submission to God. Tell Him that you want to be submissive, pliable, and responsive to His will.

Closer to You Than to Me

*Christ has called for unconditional surrender—death
to the flesh—for all who would follow Him.*

French general Monsieur le Marquis Montcalm removed his
plumed hat and bowed low before his opponent, the British
Colonel Munro. The Englishman responded with a stiff nod.
French mortars had been pounding the British in Fort William Henry
for days, and General Montcalm had called a meeting to ask for the surrender of the British. The scene was awash in the pageantry of war—in
the immaculate blue and gold uniforms and flags for the French, the red
and gold for the British, the drummers drumming, the flags snapping,
and hearts pounding. Who would yield to whom?

The French general had the advantage. His scouts had intercepted a
British messenger bound for Fort William Henry, and he read the message to Munro: "We have no men available to send to your rescue. You
are advised to seek terms for your surrender."

The shocked Colonel Munro listened to Montcalm's terms: "None
of your men will see the inside of a prison barge. They are free so long

as they return to England and fight no more on this continent. And the
civilian militia return to their farms."

When Munro asked about their arms, Montcalm replied, "They
may leave the fortress fully armed."

When Munro said, "The honors of war?"

Montcalm said, "Granted."

When Munro asked, "My colors?"

Montcalm said, "Carry them to England to your King with pride."

Such were the terms of the British surrender to the French as por-
trayed in the 1992 movie version of James Fenimore Cooper's *Last of the
Mohicans.* In a day when generals wore powdered wigs and drank from
silver tea services on the field of battle, British Colonel Munro learned
that surrender does not always lead to death. In spiritual terms, there is
both accuracy and inaccuracy in that conclusion.[1]

SURRENDER LEADS TO DEATH

On the one hand, a Christian's surrender to the lordship of Jesus Christ
does in fact mean death. A battle between flesh and Spirit is going on in
every believer, and Christ has called for unconditional surrender—for
death to the flesh—for all who would follow Him.

When we become Christians, we are "crucified with Christ"
(Romans 6:6; Galatians 2:20): our rebellious sin nature is put to
death with Christ who died on the cross as payment for those sins.
While we did not die an actual physical death with Him, the
required price for our sins was paid on our behalf in Christ's substi-
tutionary death; we died positionally. From God's viewpoint, we are
holy, positionally. Yet, Paul points out, in practical terms, "the flesh
lusts against the Spirit, and the Spirit against the flesh; and these are
contrary to one another" (Galatians 5:17). In other words, there are
still times when we don't feel like surrendering, when we refuse to
give up our independence, our individuality, and even our indecen-
cies. But Jesus draws a firm line in the sand: "Whoever does not

bear his cross and come after Me cannot be My disciple" (Luke 14:27).

Whereas General Montcalm offered Colonel Munro four terms of surrender, Jesus offers just one: the cross you died on positionally must be the cross you live on personally each and every day. Not to surrender—not to do so—means never getting close to Jesus Christ, never becoming one of His intimate friends. You may get to heaven, but you'll get there regretting all the times when you insisted on having your way instead of following His and being painfully aware of the opportunities for surrender you passed up and the quality of life in Christ you missed out on.

SURRENDER LEADS TO LIFE

The British colonel was right as well as wrong when he concluded that surrender can lead to life. For the saints of God, surrender leads to an entirely new kind of life. In fact, we are born again to a new and living hope (John 3:3; 1 Peter 1:3). But to experience that life, we have to surrender not just once but every day, if not every moment of every day. The prayer of surrender must be the constant prayer of the believer.

We find numerous examples in Scripture of saints who chose life by surrendering to God.

- Think of Job. Though he was assailed with greater calamities than most of us will ever face, he never rebelled against God. He grew impatient at times, and he even had to have his perspective about God corrected. But in the midst of his trials, a prayer of surrender was frequently on his lips: "'The LORD gave, and the LORD has taken away; blessed be the name of the LORD.' In all this Job did not sin nor charge God with wrong" (Job 1:21–22).

  The truest test of whether we are surrendered to the Lord comes in times of personal defeat. Our pride says, "Rise up and fight!" but the Spirit says, "Surrender and live." Job was wise enough to recognize the source of the two voices—and he lived (Job 42:10–17).

• Consider Joshua. When we first met Joshua, he was an assistant and commander under Moses as the Hebrew slaves were freed from Egypt. He also guarded Moses' tent and defended his position while Moses was on Mt. Sinai with God. And he and Caleb were the only two of the twelve spies who believed that God was faithful enough to give Israel victory over the Canaanites. As a result of Joshua's surrendering himself to God's will, he lived—literally! He survived the thirty-eight years of wandering in the wilderness, and the rest of his generation died.

But it was near the end of Joshua's life that we find him putting into words what it meant to him to surrender to the Lord: "Choose for yourselves this day whom you will serve. . . . But as for me and my house, we will serve the LORD" (Joshua 24:15). While not a prayer, these famous words of Joshua reflect the heart of a man for whom the prayer of surrender must have been a daily discipline. Joshua remained "the servant of the LORD" through his final days (Joshua 24:29).

• Jonah might be the surrendered saint we most readily identify with. Ultimately, he realized it was better to be submitted to God's will, but he was brought to the surrender ceremony kicking and screaming and waving his personal ensign of prideful resistance. He wanted nothing to do with God's terms of surrender: "Go to Nineveh and preach a message of judgment to the Ninevites." *Thank You, no.* Jonah had heard about those bad boys—what they did to ninety-pound weaklings like himself who dared to kick up dust in their city. So Jonah did an about-face and hopped the first ship headed for Spain. You know the story.

From the belly of a great fish, Jonah prayed his prayer of

surrender: "I will sacrifice to You with the voice of thanksgiving; I will pay what I have vowed. Salvation is of the LORD" (Jonah 2:9). Jonah's story reminds us of that old television commercial for Fram oil filters when the mechanic says, "You can pay me now, or you can pay me later." Jonah learned the hard way that it is better to surrender sooner rather than later. When he finally went to Nineveh, God used him mightily.

• Finally, the One for whom the stakes of surrender were the highest was Jesus Himself. Even as a young boy, He sensed the need to be surrendered to the will of His heavenly Father (Luke 2:49). But at the outset of His public ministry He was offered terms of surrender by the devil himself—terms He soundly rejected (Luke 4:1–13). Jesus made it to His last night on earth able to say, "I have finished the work You gave Me to do" (John 17:4 paraphrased). Yet His greatest challenge came just moments after He said those words.

  When Jesus prayed His ultimate prayer of surrender in the Garden of Gethsemane—"Not My will, but Yours, be done" (Luke 22:42)—He set the pattern for surrender for all who would follow Him into the kingdom of heaven. Bottom line, no one who says to God, "I'd rather yield to my will than to Yours" enters the kingdom of heaven. No one enters heaven who says to God, "Not Thy will, but mine be done." The ruler of hell itself earned that position with just such words as those (Isaiah 14:12–14).

❧

If Colonel Munro had stubbornly refused to surrender, he would have died an unnecessary death. Instead, he wisely surrendered, saving not only his own life but the lives of his soldiers as well. For us the stakes are greater than a fort, a battle, or a continent. The stakes are intimacy with Almighty God and eternal rewards for a life of faithful service.

But how do we accept Christ's terms of surrender, His requirement that we live daily on the cross? The only way I know is by beginning each day with a prayer of surrender:

Lord, today I surrender my life to You. I choose to do Your will, not mine. I accept Your terms for my life today, and I choose to live the crucified life which I received positionally through my faith in Christ. I ask You to give me grace to be a surrendered soldier of the Cross today. Amen.

The choice is surrendering now or surrendering later (Philippians 2:9–11). As for me (and my house), we choose to surrender today—and I pray you will too.

Signs of Life

Life Sign: Unconditional surrender to God brings me spiritual victory.

Life Verse: *Then He said to them all, "If anyone desires to come after Me, let him deny himself, and take up his cross daily, and follow Me."*

—Luke 9:23

Life in Action: Can I honestly describe my life as yielded and surrendered to God? Am I more yielded to the opinions of others or my own will than I am to my Lord? What area(s) of my life do I need to give over to God?

Love's Boundaries

*Loving the world destroys our relationship with God,
it denies our faith in Him, and it discounts
our future with Him.*

You've probably seen Andy Warhol's prints of Campbell's soup cans or celebrities like Marilyn Monroe or Elvis Presley. America's best-known pop artist was born in Pittsburgh in 1928, and he moved to New York City in 1949 to pursue a career as an illustrator for magazines and advertisements. He built a reputation as a major figure in the pop art movement and was catapulted to fame in 1968 when a woman entered his studio and shot him. The bullet passed through his left lung, spleen, stomach, liver, esophagus, and right lung. Though Warhol survived the attack, he never fully recovered.

You'd think that such an experience would have turned Warhol's thoughts toward God, but the artist's entire world revolved around the popular culture with its shallowness, fleeting pleasures, and "fifteen minutes of fame," as he famously put it. He once summed himself up like this: "I am a deeply superficial person. . . . If you want to know all about Andy Warhol, just look at the surface of my paintings and films and me, there I am. There's nothing behind it."[1]

Contrast that with the apostle John's perspective of 1 John 2:15–17:

> Do not love the world or the things in the world. If anyone loves the world, the love of the Father is not in him. For all that is in the world—the lust of the flesh, the lust of the eyes, and the pride of life—is not of the Father but is of the world. And the world is passing away, and the lust of it; but he who does the will of God abides forever.

Some people are confused by these verses, for they seem to contradict the apostle's famous John 3:16 statement that begins "for God so loved the world." If God loved the world, shouldn't we also love it? But the word *world* is used three different ways in Scripture. Sometimes it refers to the physical world with its rolling hills and churning oceans. Other times, as in John 3:16, the word is synonymous for the people in the world: God so loved all the people on earth. The third meaning has to do with the depraved culture of the times, the world system that is under Satan's control.

When we read in the Bible, "Do not love this *world,*" the word is being used in this third sense. We are not to love our world system, for it is violently opposed to Christ and all He stands for. "The whole world lies under the sway of the wicked one," says 1 John 5:19. "The world does not know us," say verses in 1 John 3, "because it did not know Him. . . . Do not marvel, my brethren, if the world hates you" (verses 1, 13).

Then, in 1 John 2:15–17, the wise apostle, like a discriminating art critic, explained the composition and perspective of the world canvas, warning Christians of three very real dangers.

THE WORLD'S PERSPECTIVE IS . . . DESIRABLE

First, John cautioned that the world system is desirable. The word *lust* (used in 1 John 2:16) literally means "desire." When we hear the word *lust* today, we usually think of its sexual implications, but this word in the Greek New Testament isn't limited to that meaning. It includes desires of all kinds. You can put the word *desire* in the place of *lust* in this verse: the desires of the flesh, and the desires of the eyes, and the pride of life. Or pleasure, possessions, and popularity.

The moment you give your life to Jesus Christ, you make a powerful enemy. Satan sets his scope on you, you're in his crosshairs, and these are his three rounds of ammunition. He uses this same strategy against everybody. Whatever the devil is doing to you or to me is some variation of this three-point tactic—the lust of the flesh, the lust of the eyes, and the pride of life. We need to learn to recognize his attacks and deflect, if not completely avoid them. . . .

Hikers and gardeners know to be alert for the blossoms of the goldenrod flower—or at least what *appears* to be merely a blossom. Closer inspection reveals a cleverly camouflaged, colorful spider. It spreads itself out, conforming to the color of the host flower, but insects that light on it expecting to find honey are pierced by the spider's strong, crablike legs and injected instead with a poison that drugs and kills them.[2]

That's the way our culture is. Its television shows, movies, magazines, trends, styles, affluence, ladder of success—behind all these things (and others) may be lurking the spider of unhealthy desire, so we must always be cautious. We must learn to be wary of the predatory allure of the world.

THE WORLD'S PERSPECTIVE IS . . . DULLING

The second danger is that the world is dulling. Just as the slow-acting poison of that deadly spider overtakes its victims, the world's pleasures, possessions, and popularity will gradually dull our spiritual responses. A prime biblical example is Demas, a man mentioned three times in Scripture. In Colossians 4:14, Paul wrote, "Luke the beloved physician and Demas greet you." In Philemon 24, Paul again sent greetings from Demas, listing him as a "fellow laborer." But in 2 Timothy, when the apostle Paul is imprisoned and facing execution, we find him writing these sad words: "Be diligent to come to me quickly; for Demas has forsaken me, having loved this present world" (4:9–10).

Demas didn't just wake up one day and have a dramatic spiritual breakdown. Something about the world's influences had been dulling his senses without his realizing how close he was to total spiritual collapse.

In his book *How to Be Born Again,* Billy Graham tells of a man in Australia who went for a haircut. His barber commented about the sore on the man's lip. "Yep," said the man. "My cigarettes have done that."

"Well," said the barber, "it doesn't seem to be healing."

"Oh, it will, it will," replied the man.

But when he came for his next haircut, his lip was split and ugly. The barber expressed alarm, but the man said, "Don't worry about it. I've switched to a cigarette holder. It'll heal soon."

The barber even showed the man pictures of similar cases of skin cancer, but the man shrugged them off.

The third month, the man failed to show up for his regular haircut. When the barber asked about him, he was told, "Oh, didn't you know? He died of cancer two days ago."[3]

Sin is like that: it's a cancer that destroys little by little, sometimes so slowly that we don't realize what's happening to us. Because of the world's desirability, we don't realize how—or how much—it is dulling our spiritual senses. The unsaved person isn't aware of the spiritual dangers that lurk among the desires of the flesh and of the eyes and the pride of life, and sometimes even we Christians are deceived. That's why the Bible warns believers against friendship with the world (James 4:4);

being defiled by the world (James 1:27); loving the world (1 John 2:15); and being conformed to the world (Romans 12:2).

THE WORLD'S PERSPECTIVE IS . . . DEADLY

Finally, the world is deadly to us spiritually. Loving the world destroys our relationship with God, denies our faith in Him, and diminishes our future with Him. The Bible tells us that one day this whole world is going up in a cloud of smoke. Only two things will prove eternal: the Word of God and the people of God. Everything else will pass away. The world and its lusts will fade to nothingness, and only those who do the will of the Father will abide forever.

When I was growing up, we used to sing a spiritual: "This world is not my home; I'm just a-passin' through. My treasures are laid up somewhere beyond the blue." We who follow Jesus are pilgrims and strangers on this earth. There are two worlds, two dimensions, two landscapes—and we Christians have a foot in each one. We're living *in* this world system, but we're not to be *of* it. We're to live by faith in the kingdom of our Lord Jesus, and our citizenship is in heaven with Him.

One more note about the world's system. In case you haven't noticed, the world front-loads its pleasures and back-loads its pain. The Christian life sometimes front-loads the pain, but it always back-loads the pleasure. And I'd definitely rather be moving toward joy than moving away from it, wouldn't you? That's why I've chosen to live my life for the Lord and to walk with Him in fellowship sweet.

To sum it up, the world is fading, not fulfilling. So don't worry about your fifteen minutes of fame. The world and its lusts are passing away, but those who do the will of the Father abide forever.

sign<small>s</small> of Life

Life Sign: My love for God is greater than my affection for anything in this desirable but deadly world.

Life Verse: *But what things were gain to me, these I have counted loss for Christ.*

—Philippians 3:7

Life in Action: Why is it important for me to have boundaries on all my affections except for my affection for God?

On Pins and Needles

*Our hearts are held together by
the pins of God's promises.*

By July 2005 more than two years had passed since the tragic loss
of seven astronauts aboard *Columbia*. NASA was preparing the
long-grounded shuttle program for an imminent lift-off.

On launch day, the three major networks set up to televise live. Early
morning clear skies yielded to ominous thunderheads. The storm passed,
but a technical difficulty arose, causing that day's attempt to be scrubbed.
The decision left anxious Americans sitting on pins and needles for nearly
two more weeks.

Pins and needles, a phrase that has been around since the 1800s, carries
two sets of meanings. It's used, for instance, to describe the physical
condition known as paresthesia, the prickling sensation that strikes our
extremities when the blood supply to them is temporarily reduced and
our arms or legs "fall asleep."

More often, however, the phrase *pins and needles* is used to describe the emotions we feel when we're nervous, unsettled, and full of worried anticipation. In 2 Corinthians 7:5, Paul said, "When we arrived in Macedonia province, we couldn't settle down. The fights in the church and the fears in our hearts kept us on pins and needles. We couldn't relax because we didn't know how it would turn out."[1]

Of course none of us can totally avoid nervous excitement and tense anticipation, but when our hearts are stitched together with the thread of scriptural truths, we shouldn't constantly live on pins and needles.

THE PINS OF GOD'S PROMISES

In fact, if you're going to live on pins and needles, why not make it the pins of God's promises and the needles of His nearness?

Do you recall watching your mother pin together pieces of cloth before sewing them into a dress? Fashion designers still put their prototypes together using pins. Likewise, our own hearts are held together by the pins of God's promises. The promises in God's Word keep our hearts from falling apart during times of stress and strain.

Dr. Donald Grey Barnhouse, a well-known preacher of an earlier day, lived with his family in France during his student days. On their dinner table sat a little Promise Box that held approximately 200 promises from the Bible. Each was printed on heavy paper and curled into a small cylinder, and the family would take one out and read it when they needed a special word of comfort.

One day Donald Barnhouse had the opportunity to lead a French girl to faith in Christ. This girl often came to the Barnhouse home, and she saw the family reading verses from their Promise Box. Unable to find one, she made her own.

During World War II, this woman found herself in real distress. No food was available except messes of potato peelings from a restaurant. Her children were emaciated, and their clothing was mere rags. In desperation, she turned to her Promise Box, saying, "Lord, O Lord, I have such great need. Is there a promise here that is really for me? Show me, O Lord, what promise I can have in this time of famine, nakedness, peril, and the sword."[3]

Blinded by her tears, she reached for the box—and knocked it over. The promises showered down around her, on her lap, on the floor; not one was left in the box. Suddenly she realized that it wasn't just one promise that was available to her, but that *all* of God's promises were for her. Joy and strength returned to her life, and she was able to trust His sufficiency in the hour of her greatest need.[2]

The same precious promises are available to you and me. In fact, they are the pins that hold together our broken heart and crippled soul in the hour of our greatest pain and need.

THE NEEDLE OF GOD'S NEARNESS

Having considered the pins of God's promises, now consider the needle of God's nearness. Needles have been around almost as long as human history itself. Needles—even ones with eyes—have been found in European caves dating back to the Stone Age. Some of the needles are so small and fine that they were evidently used with thread made from the tails of horses.

Now, as you may know about sewing, the pins hold together the pieces, and the needles join the pieces to make a single garment. In our analogy, the needle can represent the nearness of God. His nearness pierces our hearts and securely joins us to Him. The psalmist said, "It is good for me to draw near to God; I have put my trust in the Lord GOD" (Psalm 73:28).

A missionary to China, Rosalind Goforth told of a time when she and her family were in extreme danger during the Boxer Rebellion. They were surrounded by a bloodthirsty mob, and Rosalind was seized with an overwhelming fear—not of dying, but of being tortured.

Her husband, Jonathan, drew from his pocket a little book of Bible verses, and he began reading, "The eternal God is your refuge, and underneath are the everlasting arms" (Deuteronomy 33:27). He went on to read several other verses.

Rosalind later wrote this:

> The effect of those words at such a time was remarkable. All realized that God was speaking to us. Never was there a message more directly given to mortal man from God than that message to us. From almost the first verse, my whole soul seemed flooded with a great peace; all trace of panic vanished, and I felt God's presence was with us. Indeed, His presence was so real it scarcely [could] have been more so had we seen a visible form.[3]

By God's grace and due in part to the courage and composure of the missionary party, everyone escaped. Their experience was similar to that of the Lord Jesus when the people of the synagogue tried to throw Him down over the cliff: "Then passing through the midst of them, He went His way" (Luke 4:30). That same courage and composure belong to all of us whose hearts are sewn to His by the needle of God's nearness.

The Thread of God's Truth

The pins of God's promises and the needle of His nearness do little good without the thread of theology. . . .

I remember watching my mother sew. She'd go to the window where, in the brightness of the sunlight, she'd thread her needle. She often put the end of the thread in her mouth to moisten it. Then she carefully slipped it into the tiny eye of the needle. After all, it's useless to pass the needle back and forth through the cloth if the thread is unattached.

Many people today—even some pastors and church leaders—think the thread isn't that important. But there can be no personal stability, inner peace, or unwavering confidence without the thread of solid doctrine. In the old days, theology was considered the queen of the sciences, and systematic theology was the crown of the queen. Today, however, those who hold to solid biblical teaching are called dogmatic, intolerant, and outdated.

That criticism didn't faze London pastor Joseph Parker. Read what he said:

> They may be old-fashioned doctrines, but they created missionary societies, Sunday schools, hospitals, orphanages, and refuges for penitence; they gave every child a new value, every father a new responsibility, every mother a new hope, and constituted human society into a new conscience and a new trust. We cannot first sneer at the doctrine and then claim its infinite beneficence, nor can we borrow its socialism that we may quench its inspiration. Let us be very careful how we give up trees that have borne such fruit, and in whose leaves there has been such healing.[4]

I hope you're growing in your knowledge of the Bible. You don't have to be a learned theologian, but the Bible does recommend to us the example of those new Christians in the town of Berea who "searched the Scriptures daily to find out whether these things were so" (Acts 17:11).

God's faithfulness and goodness take the worry out of life, and we can trust Him with every day we live and with all aspects of our life. We Christians don't unravel like cartoon characters who snag their sweaters on a nail and walk away without realizing their clothes are disintegrating. The Lord is a trustworthy tailor who knows how to stitch together our hours and our days. He has never once failed us in the past, nor will He leave or forsake us now.

So, if you're going to live on pins and needles, make them the pins of His promises, the needle of His nearness, and the thread of His truth. That kind of life never falls apart at the seams.

signs of Life

Life Sign: My life is not plagued by worry because I am held tightly in God's hands.

Life Verse: *It is good for me to draw near to God;*
I have put my trust in the Lord GOD,
That I may declare all Your works.

—Psalm 73:28

Life in Action: What promises from God's Word can I claim in order to hold together the fraying fabric of my everyday life?

Day 20

The Potter's Hands

*Ask God to have His own way in your life as He forms—
and re-forms—you into His wonderful image.*

One day the village parson took a different route to work. Nudged by a strange impression, he walked to a different part of town where craftsmen plied their various trades. Arriving at a particular shop, he peered through the window and then entered the studio.

It was a pottery-making enterprise, and the first thing the parson noticed was the blast of heat that hit him when he walked through the door. It came from the large kiln attached to the outer wall of the shop. Workers were carefully arranging clay objects in the oven, firing them, and seasoning them for use.

The parson also noticed display shelves on the opposite wall filled with assorted pottery wares that were for sale. A couple of women were contemplating a set of clay jars. The pastor also noticed lamps, bowls, vases, and pots.

His attention, however, was quickly drawn to an old man sitting at the potter's wheel, spinning it skillfully with the foot pedals, and forming a piece of pottery with his experienced fingers. This artisan was making a drinking vessel with unique lines, ridges, and indentations. Pausing, he slowed the wheel to better look at his creation. Finding it to be marred and unsatisfactory, the potter suddenly smashed the clay into a ball, dipped his hand into a water jar, applied a new coat of moisture, and started working again.

Thinking about what he had just witnessed, the preacher turned and exited into the street. Looking up and down, he saw everywhere signs of violence, immorality, filth, poverty, and moral failure. Then this thought from God Himself came to him: "Look, as the clay is in the potter's hand, so are you in My hand, O house of Israel!" (Jeremiah 18:6). The prophet Jeremiah offered him a new perspective on God's work among His people and a new sense of hope in the Master Potter who can form and re-form our lives.

❧

The potter's wheel is an apt metaphor for God's work in our lives because we are, in a literal sense, pottery: we've been formed from clay. God physically shaped Adam from the clay of the earth and breathed into him the breath of life. We are all humans, a word that is akin to the term *humus*, meaning "earth" or "clay." Job's friend Elihu said in Job 33:6, "I also have been formed out of clay." The apostle Paul referred to our bodies as "jars of clay" (2 Corinthians 4:7 NIV).

But the Bible also tells us that God wants to shape us inwardly, to spiritually fashion us into vessels fit for His use, to mold each of us into the image of our Lord Jesus Christ. The apostle Paul says God wants to form us into "a vessel for honor, sanctified and useful for the Master, prepared for every good work" (2 Timothy 2:21).

The patriarch Job concurred: "Your hands have made me and fashioned me . . . You have made me like clay" (Job 10:8–9). These verses give us a biblical warrant to think of the events and influences of our lives as God's hands and fingers shaping us as a potter shapes clay.

His Hands Form Us

God's hands that form us are skilled hands: He knows exactly how to sculpt us into Christ's image. . . .

In biblical times, most potters learned their craft from their fathers. In cities like Jerusalem, there was even a section of shops known as the Potters' District. Families kept studios there, and the craft was passed from father to son for centuries. Entering such a shop, one would see the potter at his wheel while in the corner at a small table a child was playing with clay—and, yes, he would be covered head to toe in the gray, grimy substance. An older child might be working at a small wheel, and a couple of teens at the kiln would be proudly eyeing their creations. By the time a boy was grown, his hands were skilled, and he could alter the design of a vessel by the slightest pressure of a thumb or the scratch of a fingernail.

Similarly, God's skilled hands hold your life, and He knows perfectly how to apply pressure, when to relax His grip, how to score your life with His fingernail, how to squeeze and nudge—all of which will make you a vessel fit for His use. At times the Master Potter places us in the kiln where the fires of life turn us into stronger vessels for His use. . . .

In her little book *Why?* Anne Graham Lotz tells of a phone call that launched her into "the wild blue yonder of faith." The call was from her son, Jonathan, who said, "Mom, the doctor thinks I have cancer." Anne instinctively prayed with Jonathan over the phone, and she later wrote this:

> I was able to praise God for His divine purpose for Jonathan's life, which apparently included cancer. Although we had been caught by surprise, I knew God had known about it since before Jonathan was born. . . . Therefore I had absolute confidence that this suffering

would be for Jonathan's good and God's glory. We knew God had a plan, and apparently cancer was part of it![1]

God permitted this trial in Jonathan's life, and the Master Potter used it as a tool to further grow, develop, and conform him into the image of Christ. Romans 8:28 says that God works all things for the good of those who love Him and are called according to His purpose, and the next verse specifies His purpose: "to be conformed to the image of His Son" (Romans 8:29).

Our heavenly Father wants to use the events we encounter each day as tools to shape and sculpt us into the image of Christ. He wants to deepen our faith, develop within us the quality of perseverance, and make us watertight containers of His love, joy, peace, patience, kindness, goodness, faithfulness, gentleness, and self-control (Galatians 5:22–23).

So if you're under some sort of pressure right now, visualize the skillful hands of the divine Potter using it for good in your life. Pray as Isaiah did: "O LORD, You are our Father; we are the clay, and You our potter; and all we are the work of Your hand" (Isaiah 64:8). You can trust Your heavenly Father's dexterous and expert fingers not to harm, but to help you.

HIS HANDS ARE RE-FORMING

The Potter's skillful hands re-form as well as form us. Remember the potter from Jeremiah 18. When he saw that the vessel seemed marred, he squeezed the clay into a new lump and started to re-form it.

Sometimes we think we're unusable and even unredeemable. We've done something for which we feel shame and guilt, and we think God can no longer do much with us. Our problems are occasionally of our own making, and our pain may arise from our own stupidity. But when we bring our sin to the Lord, confess it earnestly, nail it to the cross of

Christ, and surrender it to the power of His shed blood, God can take our sins and shame from us and then mold us into a vessel that glorifies Him. . . .

Adelaide Pollard was a woman who occasionally ran away on wild-goose chases. She didn't always make wise decisions, and she sometimes became enamored by the wrong voices. But she sincerely wanted to please God, and she felt God was calling her to Africa as a missionary. She was unable to raise her financial support, however, and she became sick of heart. One night, feeling very depressed, she went to church. During the prayer meeting, a wise and elderly woman prayed, "It doesn't matter what You bring into our lives, Lord. Just have Your own way with us."

That phrase rushed into Adelaide's heart and, upon returning home, she read the story of the potter and the clay in Jeremiah 18. By bedtime she had written out a prayer of her own. We know it as the hymn "Have Thine Own Way, Lord."[2]

Today—and every day this week—make this verse from her hymn your prayer as you think of the forming and re-forming work the Master Potter does in your life. With His skilled hands, He is crafting you into a vessel of honor fit for His use. Visualize your life as a studio of the divine Potter and know that His hands are on your heart. Ask God to have His own way in your life as He forms—and re-forms—you into His wonderful image.

> Have Thine own way, Lord! Have Thine own way!
> Thou art the Potter, I am the clay.
> Mold me and make me after Thy will,
> While I am waiting, yielded and still.[3]

signs of Life

Life Sign: I am willing to be pliable in the hands of God.

Life Verse: *But now, O LORD,*
You are our Father;
We are the clay, and You our potter;
And all we are the work of Your hand.

—Isaiah 64:8

Life in Action: In what areas of my life is God molding and shaping me?

Day 21

Greater Works Than Jesus

*Our primary ministry in the world is to be conduits through
which Jesus continues to perform His miracles.*

After World War II, Berlin—the capital of Germany and head-
quarters of Adolf Hitler's Third Reich—was overseen by the
four Allied nations that had united to defeat Hitler: America,
Britain, France, and the (former) Soviet Union. Growing political differences between the Soviets and the three Allied nations, however,
caused the city of Berlin as well as Germany itself to be divided into
East (German Democratic Republic) and West (Federal Republic of
Germany). As the West German sector prospered under capitalism, resi-
dents of East Berlin, languishing under Soviet oppression, began leaving East Berlin and emigrating to the Western sector.

In August 1961, to stop the human and economic drain from East
Berlin, the Soviet government began building the infamous Berlin Wall,
dividing the city physically and ideologically. In 1953, the key East
German city of Leipzig was the site of violent protests against Communist
rule, and these protests were crushed by Communist forces. Violence

accomplished nothing when it came to trying to gain freedom in East Germany.

But in 1989 people in Leipzig tried a different approach. What became known as the Monday Demonstrations began with prayers for peace in the historic Nikolai Church in the heart of Leipzig. The prayer meetings grew into peaceful candlelight marches of ten thousand, thirty thousand, fifty thousand, and then half a million people strong. And those in Leipzig were joined by a million more in Berlin.

Finally, prayers for peace accomplished what violence had failed to do. In November 1989 the Berlin Wall was taken down. The hated symbol of the ideological Iron Curtain yielded to the power of prayer, and the people of East Germany tasted freedom for the first time in decades.[1]

☙

It is amazing that a movement begun by a tyrannical Nazi *Führer,* a movement that oppressed millions of people, was brought to an end by a movement started by another *führer*—by Pastor Christian Führer of the Nikolai Church in Leipzig. A movement that began with people on their knees in a church found ultimate expression in the feet of millions of prayerful marchers seeking freedom in the streets. As the French novelist Victor Hugo wrote, "There are moments when, whatever the attitude of the body, the soul is on its knees."[2] This was one of those moments.

Those who prayed down the Berlin Wall must have taken the words of Jesus Christ very seriously:

> Most assuredly, I say to you, he who believes in Me, the works that I do he will do also; and greater works than these he will do, because I go to My Father. And whatever you ask in My name, that I will do, that the Father may be glorified in the Son. If you ask anything in My name, I will do it. (John 14:12–14)

What did Jesus mean by saying that His disciples, on their knees, would do greater works than He had done? What could possibly be greater than healing the sick, raising the dead, stilling the storms on the sea, defeating demons, and turning water into wine? Should we expect a level of miracles beyond those?

Yes—but let me explain. Our ministry will be greater than our Lord's because it will have greater reach and greater results.

THE REACH OF OUR MINISTRY IS GREATER

The land of Israel today comprises about eight thousand square miles—roughly equivalent to the land of Palestine in Jesus' day. During the three years of Jesus' ministry, He did not cover all of that land. His ministry was confined primarily to Judea (Jerusalem) and the region of Galilee in the north. And the number of people His ministry touched could probably be numbered only in the thousands.

Compare that to the land area of the entire planet: 57.5 million square miles. The followers of Jesus have covered a land area thousands and thousands of times larger than Jesus covered Himself. And the number of people His disciples have touched during the intervening 2,000 years would number in the billions.[3]

So who has had the "greater" ministry in terms of geographic reach? As Martin Luther wrote, "For Christ took but a little corner for himself to preach and to work miracles, and but a little time; whereas the apostles and their followers have spread themselves through the whole world."[4]

The eleven disciples whom Jesus entrusted with His Gospel took it as far as their legs would carry them in their lifetime. And the people they won and trained took it even farther. In less than three hundred years, the Roman Empire was officially Christian. Jesus' own people were unconverted and scattered across the earth, but the pagan, Gentile nation of Rome was Christian.

So it is hard to dispute the notion that Jesus, working through His church, has had a greater reach than He had during His personal three-year ministry in Palestine. His promise to His disciples was, if we seek to continue the works He began, we can ask anything in His name and He will do it. With the Spirit working in and through the church, there is no limit to what can be accomplished for God's kingdom.

THE RESULTS OF OUR MINISTRY ARE GREATER

But it's not just the reach of the Gospel that will be greater through the church. The results of preaching the Gospel will be greater as well. . . .

As many Bible students have pointed out, it was wonderful that Lazarus was raised from the dead, but he ultimately had to die again. We could say the same about all the miracles Jesus performed: those who received healing ultimately had to die.

Many people to whom Jesus ministered, however, experienced spiritual as well as physical healing, but the primary role of Jesus' physical miracles was to validate His spiritual message and His ministry as the prophesied Jewish Messiah. Our primary ministry in the world is not to perform physical miracles but to be the conduits through which Jesus continues to perform His spiritual miracles.

As author John Phillips said, it's wonderful for a man's eyes to be opened physically, but it's even more wonderful for Him to see and understand the Gospel. It's a beautiful thing to see a leper made pure, but it's even more beautiful for his heart to be washed pure from the stain of sin. It's a miracle for a deaf man to hear words and music, but it's even more miraculous for him to hear and respond to the Gospel. And while a dead man might praise God when brought back to life for a few more years, a spiritually dead man will praise God for all eternity when he meets Jesus.[5]

So, in the accounting system of God's kingdom, physical, temporal results are great, but spiritual, eternal results are even greater. And Jesus promised His disciples that they would do spiritual works that exceeded His own in their geographic reach and their eternal results.

What, then, did Jesus mean when He said we could ask "anything in [His] name and He will do it" (John 14:14)? It means the same for us as it did for Him. In His own prayers Jesus always asked for God's will to be done, even in the most trying circumstances of His life: "Father, if it is Your will, take this cup away from Me; nevertheless not My will, but Yours, be done" (Luke 22:42).

The Father was glorified by the work the Son did in His name (John 17:4). Likewise, the Father will be glorified when we do His will, and Jesus commits Himself to helping us accomplish just that: "Whatever you ask in My name, that I will do, that the Father may be glorified in the Son" (John 14:13).

And the way we learn to pray according to the Father's will—praying prayers that Jesus can answer—is by abiding in Christ. Jesus made the same promise to answer prayers in John 15:7, where He said He would respond *if* we abide in Him and *if* His words abide in us. In other words, the promise is conditional: its fulfillment depends on our living intimately with the Son of God and learning to pray for the same things He prayed for, the execution of God's will. Those are prayers the Father always answers.

So if there is a spiritual mountain in your life—or a great wall of injustice and oppression that needs to come down—you will likely wear down that mountain at the same rate that you wear out your spiritual knees in prayer.

SiGNs of Life

Life Sign: I participate in personal ministry that impacts my community.

Life Verse: *Whatever you ask in My name, that I will do, that the Father may be glorified in the Son.*

—John 14:13

Life in Action: List three areas of personal ministry through which you impact your community. List one area of personal ministry that enables you to impact the world.

Rolled-Up Sleeves
Living an
authentic
Life

Rolled-Up Sleeves

*We have to roll our sleeves up if we're going to
hold our Lord up to a needy world.*

Christians have always been world changers, and our influence
has shaped society for two thousand years.

Friedrich Froebel (1782–1852), for example, was the son of a
Lutheran pastor who often helped his dad in the family garden. When
he was a young man, his Christian beliefs convinced him that children
need to learn about God and His world at an early age. One day while
hiking in the mountains, Friedrich imagined a school for young children
that would allow their minds to be cultivated by a teacher like a horti-
culturist cultivates a garden. He called his idea a child's garden. Because
of him, children have been going to *kindergarten* for the last one hundred and fifty years.[1]

In the early 1800s deaf American children had no means of obtain-
ing an education. Thomas Gallaudet, a Christian, traveled to Europe to
learn techniques to use to teach deaf children. He opened the first school
for the deaf in 1817. His son began a church and mission work with the
deaf.[2]

It's Christians who have established hospitals, started schools, begun orphanages, reformed prisons, emancipated women, abolished slavery, inspired charities, founded hospitals, clothed the naked, fed the hungry, treated the diseased, encouraged the addicted, and housed the homeless.

The Bible tells us to share the Gospel with the lost. It also tells us to bear the burdens of the needy. James wrote, "Pure and undefiled religion before God and the Father is this: to visit orphans and widows in their trouble" (1:27).

We declare Christ's love with our mouths, but we demonstrate it with our muscles. Effective Christianity means rolling up our sleeves and going to work. As John Burke wrote in *No Perfect People Allowed,* "Incarnate truth does not neglect propositional truth but presents it in love with skin."[3]

GOOD INK

Despite the good that Christians do even today, the media loves to find ways of attacking our faith, and many newspapers publish stories critical of the church. Nothing makes headlines like a pastor who falls into sin or an evangelist caught in an ethics violation. But, by God's grace, many of those same papers are searching for stories of heartwarming kindness, and such stories about Christians can make headlines too.

A local newspaper in the Cleveland area reported the formation of a school safety patrol program as a result of concerned members of one local church who saw a need at their neighborhood public school and met it.[4] A smaller paper reported that nearly 650 volunteers from 70 churches joined to form Valley Christian Clinic in Arkansas to care for medical, dental, and vision needs—free of charge—for those too poor to pay for care.[5]

One church in New Jersey got coverage in the local newspaper because of its campaign to collect Silly String for soldiers in Iraq. One of the church members heard from her son, who was serving in Iraq, that Silly String is helpful in detecting trip wires that can't be detected through other means. The three-week drive netted around 400 cans of Silly String.[6]

We're living in such a selfish age that any act of kindness is considered remarkable and magnified as noteworthy. Take the television show *Extreme Home Makeover.* Its popularity is due to its touching scenes of neighbors rolling up their sleeves to help a needy or desperate family.

In a world that is hungry for a little kindness, the Lord has provided His church, and kindness is our stock-in-trade. When we roll up our sleeves, we hold our Lord up to a needy world.

GETTING TO WORK

So what are some specific ways we can roll up our sleeves, use our muscles, and sweat out some kindness for Jesus' sake? The simplest answer is the oldest one: find a need and fill it. Ask God to show you a specific need and then to empower you in meeting it.

- Do you know someone undergoing chemotherapy who could use a meal brought in on the day of the treatment?

- Does a single mother in your neighborhood need help with lawn mowing or yard work?

- What about volunteering at your local school or hospital? Or visiting a nursing home to chat with the elderly, pray with the lonely, and perhaps organize visits by children's choirs or choral groups?

- If there's a homeless shelter or soup kitchen in your area, consider offering your time on a regular basis.

- Establish a family tradition of taking a basket of groceries to a needy home every Thanksgiving, Christmas, or Easter.

- Ask your church leaders about the congregation's benevolent ministries and find a place to help.

- Take the lead in helping your church adopt a section of local roadway to keep clean.

- Consider taking a missions trip to help build a church, give immunizations, teach VBS, or renovate an orphanage.

- Investigate the possibilities of helping refugees settle in your town or city.

- Volunteer to teach English as a second language in your church or community.

- Donate books to the local prison, linens to the local rescue mission, or tutoring time to the local school.

In the conclusion of His Olivet Discourse (Matthew 25), our Lord stressed the priority of rolled-up sleeves when He described the day when the Son of Man will come in His glory and all the holy angels with Him. The nations will be gathered before Him, and He will say to those on His right hand:

> Come, you blessed of My Father, inherit the kingdom prepared for you from the foundation of the world: for I was hungry and you gave Me food; I was thirsty and you gave Me drink; I was a stranger and you took Me in; I was naked and you clothed Me; I was sick and you visited Me; I was in prison and you came to Me (verses 34–36).

Jesus' sheep will say to Him, "Lord, when did we do these things for You?" And our Lord's reply will be short and sweet: "Assuredly, I say to you, inasmuch as you did it to one of the least of these My brethren, you did it to Me" (verse 40).

❧

When Dr. Bob Pierce, the legendary Christian humanitarian, was dying of leukemia, he still insisted on traveling the globe, trying to help meet the needs of millions of sick, poor, and hungry people. Because of his illness, he couldn't sleep, and his doctor had prescribed sleeping tablets. They were a lifesaver for Dr. Pierce as he labored.

Not long before his death, Dr. Bob visited a little riverside medical clinic in the jungles of Kalimantan, which is now part of Indonesia. This small clinic was operated by a Christian named "Borneo Bob" Williams. While he was there, Dr. Pierce noticed a girl lying outside on a bamboo mat. Asking about her, he learned that she was dying from cancer and had few days to live.

"How come this girl is lying there in the mud when she could be up there in that nice, clean clinic?" asked Pierce.

Borneo Bob explained that this girl was a jungle girl and she wanted to be near the river, where it was cooler. She had specifically asked to lie in that spot for the day. Bob Pierce's heart broke as he knelt beside the girl, rubbed her forehead, and prayed for her. The girl opened her eyes and muttered something in her native tongue. Borneo Bob translated her words. She was in great pain but was unable to sleep.

Dr. Pierce wiped tears from his eyes and reached into his pocket for his precious bottle of sleeping pills. He gave them to Borneo Bob, saying, "You make sure she gets a good night's sleep from now on."

It was many days before Dr. Pierce could replace his pills, and he suffered night after night from painful insomnia. But when he returned home, a letter was waiting for him from Borneo Bob stating that the girl had died, and one of the last things she had said was "Please thank that kind man who gave me this medicine so I could sleep."[7]. . .

❧

We may not be able to travel the world and help millions of people. We may not single-handedly open schools, orphanages, or great charitable institutions. But we can all roll up our sleeves, pitch in, help out, and become the hands of Jesus so that others might discover the heart of Jesus. That's the authentic life—and it's part of our commission. We must always remember that as we do something unto the least of Jesus' brothers, we are doing it unto Him.

SIGNS of Life

Life Sign: The world sees the heart of God through the work of my hands.

Life Verse: *Assuredly, I say to you, inasmuch as you did it to one of the least of these My brethren, you did it to Me.*

—Matthew 25:40

Life in Action: Who around me needs a special touch of Jesus' love to come through my helping hands?

Artistic Impressions

*Our lives are a canvas that captures the dominant themes
of our days.*

To introduce this chapter, I've prepared a little quiz for you. I'm going to describe what a particular artist is best known for and ask you to identify who it is. Fill in your answers and then check the end of the chapter to see how art-smart you are:

1. **Famous for his drawings of optical illusions:** people go uphill and downhill at the same time on never-ending stairs; water runs uphill; birds metamorphose into fish.

   _____

2. **The greatest artist of the Dutch school:** painted with lush, rich colors; a master of light, shadow, and human emotion; painted portraits as well as scenes from Amsterdam and the Bible (*Supper at Emmaus, The Return of the Prodigal Son*).

   _____

3. **Modern Spanish artist:** founder of Cubism; painter, drawer, sculptor, ceramicist; famous for caricatures and abstracts as well as realistic paintings; considered a rebel in the world of art. _____

4. **"The Painter of Light":** contemporary artist who paints idealistic scenes of villages, cottages, churches, lighthouses, and landscapes that evoke feelings of warmth, nostalgia, and home; noted for his portrayal of light as a reflector of values.

   _____

5. **Nineteenth-century creator of intricate woodcuts:** dramatic depictions of famous biblical scenes used in illustrated King James Bibles and biblical story and reference works.

   _____

6. **Flamboyant twentieth-century Spanish surrealist:** painted bizarre, irrational, fantastic images in meticulous renderings; famous for *The Persistence of Memory* with its limp, melting watch faces in an eerie landscape. _____

EVERYONE IS KNOWN FOR SOMETHING

So, how did you do? Are you ready to teach a class in art history?

The point of this exercise was not art per se. (In fact, I don't find the work of some of those artists particularly edifying or appealing—or even understandable!) What the exercise does point out is that artists are known for their particular style. Even just a brief description of their style was enough to trigger in your mind's eye the work of the artists I was describing.

It's probably fair to say that artists have a way of looking at the world that is reflected in their work. Their art suggests their worldview and their convictions. Certainly some artists work in more than one style, but even so, when we step back and look at their life's work, we can usually see a theme running through it.

Now let's step back from this discussion of art, because it's not just artists who are known for the theme(s) of their life's work. Indeed, everyone of us is known for something.

Imagine that I approached five of your closest friends or family members and said, "Pretend that words are paintbrushes and this blackboard is your canvas. Give me ten broad brushstrokes . . . ten descriptive words . . . that paint a picture of our friend." As I began writing down the words that came from those who know you best, a theme—maybe several—would emerge.

If I did the same exercise about the art of Rembrandt, Dali, or Kinkade, people would give me descriptive terms about their work, and certain themes would emerge. Whether we like it or not, our lives are a canvas that captures the dominant themes of our days. The question is not whether people are seeing those themes—they are! The key issue is what those themes of your life and mine are.

"HEARTISTIC" IMPRESSIONS

I've tested your art smarts. Now let's talk about your art-of-the-heart smarts. I'm going to create a "heartistic" impression with words, and you tell me the kind of person I'm describing:

> The major theme of this person's life is love. His speech, actions, thoughts, possessions, motivations—all are characterized by love. His love is emotional in expression, but rooted in choice. He loves *in spite of*, not *because* of. _____

If you wrote "Christian" in the blank, then you are probably familiar with the Bible verse that explains how followers of Jesus Christ are to be characterized in this world: "By this all will know that you are My disciples, if you have love for one another" (John 13:35). If I walk into an art

135

gallery and find a painting on the wall titled *Love,* on close examination I should find that it's a painting of you, or me, or any follower of Jesus. We Christians are to be living definitions of love; we are to be "heartistic" impressions of our Savior.

The love that is to characterize the Christian, according to Jesus, is not primarily affectionate, familial love. Important as that kind of brotherly love is, that is not the love Jesus speaks of in John 13:35. Rather, the love we are to manifest is the same kind of love God manifested toward the world by sending Jesus to die for our sins (John 3:16). That love is *agape* love, the self-sacrificing love that motivates one person to lay down his life for another. There is no greater love than *agape* love (John 15:13).

A PORTRAIT OF LOVE

Are you and I known by our love? Is love one of the first things that comes to mind when people think of us—especially those people in our world who don't know Christ? Do the depth and quality of our love make others wonder about its Source? Are they drawn to the love of Jesus when they come in contact with us?

Allow me to offer a palette of five colors of love, five ways we can leave a "heartistic" impression on those we meet that will encourage them to think of our Savior and His love for them.

1. **Words of love**—Words can build up as well as tear down. A Christian's words should "always be with grace, seasoned with salt," "like a honeycomb, sweetness to the soul and health to the bones" (Colossians 4:6; Proverbs 16:24). Reformer Martin Luther said, "When I have nothing more to say, I stop talking."[1] And our mothers told us, "If you can't say something nice, don't say anything at all." Even if you have to confront someone, make sure you speak the truth in love (Ephesians 4:15).

2. Deeds of love—God demonstrated His love for us "in that while we were still sinners, Christ died for us" (Romans 5:8). And in 1 Corinthians 13 Paul mentions sixteen ways by which love is manifested in our life. Furthermore, it is not insignificant that *love* is both a noun and a verb. In fact, while words of love are important, if they are not supported by deeds of love, they will in time sound hollow—like "sounding brass or a clanging cymbal" (1 Corinthians 13:1).

3. Thoughts of love—Our private thoughts are the building blocks of the people we become. Solomon observed that as we think in our hearts, so we become (Proverbs 23:7). Beyond the fact that our thoughts help determine our actions, they are either an offense to God or a gift of love to Him. King David desired that even the meditations of his heart be acceptable to God—and so should we (Psalm 19:14; 104:34).

4. Gifts of love—God has given to every person three things to manage for His glory: time, talent, and treasure. When God demonstrated how much He loves us, He gave His greatest gift—the life of His only Son. Jesus Himself said, "It is more blessed to give than to receive" (Acts 20:35). A synonym for *love* is *give*.

5. Steps of love—Every step we take in this life is taken in pursuit of something; everywhere we go, we are following someone or something. It's not wrong if we pursue things for ourselves; but if we are only following our own dreams, our life becomes self-centered instead of God-centered. Paul said he was pursuing something higher than the things of this world: he called it "the upward call of God in Christ Jesus" (Philippians 3:14). Steps on that path will always leave love-shaped footprints in the sand.

❦

If you didn't pass the art-smart test with flying colors, not to worry. It's the art-of-the-heart test with which we should be more concerned. Artistic impressions of love translate into "heartistic" impressions of the person of Christ wherever we go. Be sure that's the portrait you are presenting to the world.

Answers to the quiz:

1. M. C. Escher (1898–1972)
2. Rembrandt van Rijn (1606–1669)
3. Pablo Picasso (1881–1973)
4. Thomas Kinkade (1958–present)
5. Gustave Doré (1832–1883)
6. Salvador Dali (1904–1989)

signs of Life

Life Sign: The major theme of my life is love.

Life Verse: *By this all will know that you are My disciples, if you have love for one another.*

—John 13:35

Life in Action: If people who know me well were to paint a picture of who I am, what would that picture look like? What would be the theme of their paintings?

Day 24

Profiling the Mind of a Christian

*There's nothing wrong with being predictable when
it means showing up and acting like Jesus.*

C riminologist Wayne Petherick has recorded some fascinating historical details about the science of criminal profiling in its earliest stages. During World War II, for instance, the United States Office of Strategic Services (now the CIA) wanted to know more about Adolf Hitler: What kind of person was he? What made him tick? What was he likely to do in the future? What would he do in the face of defeat or death? How should we interrogate him if we captured him? They asked psychiatrist Walter Langer to develop a psychological and behavioral profile of the infamous German *führer*.

Here are a few of Langer's conclusions about Hitler: Death through natural causes was unlikely since Hitler was in good health. He would not seek refuge in another country because he saw himself as the savior of Germany. Langer ruled out assassination, coup, and death in battle, and he believed that Hitler's most likely response to defeat or capture would be suicide—which is exactly what happened in an underground bunker in 1945 when the fall of Germany was imminent. The profiling of enemy military leaders continues today as a tool for predicting and counteracting an enemy's moves.[1]

One of the most famous profiles ever was done by James Brussels, the New York psychiatrist who profiled the "Mad Bomber of New York" in the 1950s. Over an eight-year span, this criminal left thirty-two explosive packages across the city without being caught. Based on an investigation of the crime scenes and the study of a number of letters the bomber had written to authorities, Brussels developed a profile of the suspect containing the following particulars: "Heavy-set . . . middle-aged . . . foreign-born . . . single, living with a sibling . . . paranoid . . . hates his father . . . obsessively loved by his mother . . . lives in Connecticut . . . and when you find him, chances are he will be wearing a double-breasted suit, buttoned." When the bomber was finally captured, the profile was nearly perfect, right down to the buttoned-up, double-breasted suit.[2]

In the latter part of the twentieth century, the FBI developed its Behavioral Sciences Unit in Quantico, Virginia, to advance the art and science of profiling.[3] One television network had a science-based dramatic series called *The Profiler* in the late 1990s. Without question, profiling has become a critical part of Crime Scene Investigation strategy.

PROFILING: THE PRACTICE OF PATTERNS

But what about "Christian Scene Investigation"? What role can profiling play in determining whether you and I are committed followers of Christ? In the criminal world, profiling is the process of inferring specific character traits and behaviors of individuals responsible for committing crimes and then using those traits and behaviors to both track down the criminal and predict where and whether he might strike again. So how might the same concept of profiling apply in the church?

Here's an example taken from the book of Acts. If it were your job to assign financial responsibilities to, say, Barnabas or Ananias and Sapphira, whom would you have chosen? Barnabas had developed a reputation in the early church as a "good man, full of the Holy Spirit and of faith" (Acts 11:24). He was an encourager and a humble man, who was eventually willing to risk his reputation for a brother who had failed (Acts 4:36; 15:36–41). When Barnabas brought a gift of money to the early church, there is no evidence that either his motives or honesty were questioned (Acts 4:36–37). In sharp contrast, when Ananias and Sapphira gave a gift, they were immediately revealed to be greedy deceivers. They apparently had little or no history in the church since they aren't mentioned before their mortal mistake (Acts 5:1–11).

Because character is developed and revealed over time, a profiler might have accurately predicted the outcome of the two gift-giving events. It's doubtful that Ananias and Sapphira acted out of the blue. Their deceitful gift was likely a public manifestation of a private pattern of behavior—and that pattern is exactly what a profiler looks for.

PAUL THE PROFILER

The apostle Paul was a profiler of sorts. In 1 Timothy 3 and Titus 1, for instance, he profiles Christian leaders (elders and deacons) for the churches in Ephesus and on the island of Crete. If you have men among you who have displayed these characteristics and behaviors in the past, Paul wrote, they will likely make good leaders in the future. We still use Paul's profiles when choosing elders and deacons in the church today.

In addition, Paul profiles people whose lives are (Galatians 5:22–23) and aren't (Galatians 5:19–21) under the control of the Holy Spirit. The former manifest traits such as love, joy, and peace, and the latter display behaviors such as immorality, discord, and selfish ambition. The fruit of the Spirit or the acts of the sinful nature—which of these profiles is more Christlike and therefore more desirable in any Christian?

THE PROFILE OF JESUS

And that brings us to the bottom line of Christian Scene Investigation profiling: there is really only one profile that every Christian should strive after, and that is the profile of Jesus Christ. Christlikeness is the ultimate goal, and when a person is like Christ, we know what character traits and behaviors to expect from him or her.

So what can we do to develop in ourselves a profile that matches the profile of Jesus? By having what the apostle Paul calls "the mind of Christ" (1 Corinthians 2:16; Philippians 2:5). In practical terms, this means living under the control of the Holy Spirit. Just as Jesus was filled and led by the Holy Spirit in His life (Matthew 3:16; 4:1), so every believer is to be filled and led by the same Holy Spirit (Acts 2:38–39; Ephesians 5:18). And just as Jesus was motivated to speak and act by God the Father through the Spirit (John 5:30; 8:28, 42; 12:49; 14:10), so we Christians are to speak by the Spirit's leading (Mark 13:11; Luke 12:12; John 16:13). If the fruit of the Spirit (love, joy, peace, longsuffering, kindness, goodness, faithfulness, gentleness, and self-control; Galatians 5:22–23) is the profile of Jesus—and it is—and if we have the same Spirit as Jesus—and we do—shouldn't our profile be the same as His? The answer is, obviously, yes.

PROFILING AND PREDICTABILITY

Our profile—our character traits and thus our behavior—can become unpredictable when we fail to live in conformity to the mind of Christ. Our human mind can actually become debased through sin (Romans 1:28). We can pursue futile goals and vain objectives in life (Ephesians 4:17). We can set our minds on temporal, earthly things instead of on heavenly things (Colossians 3:2). And we can allow our minds—our faith and confidence in God—to be shaken by events around us (2 Thessalonians 2:2). Those traits and behaviors are not of the Spirit; Jesus never manifested any of them. So if they ever begin to characterize us, we can know that we are not under the Spirit's control and we are not living with the mind of Christ.

Crime Scene Investigation profilers might conclude, "Given our suspect's past traits and behaviors, we think he will strike again in the next six weeks." Christian Scene Investigators, on the other hand, might say something like this: "We have a tense situation developing in our inner-city ministry because of opposition from local drug dealers. We need to send in someone who is stable, courageous, winsome, and wise, but who will speak the truth in love. Who can defuse this situation the way Jesus often calmed antagonistic crowds? Whom do we know who has displayed these qualities in the past—whom can we expect will do the same again in this situation?"

While criminal profiling always focuses on others, in Christian profiling we can focus on ourselves as well. So, if you were to develop a profile of your life using the fruit of the Spirit or the characteristics of a church leader as an outline, how close would your profile come to the profile of Jesus? The goal of Christian Scene Profiling is not judgment or a guilt trip. Rather, we can let our profiles motivate us to renew our minds (Romans 12:2) and to yield to the Spirit moment by moment so we can have the mind of Christ.

There's nothing wrong with being predictable when it means showing up and acting like Jesus!

Signs of Life

Life Sign: My behavior reflects the teachings of Jesus.

Life Verse: *But the fruit of the Spirit is love, joy, peace, longsuffering, kindness, goodness, faithfulness, gentleness, self-control. Against such there is no law.*
—Galatians 5:22–23

Life in Action: In what specific ways can I more fully experience the fruit of the Spirit in my life?

Day 25

Making the "E" List

*Sometimes the smallest gesture, the simplest word, or the
shortest visit shines the light of
encouragement into someone's life.*

Once, at the end of his lecture, Greek philosopher Dr. Alexander Papaderos was asked, "What is the meaning of life?" Rather than dismissing that difficult question, he took from his pocket a small, round mirror about the size of a quarter. He told how, during World War II, he had rounded the edges of a larger piece of broken mirror from a wrecked German motorcycle in his village.

At first the small mirror was a toy for a wartime child, but it remained in the doctor's pocket as an adult. In fact, it became a metaphor for his purpose in life when he discovered that he could use the small mirror to reflect light into a dark place. That little mirror helped Dr. Papaderos realize that his life needed to be a source of light to others; he needed to reflect light into the dark places of other people's lives. Perhaps, he said, by doing so, he might not change everything, but he might change some things in some people.[1]

What I gleaned from this story about a tiny mirror is this: it doesn't take a lot to be an encourager. Far too often we think we're not equipped to be an encourager. We fear we don't have the words or the wisdom or the wherewithal to truly make a difference. We may be too discouraged ourselves to think we could encourage anyone else. But none of those thoughts are true. Sometimes the smallest gesture, the simplest word, or the shortest visit shines the light of encouragement into someone's life.

Opportunities to encourage others—"E" Opportunities, I call them—are all around us. What we need is a plan . . . a strategy . . . a little piece of a mirror always at hand by which we can shine the light of Christ's love into a dark situation. To that end, I encourage you to make an "E" List of all those people with whom you come in contact regularly and therefore could encourage.

ENCOURAGE YOUR SPOUSE

First, I believe that encouraging one's spouse is perhaps life's greatest ministry. Marriage is a perfect laboratory for encouragement. After all, it provides not only the reasons (it's easy to become discouraged in marriage) but plenty of opportunities as well (24 x 7 x 365 x the rest of your life!).

Husbands and wives have the non-optional responsibility before God to encourage each other. While scores of marriage books offer good ideas about how to be an encourager, I believe Peter's words have never been equaled. I paraphrase his words for marriage partners this way: "Husbands and wives, dwell with each other with understanding, giving honor to each other as heirs together of the grace of life" (1 Peter 3:7). I don't know of anything more encouraging than being understood and treated with honor.

And I think psychologist Abraham Maslow would agree with me. He developed a hierarchy of human needs and placed "self-actualization" at the highest level. As Christians, we might understand self-actualization as the increasing awareness of who we are in Christ, the awareness of our gifts, our new nature, our calling, and our freedom from slavery to sin. Marriage ought to be the primary place where spiritual and emotional self-actualization are encouraged as we extend and receive both understanding and honor.

Submitting to each other, serving each other, sharing in each other's deepest and innermost thoughts, dreams, fears, and joys—these behaviors are evidence of understanding and honor. While the ways these priorities are lived out will be as infinite and varied as marriages are, the result will always be the same: encouragement.

I've given the most space to the importance of spouses encouraging each other because marriage is life's most demanding and most fruitful relationship, and it sets the tone of all other human interaction. I believe that adults who are encouraged by and in their marriages will overflow with encouragement to everyone they meet.

ENCOURAGE YOUR CHILDREN

I also believe that encouraged and encouraging parents will produce encouraged and encouraging children. Living life with a "Yes!" perspective instead of the all-too-common "No!" should be our guiding philosophy with our children; we need to look for things they're doing right instead of things they're doing wrong. And we need to remember that, for children more than anyone else, love is spelled "t-i-m-e." The myth propagated years ago that it's the quality, not the quantity of time that is important in raising children has, thankfully, been debunked many times over. Children who don't think they're important enough for their parents to be with them can easily grow discouraged—especially during adolescence when the critical process of self-definition is taking place.

We can spend time with our children in many ways: in actual one-on-one activities as well as by writing notes and letters, listening, preparing favorite meals, celebrating victories, offering consolation in the face of defeat, and simply being home instead of somewhere else. The secure child is an encouraged child, and the encouraged child becomes a secure adult—and the cycle continues.

ENCOURAGE YOUR NEIGHBORS AND CO-WORKERS

If you are a Christian, you have a special God-given ability to encourage those in the world who may not know Christ. And, hopefully, you are more encouraged as a Christian than you were before knowing Christ. Not only do you know firsthand about life's discouraging moments (as we all do), but you've learned how knowing God makes a difference in life's hard times.

Many of our non-Christian friends and neighbors, however, may not know anyone with whom they can unburden their soul, and they don't know how to reach God. So God sends you and me to be "God" to them, to be as available and compassionate to them as Jesus Christ is to us. Such encouragement is a matter of seeing a need and meeting it. It may involve paying a compliment to someone at work, providing a meal for a sick neighbor, surprising a friend with a small gift of appreciation, extending an invitation to your home, or offering a listening ear over lunch. Encouragement at this level is not complicated. It's basically a matter of being willing to invest ourselves in the lives of those people God places in our path.

ENCOURAGE THOSE YOU DON'T KNOW

Maybe the most overlooked opportunities to reflect a bit of God's light into someone's life are with people we don't know personally. Think of who they are: the grocery store checkout person, the clerk in the department store, the person whom we stop to ask directions (or who stops us), the person we sit next to at a sporting event, concert, or PTA meeting, the appliance repairman who comes to our home, the mailman, delivery man, or garbage collector . . . and the list goes on. . . .

Hollywood gives us a great example of this in the romantic comedy *You've Got Mail.* I love the scene when the Tom Hanks character calms a tense situation between the Meg Ryan character and a supermarket checkout woman. By seeing the woman's name on her nametag and using it ("Hi, Rose! That is a great name. Rose."), injecting a bit of humor, wearing a smile, and wishing her a happy holiday, Hanks's character wins her over and defuses the tension.[2] All it cost him was a bit of creativity, a positive perspective, a kind word, and a warm and encouraging demeanor.

The cheapest deposit we will ever make is a simple word or act of encouragement in a stranger's emotional bank account. And it may be far more significant than we realize.

🙠

Of course you can add other categories of people to your "E" List— Christian friends in general, your closest personal friends, extended family members, church leaders, fellow church members, community and government leaders, people whom you hear or read about who have experienced some type of trouble or tragedy. . . . Our challenge is not so much identifying those who need encouraging, but developing a lifestyle of encouragement. Hopefully this chapter will spur you on toward that goal.

Be ready to make every day an "E" Day to remember!

signs of Life

Life Sign: Those who come in contact with me leave encouraged.

Life Verse: *Anxiety in the heart of man causes depression, But a good word makes it glad.*

—Proverbs 12:25

Life in Action: Here is a list of five people I will encourage this week—and an idea or two about how I might encourage each one of them.

On the Threshold of Opportunity

*You can be sure that God will open the
right door at the right time.*

A man named Walter once invited his friend Arthur to go for a
ride through some undeveloped land in Southern California.
They drove through some groves of trees and past some ram-
shackle buildings before they arrived at what looked to Arthur like barren
wasteland. Walter began telling his friend about the exciting plans he had
for this uninviting parcel of land. Walter's express purpose of the drive was
to give Arthur the opportunity to become an investor in his dream.

Walter had enough money for his main project, but he wanted to
ensure that the land surrounding his venture would be bought up at the
same time. He felt sure that within five years the whole area would be
filled with hotels, restaurants, and convention centers to serve the people
who came to visit his development. Arthur was not impressed, and
declined the opportunity.

And so Art Linkletter turned down the opportunity to buy up all the
land that now surrounds Disneyland, the dream-turned-reality of his
friend Walt Disney.[1] . . .

❦

While million-dollar opportunities rarely come along, you and I have millions of smaller open doors—opportunities that God provides—that we can walk through on a daily basis. God is constantly inviting us to trust Him and to experience ever-expanding dimensions of His faithfulness and blessing. But far too often we hang back hesitantly, not sure of what we should do.

Often, we Christians fail to walk through God's open doors because we have a faulty view of God. If we had a childlike, trusting attitude toward our heavenly Father, we would walk confidently through the doors He holds open for us just as a small child walks through doors her earthly father opens. God is trustworthy, and the more we get to know Him, the more easily we will recognize the doors He is holding open for us.

In Revelation 3:7–13, Jesus Christ speaks of an open door God has put before the church at Philadelphia, referring to the church's opportunity to be a gateway for the Gospel in Asia Minor—an opportunity the church should seize. Why? Because the God who was opening the door is holy, true, and powerful (verse 7): *holy* refers to God as the Almighty; *true,* to God as trustworthy; and *powerful,* to God as able.

God is the Opener and Closer of all doors in life. When He opens a door—when He sets an opportunity before us—we should walk through it. But I will be the first to admit that walking through some of God's open doors can definitely challenge our faith.

❦

After years of watching Christians miss opportunities God has set before them, though, I can offer four observations about why we don't walk through God's open doors.

First, opportunities are often disguised as problems. It was the brilliant cartoon philosopher Pogo who once observed, "Gentlemen, we are surrounded by insurmountable opportunities."[2] Too often what we perceive as obstacles—no money, no machinery, no methodology, no manpower—are God's opportunities in disguise.

Two decades ago, in the days before multi-venue simulcasts, my church was responsible for worship services being held in three different locations. We knew we needed larger facilities at our main location, and we eventually were able to build our current worship facility. But before that happened, we were stymied in our building program. Each time we began to discuss building plans, the three locations were at odds with one another over the allocation of resources and other matters. So we wrestled with that "problem" for several years.

Eventually, the problem became an opportunity. While we were stuck in our "no building" mode, the Lord showed us another way to reach more people—even more than if we had huge new facilities at all three locations. We began Turning Point Ministries, and now we send the Gospel out over radio, on television, and in print. If we had not been stuck with the building "problem," I don't know if we ever would have gone into radio and television. I know now that the media ministry was an opportunity disguised as a problem with our building program.

Don't miss an opportunity because it's dressed up in a misleading costume and is looking like a problem.

Second, opportunities are often time sensitive. When Walt Disney was planning Disneyland, he offered a friend the opportunity to buy up the scrubland surrounding the site, land that he knew would dramatically increase in value. The friend said he'd think about it. Because Disney needed an answer quickly, his friend lost the opportunity and tremendous wealth besides. If you fail to seize an opportunity God puts before you, it doesn't necessarily mean God is finished with you. But it probably means He will turn to someone else who will jump at the opportunity.

Do you remember what Jesus told the Jewish leaders when they failed to grasp that He was their long-awaited Messiah? "Therefore I say to you, the kingdom of God will be taken from you and given to a nation bearing the fruits of it" (Matthew 21:43). As a result of Israel's reluctance to walk through the door of salvation before them, God turned to the Gentiles and offered them the Gospel. Israel will yet have an opportunity to embrace Jesus, but only many long, sad centuries after missing their first opportunity (Zechariah 12:10).

Don't let hesitation become procrastination that leads to devastation.

Third, opportunities are often tested by opposition. Some people have gotten halfway through an open door and turned around when they encountered opposition. They thought, "We must not have heard God correctly. This opposition can't be from God." If Paul anticipated opposition when going through God's open doors, we should too (1 Corinthians 16:8–9). Opposition can actually be a sign that you heard God correctly and that Satan is doing all he can to discourage you and cause you to turn around.

Paul and Barnabas warned the churches in Asia Minor, "We must through many tribulations enter the kingdom of God" (Acts 14:22). Entering the kingdom refers not only to enjoying eternal salvation, but also to experiencing all the blessings God has in store for those who love Him (1 Corinthians 2:9). If God wants you to prosper in any way, you can be sure Satan does *not*. And your enemy will not sit idly by and watch you be blessed by your generous heavenly Father.

Don't miss a blessing-filled Christian life by trying to have a problem-free Christian life.

Finally, opportunities are usually missed because of fear. I can't think of a God-given opportunity I ever received without trembling hands. But let me assure you that I have often reached out and taken

God's steady hand as I walked through His open door—and so can you.

All opportunities and all open doors have one thing in common: they focus on the future. And when we're looking toward the future, we have two choices—to walk by faith or to walk in fear. God has not given us a spirit of fear (2 Timothy 1:7), but He has promised to go with us wherever we go in His will (Hebrews 13:5). God loves to get us to the place where our strength is little so that we can see His mighty power. The church in Revelation was told that an open door was before them "for you have . . . little strength" (Revelation 3:8), and God told Paul that His power was made perfect in human weakness (2 Corinthians 12:9).

So is there an opportunity in front of you at this very moment that makes you nervous, scared, weak, and faithless? Wonderful! You are right where you need to be to see God hold the door open for you as you walk through. I encourage you not to let fear dampen your anticipation of a victorious future.

Wherever there is a fearful response on our part, there is a faithful reassurance on God's.

Friend, you don't have to worry about how or when or where the next door in your life will open. The doors God opens for you only have doorknobs on one side . . . His! So you can be sure the true, holy, and powerful One will open for you the right door at the right time. The knob is in His hands.

That door may involve your job, where you live, your education, a partner in marriage, or an opportunity for ministry. Don't limit God! Develop eyes of faith that are constantly looking for doors He is opening. Use the four checkpoints above to evaluate any current opportunities and see if God is trying to get your attention. If you conclude that He is, then take a step of faith and seize the opportunity. Once you cross the threshold of that open door, you'll discover God's hand reaching out for yours on the other side.

SIGNS of Life

Life Sign: I courageously walk through the open doors God puts before me.

Life Verse: *And the LORD, He is the One who goes before you. He will be with you, He will not leave you nor forsake you; do not fear nor be dismayed.*

—Deuteronomy 31:8

Life in Action: What opportunity—set before me right now—do I need to seize?

The Ripple Effect

*We have the assurance of our salvation today
because of ripple effects set in motion
by others' faithfulness years ago.*

At 5:16 p.m. on November 9, 1965, events were set in motion that brought one of the richest, most industrialized, and highly populated areas of the Western world to a complete standstill. A back-up electrical relay switch was tripped at the Sir Adam Beck Power Station in Niagara Falls, Ontario, Canada. The switch had not been updated to keep pace with the increasing power transmission, and in less than three seconds the entire northeastern power grid, affecting both Canada and the United States, went down.

The results were unimaginable. There was no electrical energy to heat, to light, to communicate, to power any kind of machine, to operate pumps that move sewage, water, and gas, or to run life-support systems at many hospitals. An estimated 800,000 people were trapped in subways. Only half of 150 hospitals had emergency power systems available. The 250 flights arriving at John F. Kennedy Airport had to be diverted—and some planes were landing right as the runway lights went off. Without any light, heat, or phone system, 30 million people found themselves in a dark, silent, and frightening world. All because a spindle on a little metal cup in a small box touched a metal contact.

This anecdote is one of hundreds cited by British author and historian James Burke in his *Connections* books and video series.[1] He has made a career out of demonstrating the ways that history reveals life's connections in the most unexpected ways—how the smallest act or incident can set off a ripple effect far beyond expectations.

Fortunately, not all ripples are negative. Both Scripture and post-biblical history are filled with examples of ripple effects that helped spread the gospel of Jesus Christ throughout the world. To understand the power of spiritual ripple effects is to become empowered to take advantage of opportunities to set in motion events that result in the Gospel being shared and people being saved for eternity.

The reality of the spiritual ripple effect should compel every Christian to ask, "What kinds of ripples and waves am I setting into motion by my words and works for Christ?" People who toss stones into a pond don't always see who or what is touched by the waves their stones cause, but the waves go forth nonetheless. Similarly, we won't always know who is touched by our words and works for Christ. Our job, however, is not to question whether our words and works are having a certain impact. Instead, our job is to continually cast ourselves upon the water and put in motion those waves that God can direct in His perfect way in order to accomplish His perfect results.

Think for a moment about the greatest ripple effect in history—the impact of the "One Solitary Life" of Jesus of Nazareth. The author of that famous bit of prose—written in the last century—said it so well:

> Here is a man who was born in an obscure village, the child of a peasant woman. . . . He never owned a home. He never wrote a book. He never held an office. He never had a family. He never went to college. He never put His foot inside a big city. He never traveled two hun-

dred miles from the place He was born. . . . When He was dead, He was laid in a borrowed grave through the pity of a friend. Nineteen long centuries have come and gone, and today He is a centerpiece of the human race and leader of the column of progress. I am far within the mark when I say that all the armies that ever marched, all the navies that were ever built, all the parliaments that ever sat, and all the kings that ever reigned, put together, have not affected the life of man upon this earth as powerfully as has that one solitary life.[2]

The Christian Gospel is the story of the life, death, and resurrection of one Man two thousand years ago, and since that time the account of Jesus' victory over sin and death has been embraced by hundreds of millions of people. You and I are beneficiaries of this ripple effect of the Gospel. Those of us over whom the waves of God's grace have washed are responsible for infusing the Gospel with new power and causing the ripple effect to continue and to impact others.

We don't find the specific words *ripple effect* in the four Gospels, but it seems abundantly clear that Jesus' own ministry did indeed have a ripple effect. One example of ever-expanding circles of influence (picture the stone cast into the pond) begins with the disciple John, who seems to have had the closest relationship with Jesus (John 13:23, 25; 19:26; 20:2; 21:7, 20). John's influence seemed to impact Peter and James (John's brother), and the three of them formed an inner circle within the Twelve (Matthew 17:1; Mark 5:37; 13:3; 14:33). Next was that circle of twelve disciples who traveled and ministered with Jesus for three years. They were the core of the larger post-Resurrection group of 120 who gathered in Jerusalem to await the gift of the Holy Spirit (Acts 1:1–8, 15). As a result of the pebble from the pulpit that Peter tossed into the sea of Jews gathered in Jerusalem at Pentecost, the waves of the Spirit washed over 3,000 souls, a number which shortly grew to 5,000 men and undoubtedly many more women and children (Acts 2:41; 4:4).

So, at least in terms of influence if not chronology, Jesus had one disciple, then three, then twelve, then 120, then 3,000, then more than

5,000 . . . and the rest, as they say, is His-story. Following Jesus' own instructions in Acts 1:8, the disciples made waves with their Gospel message, and this good news left Jerusalem and washed over all Judea and Samaria, then Damascus and Antioch (modern Syria), Galatia (Asia Minor), Macedonia (Greece), Rome (Italy), and from there possibly into Spain (Europe) (Romans 15:24, 28). And, being used as John was, the apostle Paul kept the ripple going through those whose lives he touched.

"Yes," many Christians say, "I can well understand the impact of John, Peter, James, the Twelve, and Paul. They were apostles! But my life will never set off those kinds of ripple effects."

Wait! What were these people before they were apostles? They were—like you and me—commoners of the most ordinary sort. They were people whose names would never have garnered a footnote in history had they not responded to Christ's call.

But how different history would be if an ordinary man named Andrew had not gone to find his brother, Simon (Peter), and said, "We have found the Messiah" (John 1:40–41). What if another ordinary man named Philip had not sought out Nathanael and told him, "We have found Him of whom Moses in the law, and also the prophets, wrote—Jesus of Nazareth, the son of Joseph" (John 1:45)? And what if an ordinary fisherman named Peter had not responded to the request of a Gentile named Cornelius and gone to his house to share the Gospel (Acts 10:1–48)?

What if a five-year-old child named John Wesley had not been snatched from a burning house? And what if his brother Charles had not taken ill and, during that time, read Luther's commentary on Galatians and learned of salvation by grace through faith? What if they had not had their godly mother, Susanna, teaching each of her nineteen children the things of God and praying for them?

What if martyrs and reformers like Polycarp, Ignatius, Huss, Savonarola, Latimer, Ridley, and Cranmer had recanted their faith in the face of the flames? What if an unknown Sunday-school teacher named Edward Kimball had not pursued a recalcitrant lad named Dwight L.

Moody, ultimately winning him to Christ in a Chicago shoe store? What if a dairy farmer in Charlotte, North Carolina, had not faithfully taught his young son, Billy Graham, the Gospel from an early age? You and I have the assurance of our salvation today because of the ripple effects set in motion by other people's faithfulness years and even generations ago. But what about those people who have yet to hear the Gospel? Who will speak the words and do the works that will set in motion the events that will lead to their being saved? By God's grace and through our obedience to the Holy Spirit's promptings, you and I will set those ripples in motion.

INITIATE POWERFUL RIPPLES

To great effect, twentieth-century missionaries and evangelists took advantage of a dynamic presented in Scripture, and that dynamic is *oikos,* evangelism. Actually, *oikos* is the Greek word for "house" or "household," and it refers to the way the Gospel tends to travel along familial and relational lines. The jailer in Philippi, for example, brought his whole family to the Lord as soon as he heard the Gospel (Acts 16:31–34). Likewise, many around the world are won to Christ from within a circle of influence, an *oikos,* which the Gospel has penetrated.

Now take a fresh look (below) at the ever-widening pools of influence across which the ripple effect started by God being at work in your life can spread when you take advantage of God-given opportunities to speak and act in the name of Christ:

1. Family—Those within your immediate family are the most fertile ground for planting seeds of the Gospel.

2. Extended family—Relatives with whom you have contact and who can observe your life may need to hear the Gospel—from you.

3. Close personal friends—These can develop from many sources, but it is the trust and intimacy you share which makes your influence significant.

4. Work associates—Family is at the top of the list, but we spend the next greatest amount of time with other people in vocational and educational contexts.

5. Neighbors—The greatest untapped harvest fields in modern America are our neighborhoods. When will we take the time to open and establish lines of communication along which the Gospel can spread?

6. Civic and community contacts—Manifesting biblical values of integrity, compassion, and generosity at the community level will open unexpected doors of opportunity.

7. Strangers—"Divine appointments" which appear insignificant to us can have a life-changing impact on one who meets Christ in us.

The question for every Christian is not whether our lives have a ripple effect on the people around us—but what *kind* of effect we are having on those people. I challenge each of you—as I challenge myself—to ask God for a year of making powerful ripple effects for His Gospel. You may not see the shore on which each wave lands, but the shore where you stand at this moment is where the wave must begin.

signs of Life

Life Sign: My life makes waves in the hearts of those around me.

Life Verse: *Let no one despise your youth, but be an example to the believers in word, in conduct, in love, in spirit, in faith, in purity.*

—1 Timothy 4:12

Life in Action: What ripples and waves am I setting in motion with my words and my works for Christ?

Day 28

Jesus' Rolled-Up Sleeves

*This humble Man was willing to lead by example,
willing to put others before Himself.*

The story is told of a soldier who lay dying and the preacher who came to attend to him. "Can I help you in any way?" the young preacher asked.

"I'm cold," snapped the dying man. In silence the minister took off his overcoat and spread it over him.

The dying man glared at him awhile. "My neck is hurting," he snarled in pain, and off came the minister's suit coat to serve as a pillow.

A few more moments of glaring and then the voice came in a softer tone: "I'd sure like a cigarette." The preacher found a cigarette, lit it, and put it in the soldier's mouth.

Finally the soldier said to the compassionate preacher, "Mister, if you've got anything in that Bible that makes you act like this, read it to me."[1]

That story reminds me of something that happened to a friend of mine when he was a seminary student in Dallas, Texas. As part of his course in pastoral ministry skills, he was required to spend a Saturday night in the busy emergency room of a large hospital near downtown Dallas. Under the supervision of the hospital chaplain's staff, my friend was to minister in whatever way he could—prayer, encouragement, counsel— to those coming into the emergency room and to their families.

Late that Saturday night an ambulance brought in a woman to the emergency room who had attempted to take her own life by cutting her wrists. She was past middle age and very thin, and her face indicated years of despair and hard living. Her wrists were bandaged and the medics had stabilized her, so she was in no danger of dying. But she was in a highly agitated state and needed someone to comfort her. So my friend stood by her side as doctors worked on her wrists—wrists that bore the scars of numerous previous acts of desperation.

After the doctor was finished and left the room, my friend began listening to the woman's story with a measure of compassion that was no doubt strange to her. No judgment, no trying to evangelize her, no trying to point out where she was wrong. My friend loved her by just listening to her. When he did have the opportunity to speak, he told her how much God loved her, cared about her, and understood the pain she was feeling.

When it was time for the woman to leave the treatment room, she looked up at my friend and asked, "Are you Jesus?"

THE JESUS WHOM PEOPLE LOVE

Lots of people in the world don't like religion in general or Christianity (or Christians) in particular, but it's hard to find anyone who has anything bad to say about Jesus. What could they say? Jesus was kind, humble, wise, strong, sacrificial, gentle, and willing to associate with everyone. There is no record anywhere of Him doing anything untoward or unkind. Even when He spoke or acted forcefully, people agreed that His actions were needed and justified (Matthew 23:1–39; John 2:13–16).

The only people in the Bible who didn't like Jesus were those who were jealous of His popularity with the common people. These people sensed something good in Jesus. He was the kind of person anyone would have loved to hang out with, to use our modern language; He was the kind of person anyone would want as a friend. Women were touched by His kindness, men were amazed at His strength, and children found comfort and love in His arms.

While there were lots of day-to-day reasons to be attracted to Jesus, something He did for His disciples on the night before His crucifixion has come to define who He was: a humble servant. You may be very familiar with the scene . . .

Jesus and the Twelve had gathered to celebrate the Passover meal. When Jesus mentioned that one of those present would betray Him, a discussion immediately ensued as to who the guilty one might be. And that, not surprisingly, led to an argument among them as to who the greatest might be—that is, who would be the least likely to ever betray the Master (Luke 22:22–24). No doubt, this was not a case of the disciples commending one another. Instead, they were probably each pointing to himself as the greatest—the least likely to commit an act of betrayal, the kind of act Peter would commit later that night (Matthew 26:33; John 18:25–27).

Now this was not the first time the Twelve had engaged in such grand speculations about their personal sanctity and worthiness. Earlier in Capernaum, Jesus discovered the disciples arguing about who among them was the greatest. Interestingly, this argument also followed Jesus' teaching that He would one day be betrayed and killed (Mark 9:30–34). At that point, the disciples seemed intent on proving they would serve Jesus until the end. After this first argument about greatness, however, Jesus sat them down for a talk: "If anyone desires to be first, he shall be last of all and servant of all" (Mark 9:35).

But let's return to the Passover celebration. When the argument about greatness broke out this time, Jesus took a different approach. Instead of *talking* to the disciples about servanthood, He *showed* them.

Since no household servant was present, Jesus Himself took on that role (as the apostle Paul later explained in Philippians 2:7). The Son of God took a towel and a basin of water and began washing the dust and grime from His disciples' dirty feet. While the echoes of the word *greatness* were still reverberating in the room, Jesus showed His disciples that the nature of true greatness is . . . humble service.

Even by the dim lamplight in that darkened room, I'm sure the beet-red faces of the disciples were plainly evident. Can you imagine anything more embarrassing than to be proclaiming one's own greatness right before the Son of God washes your smelly, calloused feet?

But that's why people love Jesus; that's why Jesus was truly great. There was no pretense or presumption about Him. This humble Man was willing to lead by example and willing to put others before Himself. What is there not to like about Jesus?

BEING LIKE JESUS

It would have been convicting enough for Jesus to wash the disciples' feet without saying a word. But when He finished, He said to them, "If I then, your Lord and Teacher, have washed your feet, you also ought to wash one another's feet. For I have given you an example, that you should do as I have done to you" (John 13:14–15).

It is perfectly clear that Jesus wanted His disciples (and that includes us) to be like Him. He was not calling us today to perform the same act of servanthood that was a custom in His day. Instead He was calling you and me to be people who are not above serving others. In the twenty-first century, what would such service look like? Cutting a neighbor's grass? Changing the diapers of an incontinent, aging parent? Cleaning up the church grounds after a windstorm leaves the property littered with tree limbs and debris? Stepping up to serve in the church nursery when there is an unexpected shortage of workers? Doing a spouse's chores when you know he or she has had a particularly hard day?

There is an infinite number of ways for us to serve as our Savior served. Some of the ways we can plan, and those are the "easy" opportunities. More challenging are those situations for which we don't plan—those divine appointments that we find God has arranged, like the encounter my friend had with the desperate woman in the hospital emergency room. In such situations we find people desperately longing for someone to help them, to serve them, like Jesus would. In those situations we find the world hungry not for religion or Christianity, but for Jesus Himself.

Jesus didn't love us just because we need to be loved. He loved us also that we might learn to love (serve) one another (John 13:34). Henry Drummond, in his classic sermon "The Greatest Thing in the World," explained how such a transformation takes place: If a piece of ordinary steel is attached to a magnet and left there, after a while the magnetism of the magnet passes into the steel so that it too becomes a magnet. The way we learn to love others, then, is by staying so close to Jesus that His love becomes our love for others.[2]

The Jesus in you may be the only Jesus someone ever meets. Make sure they see the Jesus people have always loved.

siGns of Life

Life Sign: Humility is the hallmark of my service.

Life Verse: *For I have given you an example, that you should do as I have done to you.*

—John 13:15

Life in Action: What actions could I take to—like Jesus—live with humility in front of the people around me?

Open Hands
Living a
GENEROUS
Life

Open Hands

You can successfully live life with an open hand.

According to tradition, the custom of shaking hands began among ancient German duelists as a sign of peaceful intentions. The men couldn't draw swords when their hands were outstretched, so an open hand signified that they were meeting as friends.[1] Conversely, a closed or clenched fist is a universal sign of greed and selfishness. Furthermore, a closed hand often means a closed heart.

In light of those facts, I'd like to suggest making this The Year of the Open Hand. And the first step to making that happen in your personal world depends on how you answer the question God asked Moses in Exodus 4:2: "What is that in your hand?" When Moses told Him—it was his shepherd's staff—God commanded him to open his hand and release it. As Moses relinquished it, the Lord returned it to him with fresh power and purpose.

What is in *your* hand? Are your fingers open, hands lifted upward, releasing everything to God and ready to receive all He wants to give you? Or are you grasping onto life with a death grip?

Be warned! A trapper in the African Congo devised a clever

monkey trap using a hollow gourd into which peanuts were poured through a small hole. The monkey would reach in and grab the peanuts, but the hole was too small to remove his closed hand. Unwilling to release his treasure, the monkey would be caught.[2]

What are you grasping tightly. . . trying to keep under your control . . . unwilling to give to the Lord? Perhaps it's a relationship? a possession? a plan, a goal, or a dream? Maybe it's an attitude of bitterness you should have released months ago? Perhaps God isn't able to bless you because your hand isn't open to receive His blessings.

A closed hand is based on the faulty assumption that we know more about what's best for us than our all-knowing God whose wisdom is unfathomable. An open hand, however, reflects the humble awareness that the Lord Jesus can do more than we can do and that His plan for us is better than any we can devise. An open hand says, "Lord, You know how precious this thing is to me, but I acknowledge You as *more* precious. You have a greater plan for my life, and I don't want to miss it by clinging to my own tarnished treasures. I'm opening my hand to You in surrender and trust."

A retirement fund executive I know recently spoke of the years when his son was away from the Lord. "I finally realized I had to open my hands and let him go," said Bill. "For a while I tried to control, to manipulate, to pressure, to influence events, but my efforts only drove him further away. I finally just opened my hands and released my son into God's care and keeping. I knew the Lord was able to do more than I could. In time, the Lord brought my son back to Himself and back to us."

Are you, like Bill, burdened by a difficult problem? Open your hands and release that problem to the Lord. His hands are bigger than yours, and He can do far more than you can do. So give to Him all your fears, all your worries, all your anxiety. Cast all your cares on Him, for He cares for you (see 1 Peter 5:7).

Also give God those sins that you can't seem to beat. Confess them and ask Him to forgive and cleanse you. And give Him those precious people and things that you're clutching. An open hand signifies willingness—your willingness to part with your sins, your struggles, yourself. Missionary E. Stanley Jones wrote, "In self-realization you try to realize your self, for all the answers are in you. In self-surrender, you surrender your self to Jesus Christ, for all the answers are in Him."[3]

GENEROSITY

Besides reflecting a humble trust in God, our open hand also signifies generosity. Deuteronomy 15:7–8 tells us that whenever we encounter a "poor man of your brethren," we should not harden our hearts, "but you shall open your hand wide to him and willingly lend him sufficient for his need, whatever he needs." The wise woman in Proverbs 31 "opens her hand to the poor, and reaches out her hands to the needy" (verse 20 RSV).

My mother was such a wise woman. One of my greatest childhood memories involves something she did every Saturday night. She got out all the bills and put them on the table. Then she opened the checkbook, and the first check she wrote was always to the church. I saw the box of offering envelopes sitting there, and I watched her week after week give the firstfruits to the Lord. She was like the woman in Proverbs 31, and I grew up with that living testimony in front of me.

Will your children have similar memories? Listen to the way the *Amplified Bible* renders 2 Corinthians 9:7: "Let each one [give] as he has made up his own mind and purposed in his heart, not reluctantly or sorrowfully or under compulsion, for God loves (He takes pleasure in, prizes above other things, and is unwilling to abandon or to do without) a cheerful (joyous, "prompt to do it") giver"—whose heart is in his giving.

Spiritual giving begins in the heart with "I want to." It's translated to the head where it says, "I will." Then it opens the hand and says, "I'm doing it." This open-hearted, open-handed giving can characterize your very next act of obedience and service.

RECEPTIVITY

An open hand implies receptivity as well as generosity, for it's hard to receive a gift when your hands are closed. God's hands, after all, are open and stretched in our direction: He is ready to give all that we need—and more. As Psalm 145:16 puts it: "You open Your hand and satisfy the desire of every living thing."

Jesus' hands offer the most stirring example of open hands in human history. The sinless Lamb of God had His arms stretched out along the crossbeam of Calvary and His hands wide open to receive the nails that affixed Him there for us. It is Jesus' nature to give with open, nail-pierced hands. Consider how often the verb *give* is connected to the nouns *God, Jesus,* and *the Lord* in the Bible.

> If you then, being evil, know how to give good gifts to your children, how much more will your Father who is in heaven give good things to those who ask Him! . . . God so loved the world that He gave. . . . Christ also loved the church and gave Himself for her. . . . [He] gave Himself for our sins . . . and gave Himself for me. . . . He who did not spare His own Son . . . how shall He not with Him also freely give us all things? . . . [He] gives us richly all things to enjoy (Matthew 7:11; John 3:16; Ephesians 5:25; Galatians 1:4; Galatians 2:20; Romans 8:32; 1 Timothy 6:17).

These biblical truths cut to the heart of our relationship with God through Christ Jesus our Lord. Jesus wants the treasure you're grasping so tightly; He wants you to open your hands so He can bless you. What might God be wanting to give you that He can't because your hands are closed? What could you be releasing to Him? Your open hands will mean endless possibilities; closed hands, none.

Think of the woman Jesus met at the well (John 4). Evidently Jesus intentionally traveled through Samaria and stopped at Jacob's well because, in His omniscience, He knew that there was a woman there whose hands—and heart—were ready to open themselves to Him. And Jesus was ready to abundantly give. "Whoever drinks of the water that I shall give him will never thirst. But the water that I shall give him will become in him a fountain of water springing up into everlasting life," He said (verse 14). And the woman replied, "Sir, give me this water" (verse 15).

The Lord wants to give us more peace, more grace, more love for Him, more love for others, more patience, more joy, more self-control. He longs to give you a new start in humility, generosity, and receptivity. But He is waiting for you to hold out your empty hands—and He'll help you do that. Just ask Him! Simply say, "Lord, I can't open my hands by myself, but with Your help, I'm willing to stretch out my fingers to You."

Like a good Father, He will help you unclench your fist. Then He'll fill your world with His goodness. He can help you live life with an open hand.

> *The Lord spread out His hands for me,*
> *Outstretched on cruel Calvary.*
> *May I this year return the sign:*
> *A hand unfurled by grace divine.*

SIGNS of Life

Life Sign: I look for ways to generously give to others.

Life Verse: *If there is among you a poor man of your brethren, within any of the gates in your land which the LORD your God is giving you, you shall not harden your heart nor shut your hand from your poor brother, but you shall open your hand wide to him and willingly lend him sufficient for his need, whatever he needs.*

—Deuteronomy 15:7–8

Life in Action: What resources do I have that I can give to help others?

Empty-Pocket Living

In the kingdom of God, empty pockets are praised.

Sometime in the 1700s, pockets as we know them today came into being. But they are very different from an early form of pocket that was a small bag, or purse, hung from one's belt or even around one's neck. But . . .

- **Problem:** Pockets hanging from the belt were an easy target for thieves.

- **Solution:** Hang pockets from the belt, but on the *inside* of the clothes rather than the outside.

- **Problem:** This solution foiled thieves, but it also kept the owner from easily retrieving anything from the pocket.

- **Solution:** Cut a slit in the side of the pants (pantaloons) to allow access to the pocket.

- **Problem:** Reaching through the slit and trying to open the pocket from inside the clothes was much too cumbersome.

- **Solution:** Someone suggested sewing the pocket right inside the slit in the pants so that one's hand went directly into the pocket. Brilliant![1]

THE LAW OF THE POCKET

If no one has come up with this spiritual law before, I'll call it Jeremiah's Law of the Pocket and introduce it right now: "Personal possessions expand to fill the empty space in all available pockets." As I use the pocket as a metaphor for our lives, see if you don't agree.

It seems to me that the more room we have (the more pockets we have) in life, the more stuff we accumulate to fill up that room. For instance, think about how families progress through life. Their first house is usually small, and the young couple barely has enough furniture to fill it up. But eventually they do, and pretty soon, as children come along, they need more room. So their next home is larger—perhaps it has a basement, a walk-in attic, or a spare bedroom—and all the regular rooms are much larger. They laugh and joke, shouting "Hello-o-o-o" as their voices bounce around the empty rooms. "Wow, we'll never fill this place up!" they predict. Then before they know it, their two cars are parked in the driveway because the double-size garage is full of stuff, and every room on the inside is packed to overflowing too.

None of us means for this to happen, but it just does. It's Jeremiah's Law of the Pocket: "Personal possessions expand to fill the empty space in all available pockets."

From the very beginning, the most important purpose for pockets was to carry one's money. After all, people didn't have all the gadgets and papers and things to carry around that we have today. With easy money to be made with a cunning hand, thieves—pickpockets—made pockets their target. But, as we move through life, instead of our pockets getting filled with more and more money that we can use to build up God's kingdom, our pockets fill up with the things money can buy. We dig deeply in order to give to the Lord's work, but there just doesn't seem to

176

be a lot there. Somehow we always seem strapped when it comes to giving money to God.

Let me therefore suggest that all of us have—or should work toward having—five different kinds of money in our pocket that we can use as God directs.

PARTITIONS IN YOUR POCKET

First is, in a sense, *invisible money.* This is money that you have, but you don't have it to spend as you would like. Think about the $5 your mom gave you when you went on a field trip in elementary school: "Now, David, don't lose this money or spend it. Take it to school and give it to your teacher. Understand?" For a brief time, that money was in my possession, but it was not mine to spend as I wished. It was designated for a purpose. Ultimately I received the benefit of the trip, but when I handed the money to my teacher, I lost control of it.

Ten percent of a Christian's money (income) should be *invisible money.* It's in your possession for a while before you turn it back over to the Lord. It's God's tithe: it's the tenth of all that He gives us—and it belongs to Him anyway (Leviticus 27:30; Deuteronomy 14:22–23; Malachi 3:10; Luke 11:42).

Next is *pocket money.* We usually think of pocket money as the change, the coins, we carry in our pocket or purse. It doesn't usually add up to a lot of money, and it's money we are comfortable giving on a moment's notice—like the one-time gift the Philippians sent to the apostle Paul (Philippians 4:10–20).

There ought to be this category of money we give above and beyond our tithe, money that we feel free to give generously and willingly whenever a need arises. Perhaps a collection is being taken up to help meet the needs of a Sunday-school class member, or a love offering is being collected for a visiting missionary. Or perhaps a neighborhood child comes to your door selling candy or wrapping paper to help her school. This *pocket money*—and the amount will vary for each of us—is money that we're free to say, "Sure, I'd be glad to help" when someone is in need.

Third is *wallet money.* I'm referring to a wallet because that's where we keep bills . . . folding money . . . the presidential paper. This is a bit more serious money than *pocket money;* it takes a deeper commitment to spend *wallet money* than *pocket money.*

In my mind, this is the kind of money the Corinthians set aside at the first of every week to prepare for the collection Paul was taking for the needs of the church in Jerusalem (1 Corinthians 16:1–4). It was a long-term commitment, not an impulsive gift. *Wallet money* is probably a sacrificial gift, one that requires you to choose to give up one thing in order to accomplish another.

The next category is *check money*—money that we don't carry around with us but which we spend by writing a check. This is giving that costs at a higher level altogether.

Maybe, for instance, you pray about making a two-year commitment to support a missionary every month—a decision that represents several thousands of dollars. Or you hear about a widow in your church whose furnace has just broken down in the middle of winter and must be replaced. You and a friend decide the Lord wants you to meet her need. The gift won't be tax-deductible; it will mean putting off a repair on your own house—and there will be no public praise involved. But you give beyond what you would ordinarily give for the sake of someone who is in need—just as the Macedonians did when they learned that their brothers and sisters in Jerusalem were suffering (2 Corinthians 8:1–7).

Finally, there's *serious money.* That's not to say that the previous four categories aren't serious. All money belongs to God, so all of it is serious. But when you give *serious money,* you are saying, "Lord, it all belongs to You. As a slave of Jesus Christ, I acknowledge that all I have comes from

You and is Yours to spend. Feel free to ask for any or all that I have, and I will obey."

David gave *serious money* when he emptied his personal treasury to build the first temple in Jerusalem (1 Chronicles 29:1–20). And Paul left behind *serious money*, along with everything else in his world, when he made knowing Christ the sole goal of his life (Philippians 3:7–14). For the individuals who have given their life to Christ, Paul says, giving up earthly things to gain heavenly things is a sign of maturity (verse 15).

WHAT'S IN YOUR POCKET?

The world we live in says that full pockets are a sign of intelligence, diligence, and prosperity. But in the kingdom of God, it's empty pockets that are praised. Jesus never praised the rich for having full pockets after giving, but He did praise a poor widow whose pockets were empty after she gave her last two pennies (Luke 21:1–4).

If we are generous people before the Lord, we will commit to giving Him our *invisible money.* Then sometimes He will ask us to give *pocket money,* sometimes *wallet money,* occasionally *check money,* and then that one-time gift of *serious money.* In fact, if we reverse the order and give God our *serious money* first—if we give Him all that we are and all that we have—the rest of the giving will flow like a stream of living water through us to others.

So talk to God today about your pockets and what's in them. Ask Him for grace to live with pockets that are empty—or with no pockets at all!

signs of Life

Life Sign: I give to others because God has given richly to me.

Life Verse: *Command those who are rich in this present age not to be haughty, nor to trust in uncertain riches but in the living God, who gives us richly all things to enjoy. Let them do good, that they be rich in good works, ready to give, willing to share, storing up for themselves a good foundation for the time to come, that they may lay hold on eternal life.*

—1 Timothy 6:17–19

Life in Action: How do I view money? Do I see it as what God has given to me *or* as what God has given to me to give to others?

Day 31

Rich Man, Poor Man

Christian discipleship is radical.
Live as a servant of Christ!

While many Christians know *of* Dr. Bill Bright, the late founder and president of Campus Crusade for Christ International, far fewer know *about* Dr. Bright and his wife, Vonette. And what I want to tell you about them, I tell you as their friend because of my admiration for them. Dr. Bright and Vonette stand as sterling examples of people who decided never to let the things of this earth interfere with their pursuit of heaven.

Dr. Bright was a prospering young businessman, well on his way to financial success, when he and Vonette met Christ. As they grew in their faith, they were struck by the total commitment of Jesus' disciples and decided they should live their lives the same way. So they drew up written contracts with Christ, promising to turn over all their possessions—including their gifts, abilities, and dreams for their future—to Him to be used in His service. In this written document, they literally gave up everything they owned and became slaves of Christ (Romans 1:1). Within twenty-four hours of that decision, Bill Bright received inspiration from the Lord to start the organization that became Campus Crusade for Christ International.

And Bill Bright never looked back on that commitment. A 1997 *Christianity Today* article explores how the Brights, as slaves of Christ, handled money. That year Campus Crusade had revenues of over $300 million, but Bill and Vonette Bright drew combined salaries of $48,000, raised from individual supporters like all other CCC staff. When he won the Templeton Prize for Progress in Religion in 1996, Dr. Bright donated the entire prize—more than $1 million—to help develop a worldwide ministry for teaching about prayer and fasting. He invested $50,000, nearly all his modest CCC retirement account, to start a discipleship training center in Moscow. All the royalties from his numerous books go to Campus Crusade; he accepted no speaking fees and had no savings account. The Brights owned no car or real estate, and they paid monthly rent to live in a condominium donated to Campus Crusade as a gift.[1]

I publicize this information about Dr. and Mrs. Bright only because it has, with their permission, previously been made public. Even so, I recount these facts with some hesitation: I'm aware of the danger of inviting comparisons when we focus on the life of an individual Christian who has accomplished extraordinary things. But I call attention to my friends' lifestyle because it illustrates the right response to what Jesus told a rich young ruler to do—but he could not do it. Jesus' statement to this man was so radical that he simply would not follow through. But I believe Jesus Christ spoke the same challenge to Bill and Vonette Bright—and they obeyed.

Christian discipleship is radical. Living as a servant of Christ is radical. And that radical perspective is missing from much of Christianity today. When Jesus Christ asked the wealthy ruler to give up everything he had and follow Him, he hesitated and was lost. Bill Bright didn't hesitate, and I believe the Brights' example is worthy of notice in a day when the earth stands in the way of heaven for so many disciples.

A RADICAL QUESTION

It is significant that Matthew, Mark, and Luke all record the story of the rich young ruler (see Matthew 19:16–30; Mark 10:17–31; Luke 18:18–30). The account starts off as a touching inquiry by one who has heartfelt concerns about eternal life, but it ends as a tragedy: the man loses the kingdom because of his love of materialism.

By combining all three Gospel writers' accounts, we get a 3-D image of this encounter. A young Jewish ruler (an official of some kind), whom we learn is very rich, falls to his knees before Jesus and asks what he must do to inherit eternal life. Jesus' first answer—based on the Decalogue, the Ten Commandments—is that he must keep the six commandments having to do with loving one's neighbor (Exodus 20:12–17). The young man acknowledges that he has kept these commandments from his youth, probably meaning since his *bar mitzvah* ("son of the commandment") at age 13. He is not responding arrogantly or pridefully; he is simply saying he has been focused intently on the external keeping of the laws of God, much as Paul the apostle had been doing (Philippians 3:5–6).

The young man's answer prompted a response of *agape* love from Jesus—probably a response of compassion for someone who had spent his whole life focused on the wrong priority. The young man had kept the external requirements of the law, yet sensed in his heart that it wasn't enough to gain eternal life. Jesus loved him for his honest search and transparent inquiry.

But when Jesus moved the conversation from external proficiencies to internal priorities, the young ruler's face fell. Jesus had focused on the weakest link in the chain that the young man had hoped would anchor him to heaven's gate.

JESUS' RADICAL ANSWER

Many Jewish leaders would probably have answered as the young ruler had, saying that they had faithfully kept the laws of God. Again, we have

Paul's testimony that he was blameless as to the Law, and others undoubtedly held themselves in the same high regard. But when Jesus issued the next requirement for eternal life, He knocked the young ruler's foundation of rule-keeping right out from under him: "One thing you lack: Go your way, sell whatever you have and give to the poor, and you will have treasure in heaven; and come, take up the cross, and follow Me" (Mark 10:21).

To be honest, most Christians' unspoken response to that command is probably exactly like the young ruler's: "Is He serious?" The synoptic writers tell us the young man went away crestfallen, "for he had great possessions."

Apparently this young man would allow Jesus to have everything in his life—his sexual temptations, his desire to take vengeance, his murderous anger, his inclinations to lie, his need to honor his parents— everything except his possessions. The wealth was his—and he would use it for good things. He would use it to keep the Law. He would give some of it away as offerings. But he wasn't going to give it up. He wasn't going to go from being a man with riches to a man without riches. And he didn't say why he wouldn't. He just took his wealth and walked away.

And Jesus said to His disciples (that's us too), "How hard it is for those who have riches to enter the kingdom of God!" (Mark 10:23).

OUR ANSWER: RADICAL OR REGRETFUL?

Was Jesus serious? We know He was: Jesus didn't lie or say anything He didn't mean. But maybe that test was just for that one young man? Do you think? I'm thinking not. In Luke 14:26–27, Jesus addressed a large crowd of followers and said basically the same thing: if you're not willing to leave everything behind, you "cannot be My disciple."

If you and I were conversing personally about this, at this point we'd both be looking for something profound to say. Our mutual silence would be an echo of the young ruler's silence when he turned and walked away. There's little to say in the face of such radical simplicity: "Give up your wealth and possessions—all of it—and follow Me."

Are you and I answering Jesus radically ("Yes, Lord") or regretfully ("No, Lord")? I can't tell you at what point things have to leave your hand or your home in order for you to know you're not letting earth stand in the way of heaven. You'll have to get before the Lord and do what Bill and Vonette Bright did—say, "Lord, I am Your slave. Everything I have is Yours. Now show me what to do with it as Your faithful servant." If you ask Him to show you, He will.

Make a commitment to get earth out of heaven's way. Turn your wealth, gifts, abilities, and dreams over to God to use in His service. As the radical missionary Jim Elliot said, "He is no fool who gives what he cannot keep to gain that which he cannot lose."[2]

SiGNS of Life

Life Sign: Nothing stands in my way of following Jesus.

Life Verse: *How hard it is for those who have riches to enter the kingdom of God!*

—Mark 10:23

Life in Action: Are there any aspects of my life that are standing in the way of heavenly pursuits? What can I do to be more heavenly minded?

Making a Way

*It's impossible to know every Christian intimately,
but we can open our hearts to anyone
who claims the name of Christ.*

The names of people who have served God in important, sometimes illustrious, ways appear throughout the Bible. You've read their stories yourself or heard of their legendary feats . . . I'm thinking of Abraham, Moses, Deborah, Esther, David, Peter, John, Mary Magdalene, Gaius, and Paul, just to mention a few.

Wait a minute. Gaius? Who's Gaius? Glad you asked! Gaius can be characterized as a very ordinary person in most respects, but it's not by chance that someone gets mentioned in the Bible. A name appears or is omitted on purpose. Some folks are cited for their good works; others attain eternal notoriety because of their disobedience to God. And some people who lived otherwise obscure lives are mentioned in the Scriptures because of a single exemplary act of faith.

Gaius's name appears in the Bible as a testimony to his spiritual acts of service. Perhaps you aren't familiar with him, but without a doubt his kingdom work was vital and important. In fact, a whole book of the Bible revolves around this man's service to God. What outstanding act of obedience earned Gaius a mention in God's Word?

To put it very simply, Gaius was a man who made a way. He wasn't a preacher, pastor, or missionary himself, but he learned how to make a way for those who were. Gaius is mentioned in the Bible—and we still talk about him today—because he epitomizes the kind of servant that we should be for God.

Gaius empowered others for ministry, and so can you.

THE GAIUS WAY

Gaius was a common Roman name, so we occasionally come across it in the Bible. But this particular Gaius, a Christian in one of the churches of Asia Minor, is referred to in 3 John. John addresses this letter to Gaius, calling him "beloved" and openly declaring his love for him (3 John 1). John obviously held Gaius in highest regard because Gaius unreservedly exercised the gift of hospitality on behalf of the itinerant preachers who traveled through. In so doing, Gaius accomplished much more than providing bed and breakfast for a passerby. He helped pave the way for the Gospel.

There's no suggestion in this passage that Gaius ever went to the mission field himself, but his support of those who did empowered them for ministry. He kept the door of his home open for traveling Christians who passed his way. While others were not nearly so hospitable—John made a point of later mentioning someone who failed the brethren in that regard—Gaius's simple ways of expressing his love for God had significant impact on the kingdom work.

We can't all go to the mission field. Nor does God call every one of us to be a career missionary. But any of us—literally any one of us—can follow Gaius's example: we can pave the way for others.

Here are some things you can do to support God's messengers.

OPEN YOUR HANDS

There's no getting around it. It is the Christian's responsibility to provide a financial base for the sharing of the Gospel. The secular world will never pay to be evangelized.

In his letter, John points out that the preachers coming Gaius's way left their secular world, the world of the Gentiles, and went forth in Christ's name, taking nothing with them (3 John 7). The same case can be made for today's missionaries and other ministers of the Gospel. Most of them have surrendered opportunities for careers, possibly lucrative ones, in order to serve God. So the church of Jesus Christ must ensure that the needs of these teachers and preachers are met while they are in town. Gaius opened his own hands as he sacrificed financially for them.

You may not have had the opportunity to visit a foreign mission field. But by giving financial support, you can make a way for others. And by extending help to those who do go, you become an ally of the truth and a co-laborer with the messengers there. It's as if you're proclaiming the truth to the lost yourself just as God desires. First Corinthians 3:9 says that "we are God's fellow workers." When we open our hands, the gifts we give literally allow us to become direct participants in the Gospel.

OPEN YOUR HEART

In this very brief letter from John to Gaius, the word *love* or a derivative of it appears several times. John and Gaius apparently formed a close bond in the Lord. That's one of the benefits of opening your heart to others. Christians who have never met before or who may never see each other again can experience a kind of closeness as they bond through the Gospel of Jesus Christ.

Although these itinerant preachers were strangers, as 3 John 5 describes them, Gaius welcomed them. He didn't personally know them, but he loved them with God's love. Not only were his doors open, but his heart was open too. Gaius's love for God was so great that it extended to those who loved God and whom God loved.

In a world teeming with people, we can't possibly know every Christian intimately. But we can open our hearts to those people who name Christ as Lord and give them immediate access to our affections. Furthermore, by praying for them intelligently and regularly, we can figuratively go with those who are called to mission fields that we will never impact by being physically present. This kind of heartfelt service produces its own rewards. Foremost, it pleases God. John praises Gaius in 3 John 5 for his ministry. God doesn't just approve the efforts of preachers or singers. Those who want to hear "Well done, thou good and faithful servant" may hear it for following Gaius's example of supporting fellow workers in the kingdom.

Such a willingness to serve fellow believers produces joy in the hearts of leaders. As a pastor, I can vouch for the joy that results from watching people serve. I've seen people with such an open heart for the Gospel that, despite holding full-time jobs, they pour themselves into the work of ministry at every opportunity. Sometimes I want to tell them, "Hey, enough." But deep down in my heart I get great joy from watching them. There's no human way I could motivate them to open their hearts to others as they do. Their efforts are prompted by their love for God.

OPEN YOUR HOME

Gaius used his gift of hospitality and opened his home when it was needed. His expression of love wasn't just heartfelt or simply financial. It got practical and personal. He took people in right under his own roof and fed them and gave them shelter.

Perhaps you're already saying to yourself: "Whoa! Hold on! I just don't have the gift of hospitality." Maybe not. But remember that the Bible instructs us on the subject of hospitality, and God does not exclude those without a special spiritual gift for it. First Peter 4:9 tells us all to "be hospitable . . . without grumbling." (How often we forget that last part!) Romans 12:13 tells us to be "given to hospitality." There is no escape clause for those without a special spiritual gift, and the need for that kind of hospitality is just as important in today's world as it was in the time of Gaius.

And I can attest to the fact that such hospitality brings blessings. When we first started home Bible studies at Shadow Mountain Community Church, we needed hosts and hostesses to help us. One woman came up to me as we got organized. "I need to give my house to God for ministry," she said. Recently widowed, the woman was lonely and searching for ways to overcome her loneliness. I still see this woman frequently, and the smile on her face tells me that she has been blessed in return.

EMPOWERING OURSELVES

Gaius's way is God's way—and it can be our way. When we selflessly refuse to look out just for ourselves or for our own property, we give God the freedom to prosper our souls. When we serve in whatever capacity we find, not only do we empower others for ministry, but we receive the benefit of knowing we have obeyed our loving Father.

Sometimes we hold back for fear that we are barely managing to take care of ourselves. Our own pressing needs and those of our family members force us to try to keep something in reserve. Or we become so used up by the busyness of our lives that it seems we have virtually nothing left over to give.

I've learned, however, that the very nourishment that our own impoverished souls need may be to offer whatever we do have left to someone else. We may need to be like the Old Testament widow, down to her last drop of oil, who gave what she had to Elijah. But then, just as the widow learned, God replenishes.

I've also discovered that it actually seems to please God when we feel that we have nothing to offer because then He works through us, and we don't get confused about who's doing what. In our emptiness, God uses us.

❧

It definitely takes a special calling to be a career missionary or a pastor. But the power behind those messengers of God is fueled in part by faithful people like Gaius, people who look so ordinary in many respects . . . until you notice their open hands, open hearts, and open homes all helping to make a way for the Gospel.

signs of Life

Life Sign: God is free to use any area of my life to do His will.

Life Verse: *Distributing to the needs of the saints, given to hospitality.*

—Romans 12:13

Life in Action: What can I do to make myself more available for ministry, both personally and through my church?

Day 33

Monopoly: The Pursuit of More

*The vacuum in the human heart is not
money-shaped, but God-shaped.*

In 1934 the American people had a monopoly on depression. The stock market had crashed in 1929, and millions of workers were jobless. Creativity took over as industrious citizens tried to find ways to feed themselves and their families.

Charles B. Darrow of Germantown, Pennsylvania, for instance, took a board game to the executives at Parker Brothers, a company almost driven out of business by the Great Depression. Darrow called the game "Monopoly®," but Parker Brothers rejected it because of "52 design errors"!

Undaunted, Darrow, with the help of a printer friend, produced five thousand handmade sets and sold them to a Philadelphia department store, where it became an overnight sensation. In 1935, Parker Brothers came to its senses and began producing the game. Since then, an estimated 500 million people around the world have played this most famous of board games.[1]

So here's some Monopoly trivia to share the next time you're trying to keep your opponent from noticing he's landed on Boardwalk or Park Place:

- More than 200 million games have been sold.

- More than five billion little green houses have been produced.

- A game with solid gold houses and pure silver hotels once sold for $25,000.

- The longest game in history lasted seventy days.

- A game played underwater lasted forty-five days; an upside-down game lasted for thirty-six hours.

- The total amount of Monopoly money in a set is $15,140.

How fitting that a game about living the high life as a successful financier was introduced at a time when the country was trying to rebound from its worst-ever economic depression. Even with their very real financial struggles people somehow found the two dollars to get in on the newest craze. Parker Brothers went into around-the-clock production and sold 20,000 sets per week![2] People probably thought, "If I can't have money and property in real life, at least I can pretend by playing Monopoly."

While we may think it understandable for people to dream and fantasize about material wealth in times of economic depression, what about during more comfortable economic times? Is any one of us completely free from materialistic longings? Haven't we all been tempted to think that money, wealth, and power might be the answer to all of life's problems?

HOW MUCH DOES IT TAKE?

A 1987 poll conducted by the *Chicago Tribune* revealed that people who earned less than $30,000 a year said that $50,000 would make them happy. However, people who earned $100,000 a year said they would need $250,000 to be completely satisfied.[3] These findings support what psychologists call the "escalation of expectations." If people work to attain a certain level of prosperity, thinking they will be happy when they reach it, they quickly become accustomed to their prosperity, grow discontent, and start striving for the next level. The bar indicating what it will take to make us happy is continually raised as our expectations escalate.

Church-growth strategists and missions experts have found this same phenomenon occurring on the mission field. Within three generations of the acceptance of the Gospel by a primitive culture, which resulted in increased wealth and higher standards of living, people start losing interest in the very spiritual truths that pulled them out of poverty. A little bit of money creates a longing for more. And that's true even for those with a lot of money.

At a time when John D. Rockefeller was the world's richest man, he was asked, "How much is enough?" His reply validates the "escalation of expectations" phenomenon: "Just a little bit more."[4]

What Solomon Discovered

Solomon reminds us in Ecclesiastes that "there is nothing new under the sun" (1:9), and that includes the fact that wealth does not—indeed, cannot—satisfy the deepest longings of the human heart. And yet he tried to make it happen.

We might say that Solomon exercised one of the first monetary monopolies in human history. As king of Israel, he controlled most of the wealth and commerce of the Middle East. He accumulated fabulous amounts of gold and silver from his trading ventures with nearby nations (1 Kings 10:14–15). His ships traveled the seas (2 Chronicles 8:17–18) and returned with "gold, silver, ivory, apes, and monkeys" (1 Kings 10:22). Foreign rulers came to see the magnificence of his kingdom and brought even more wealth and exotic gifts (2 Chronicles 9:1–12, 22–24).

To put it in Monopoly terms, Solomon owned all the property, utilities, and railroads; he had hotels spilling off the board; and his stacks of money threatened to obscure the board from his opponents' view.

And here's the irony: Solomon, in spite of his wealth, was a dissatisfied soul. He discovered that money and power are not the secrets to happiness. He had escalated his expectations higher than anyone in history and fulfilled them all . . . only to find that money could not meet his expectation for happiness.

Because Solomon could buy anything, he did. He tried satiating himself with wine and exotic food served in solid gold vessels, but that didn't work (1 Kings 4:22–23; 2 Chronicles 9:20; Ecclesiastes 2:3). Then he tried to find happiness by spending money on building projects: he built houses; planted vineyards, gardens, and orchards; and built reservoirs from which to water them (Ecclesiastes 2:4–6). Still nothing. So he started accumulating stuff: servants, wives, a harem of concubines, flocks, herds, choirs of singers, and, of course, more gold and silver (1 Kings 11:3; Ecclesiastes 2:7–8). But the dull ache of emptiness just wouldn't go away.

As the French philosopher Pascal noted in the seventeenth century, the vacuum in the human heart—in King Solomon's heart as well as in yours and mine—is not money-shaped, but God-shaped. When Solomon tried to fill that vacuum with everything except God, he grew more and more dissatisfied. The book of Ecclesiastes recounts Solomon's sorrowful search for meaning in life and his final realization that meaning can be found in God alone (Ecclesiastes 12:13–14).

CLASSIFYING CURRENCIES

What, then, is the purpose of wealth? If God is supposed to fill our hearts, what are we supposed to do with money?

First, let's be biblically clear: It is not money that is the root of evil. It is the "love of money" (1 Timothy 6:10). Nowhere does the Bible say that money is evil or that to have it, even in large quantities, is inappropriate, much less a sin. Money is amoral—neither good nor bad.

What we think of as money, the paper currency we all use, is nothing more than a manmade means of exchange. To tell the truth, it only exists and it only works because we all have faith in the system that says if I give you two pieces of green paper, you'll give me a loaf of bread. You then give the pieces of paper to the farmer for flour so that you can make more bread. He then gives pieces of paper to the seed company for more seed—and on it goes. It's the bread, flour, and seed that have value, not the pieces of paper—and there's nothing wrong with having those pieces of paper. They are the currency of this world and temporal in nature.

Second: The problem comes when we try to use temporal currency (money) as a medium of exchange in the eternal kingdom. As citizens of an eternal kingdom, we need an eternal currency. We use money to do business in the world's temporal kingdom. What do we use to do business in an eternal kingdom?

The currencies in the kingdom of God are love, joy, peace, longsuffering, kindness, goodness, faithfulness, gentleness, and self-control. You recognize these as the fruit of the Holy Spirit (Galatians 5:22–23). And they come only from God.

Economists refer to "guns and butter" as the staples or chief commodities of this world, and they can only be obtained with money. But the staples of God's eternal kingdom—treasure that moths, rust, and thieves can never threaten—can only be "purchased" with the fruit of the Holy Spirit (Matthew 6:20).

SOLOMON'S SYNDROME

To do business in the world, you need a wallet full of money. But to do business with God, you need a heart full of love, joy, peace . . . the fruit of the Holy Spirit. When we confuse currencies and try to purchase peace with money . . . well, that's when we end up with Solomon's Syndrome.

I use the term *Solomon's Syndrome* to refer to that affliction of the soul whereby eternal things are sought after with temporal means. I strongly urge you not even to try, or you'll end up as unhappy as that long-ago king himself did.

So don't try to monopolize anything of which there is a finite supply, like money. Because the fruit of the Spirit is limitless, however, you and I are free to accumulate all we can! That attempt at a monopoly is perfectly legal in God's kingdom.

Signs of Life

Life Sign: I am a faithful steward of all God has given me.

Life Verse: *He who is faithful in what is least is faithful also in much; and he who is unjust in what is least is unjust also in much.*

—Luke 16:10

Life in Action: In what ways can the preoccupation with money interfere with my relationship to God?

Day 34

Nugget-Faith Living

*We're not rich just because of God's blessings;
we're rich because of God Himself.*

If you ever find yourself driving behind a car with California license plates reading "GLD FVR," you'll know it belongs to modern-day gold prospectors Don and Annie Robinson. Seems the California Gold Rush isn't over. Nobody knows for sure how many practicing full-time gold miners are currently in California, but the best estimates put the number at 5,000—and 50,000 more are classified as "hobby prospectors." These enthusiasts ferret out possible gold strikes, dive into mountain lakes looking for flickers of the precious metal, and use specialized metal detectors to search out hidden veins in the hills and valleys.

"It's kind of like a euphoria," said a modern-day prospector. "Your blood starts to run. You can feel your pulse quicken. I don't know if I've broken out into a sweat yet, but I've seen people with gold fever get light-headed and dizzy."[1]

Who wouldn't be excited to find gold? One good nugget can lead to another—and another. The 1849 Gold Rush started the whole thing, and it's remembered as one of the largest mass migrations of people in history, with over 300,000 people thundering westward to California. The lure was almost irresistible, and it changed the demographics of America. "When California discovered gold," said one historian, "the world discovered California."[2]

What if our *God Fever* matched our *Gold Fever?*

The book of Ephesians describes the gold mine of knowing God. It talks about "the riches of His grace" abounding toward us, "the riches of the glory of His inheritance in the saints," "the exceeding riches of His grace," and "the unsearchable riches of Christ" (1:7, 18; 2:7; 3:8).

We're not rich just because of God's blessings; we're rich because of God Himself. *He* is our treasure and our exceeding great reward. None of us can take a single coin into eternity, and even the most beautiful metals on earth are temporary and perishing. But our Lord Jesus is the Alpha and the Omega, the Beginning and the End, the One whose goings forth are from everlasting. He's our eternal treasure. Shouldn't we have a holy craving for Him? Shouldn't our yearning for the Lord be greater than our longing for any earthly thing?

Let's consider how we can mine the depths of God's grace. Here are four nuggets to whet your "God Fever."

PRAYERS OF AFFIRMATION

First, offer God prayers of affirmation: rededicate yourself to the Lord every day, tell Him of your love for Him, and ask Him to help you desire a deeper relationship and a closer walk with Him. And then seek His face so that you, like the psalmist, will say, "When You said, 'Seek My face,' my heart said to You, 'Your face, LORD, I will seek'" (Psalm 27:8).

When I read some of the prayers offered by spiritual heroes of the past, I'm ashamed of the shallow praying of our own day. Listen to this prayer offered by Henry Martyn (1781–1812): "Oh, send Thy light and

Thy truth, that I may live always near to Thee, my God. Oh, let me feel Thy love, that I may be, as it were, already in heaven, that I may do all my work as the angels do theirs."[3]

Another saint of old, Ashton Oxenden, wrote this prayer: "Warm my cold heart, Lord, I beseech Thee. Take away all that hinders me from giving myself to Thee. Mold me according to Thine own image . . . I would not live unto myself, but unto Thee."[4]

Your God Fever might grow if you composed some prayers like that, affirming your love for Him—and then record your prayers in your journal. We seek the Lord best during our times of prayer, and we find Him easiest when we're on our knees. When our prayers grow deeper, we grow richer in our Lord.

HYMNS OF ASPIRATION

We need to consider the gold mine of our hymnals and rediscover the joy of singing and making melody in our hearts to the Lord. If you thumb through some old hymnbooks, you'll find a section entitled "Hymns of Aspiration." Listed there will be hymns that reflect the desires of the longing soul for a deeper walk with the Lord. A good example is the old song "Higher Ground," which says this:

> I'm pressing on the upward way,
> New heights I'm gaining every day;
> Still praying as I'm onward bound,
> Lord, plant my feet on higher ground.[5]

I think it's a good idea for every believer to have a hymnbook nearby. As more churches project the words of praise songs on screens, more of us individual Christians should keep the hymnbook with our Bible. Nothing enriches one's personal devotional time like singing a hymn quietly in the Lord's presence; and when it's a hymn of aspiration, it helps us express the desire of our hearts to grow closer to Him.

WORDS OF CONTEMPLATION

We can also find some rich nuggets in the writings of the great devotional writers of Christian history. I read a lot of new books on current subjects, but I also like to return to the classics—to those works that have stood the test of time.

Consider, for instance, this piece of advice from William Law (1686–1761): "If anyone would tell you the shortest, surest way to all happiness and all perfection, he must tell you to make it a rule to yourself to thank and praise God for everything that happens to you. For it is certain that whatever seeming calamity happens to you, if you thank and praise God for it, you turn it into a blessing."[6]

It's a good idea to find a quiet spot every once in a while, order a cup of tea, and feed on this kind of wisdom from saints of the past, for they knew something about pressing through to the higher life. They knew how to mine for God, as it were.

Need some suggestions about where to stake a claim? Try mining in John Bunyan's *Pilgrim's Progress,* the sermons of Charles Spurgeon, *The Practice of the Presence of God* by Brother Lawrence, Hudson Taylor's *Spiritual Secret,* the prayer books of E. M. Bounds, and a bevy of old devotional books like *Streams in the Desert* and *Daily Strength for Daily Needs.* Build a little library of spiritual classics, and you'll find they make good picks, axes, and shovels as you dig for spiritual gold.

TIMES OF MEDITATION

No other aspect of mining, however, compares to the direct practice of meditating on Scripture. The psalmist wrote, "The law of Your mouth is better to me than thousands of coins of gold and silver. More to be desired are they than gold, yea, than much fine gold. . . . I love Your commandments more than gold, yes, than fine gold!" (Psalm 119:72; 19:10; 119:127). Every verse in the Bible is a glittering nugget, and when we meditate on God's Word, we're storing up gold in the treasuries of our hearts.

❧

When missionary Geoffrey Bull was imprisoned by Chinese Communists, they took his Bible and subjected him to mental and psychological torture. He later talked about the one thing that kept him from losing his mind. Although Geoffrey had no Scriptures while he was in prison, he had studied the Bible all his life. So he began to systematically review the Word in his mind. It took him about six months to go all the way through the Bible mentally. He started at Genesis and recalled each story and every incident as best he could, first concentrating on the content and then musing on certain points, always asking God in prayer to shine His light on his efforts. Geoffrey continued through the Old Testament, reconstructing the books and chapters as best he could, and then he began on the New Testament right through to Revelation. Then he started over again. He later wrote, "The strength received through this meditation was, I believe, a vital factor in bringing me through, kept by the faith to the very end."[7]

Nothing is more advantageous in our Christian growth than consistent, daily meditation on Scripture—and by that I don't mean just reading God's Word or studying it, but hiding it in our hearts, storing it in our minds, mulling over it, visualizing it, and personalizing it until it works its way into our daily lifestyle.

Longing for Christ and trusting Him and His Word are some of a Christian's genuine treasures, and we should always be mining for the next nugget. It's great to glance back at what we've accomplished, but we have to focus on the present and press on to the future, going deeper, higher, and further for Christ.

So go for the gold in your Christian life! Don't be content with where you are, but reach forward and press onward toward the goal of the prize of the upward call of God in Christ Jesus.

signs of Life

Life Sign: I take time each day to mine God's Word.

Life Verse: *The law of Your mouth is better to me*
Than thousands of coins of gold and silver.

—Psalm 119:72

Life in Action: In which areas of my life should I be making more of an effort to mine for treasures that will last for eternity?

Day 35

Life in Your Golden Tears

The greatest secret is keeping our passion, our burden, and our
tears for the needs of those around us and
for the entire world.

Former First Lady Barbara Bush tells of a group of older women who were playing bridge. One said to the other, "I have enjoyed this so much, I'd like to call you so we could plan another game, but I'm afraid I can't remember your name."

The other woman paused a moment and then asked, "Do you have to have it right now?"[1]

As we grow older, we worry about losing our physical and mental powers, but I like the attitude of the poet who wrote this little poem:

> Gone, they tell me, is youth;
> Gone is the strength of my life.
> Nothing remains but decline,
> Nothing but age and decay.

Not so, I'm God's little child,
Only beginning to live.

Coming the days of my prime,
Coming the strength of my life,
Coming the vision of God,
Coming my bloom and my power![2]

Dr. V. Raymond Edman used to say, "It's always too soon to quit,"[3] and that's good advice as we grow older. After all, according to the Bible, we may be outwardly perishing, but we're inwardly renewed day by day.

⁓

In 1990 Robertson McQuilkin resigned from the presidency of Columbia Bible College in order to care for his ailing wife, Muriel, which he did until she died in 2003. His motivation was his belief that God has planned the strength and beauty of youth to be physical, but the strength and beauty of age to be spiritual.[4] We gradually lose the strength and beauty that is temporary, so we'll concentrate on developing the strength and beauty that lasts forever.

We might lose some of our vigor, but none of our zeal. Our strength may ebb, but our enthusiasm for the kingdom should grow stronger with time. We might have some golden years and some golden tears, but remember that gold is precious and highly valued.

Missionary Bertha Smith served the Lord faithfully in China until, at age seventy, she was forced to retire because of the policy of her mission board. She wasn't at all ready to retire. "What a pain!" she wrote. "I never dreamed that anything in this life could ever hurt like giving up work with the Chinese and returning home. I was still doing about fifteen hours of work a day, and I never became too tired to get up rested the next morning."

Bertha accepted her retirement as from the Lord, but she was convinced that God had a new work for her to begin. It wasn't long before invitations flooded in for her to speak and share the principles of revival that she had learned and observed in China. So Bertha traveled far and wide across America and around the world, carrying on an exhausting ministry of telling the story of revival. For almost thirty more years, she served the Lord during her retirement ministry, and then she passed into glory just five months shy of her one-hundredth birthday.[5]

She reminds me of the writer of Psalm 71 who prayed, "When I am old and gray headed, O God, do not forsake me, until I declare Your strength to this generation" (verse 18).

❧

The *Florida Baptist Witness* recently carried the story of Virginia Tebby, a ninety-five-year-old grandmother who still goes out with a church visitation team to witness for the Lord. When her church pioneered a new outreach program, she attended every training session and started making visits with her team every week. "I just love it all," she said, especially when "you visit and revisit someone, and then they come to church. I'm just glad I'm still able to do all of this."[6]

John Wesley would have agreed. On his seventy-first birthday, he wrote, "How is this, that I find just the same strength as I did thirty years ago? That my sight is considerably better now, and my nerves firmer, than they were then?" Nine years later, on reaching the age of eighty, he said, "Lord, let me not live to be useless."

And Wesley remained useful to the Master until his last days, dying at age eighty-seven. His final years were his fullest, and those who saw him were deeply moved by the beauty of his face, the brightness of his eyes, and his long, white hair falling over his shoulders.[7]

❧

The greatest secret to living a fulfilling life as a senior saint is to keep our passion, our burden, and our tears for the needy people around us, as well as for the entire world. Psalm 126:5–6 says this:

> Those who sow in tears
> Shall reap in joy.
> He who continually goes forth weeping,
> Bearing seed for sowing,
> Shall doubtless come again with rejoicing,
> Bringing his sheaves with him.

- Propelled by passion and constrained by the love of Christ, the apostle Paul kept going to the very end of his life.

- Bob Pierce, the founder of World Vision, prayed, "Let my heart be broken by the things that break the heart of God."[8]

- During the Great Depression, missionary J. G. Morrison spoke to his Nazarene denomination, pleading with them, and asking, "Can't you do just a little more?"[9]

If you're anxious about growing older, I'd like to encourage you to ask the Lord for a specific promise to reassure you during this period of golden tears. In his autobiography, the popular Bible teacher Warren W. Wiersbe describes feeling troubled one drizzly day when he was suffering the pangs of arthritis. Somehow it reminded him of the creeping consequences of getting old. During his devotions that day, he asked the Lord to give him a promise to sustain him through his "declining" years, as he put it. In the course of his regular reading that morning, he came to Isaiah 58:11. Wiersbe read it and said, "That's it! Thank You, Lord!"[10]

Isaiah 58:11 says this:

> The Lord will guide you continually,
> And satisfy your soul in drought,
> And strengthen your bones;
> You shall be like a watered garden,
> And like a spring of water, whose waters do not fail.

Then Wiersbe wrote this:

> After I've attended my last meeting and preached my last sermon,
> written my last book and answered my last letter, told my last joke
> and said my last good-bye, and I wake up in the presence of my
> Lord, I want to be able to say to Him what Jesus said when He came
> to the end of His earthly ministry: 'I have glorified You on the earth.
> I have finished the work which You have given me to do' (John
> 17:4).[11]

Amen!

We easily realize that our earthly resources are limited and precious. Our
days are numbered, so we need to spend them more wisely. Our money
isn't going to heaven with us, so we are wise to invest more in eternal
works. Our energy is less, so we need to concentrate on the essentials of
God's will for us. But if we have a broken heart, a passion for souls, and
a commitment to Christ, we'll make investments that we'll never regret;
and our golden years and tears will be tools fit for the Master's use.

The film *Schindler's List* chronicles the heroic efforts of a German industrialist during World War II, who, having learned what was happening
at Auschwitz, began a systematic effort to save as many Jews as he could.
He found that he could "buy" Jews to work in his factory, which was
supposed to be a part of the military machine of Germany, though
Schindler was deliberately sabotaging the ammunition produced in his
plant. As a result, he entered the war as a wealthy industrialist, but by
the end of the war he was basically bankrupt.

When the Germans surrendered, Schindler met with his workers
and declared that at midnight they were all free to go. When he said
good-bye to the financial manager of the plant, who was a Jew and a

dear friend, he embraced the man and began sobbing. "I could have done more," he said.

Looking at his automobile, he asked, "Why did I save this? I could have bought ten Jews with this." Taking another small possession, he cried, "This would have saved another one. Why didn't I do more?"[12]

Those are poignant questions for all of us. After all, one day Jesus is going to split the eastern sky and come for His own. It will not matter then how much money we have accumulated or how many houses we own, but whom we have rescued for the kingdom.

So ask God to use you—whatever your years or tears or fears. Ask Him not to forsake you until you've declared His praise to the next generation and borne fruit for His kingdom in your old age. Stay passionate for Him throughout all the days He has allotted to you. After all . . .

> For this one life will soon be past;
> Only what's done for Christ will last.

signs of Life

Life Sign: There is always more I can do for God's kingdom.

Life Verse: *Those who sow in tears*
Shall reap in joy.
He who continually goes forth weeping,
Bearing seed for sowing,
Shall doubtless come again with rejoicing,
Bringing his sheaves with him.

—Psalm 126:5–6

Life in Action: I want to wear out—not rust out—in my service for the Lord, so today I will ask Him to show me who needs me today.

Outstretched Arms

Living a compassioNate Life

Day 36

Outstretched Arms

*The way the world will know the compassion of Christ
is by seeing the outstretched arms of
His followers.*

When a man I know was a young pastor, someone in his congregation gave him a trip to the Holy Land. It was his first trip overseas, and he found himself unprepared for the radical differences between his own affluent lifestyle in America and what he encountered in the Middle East in the early 1980s.

One day when his tour group was in Jerusalem, he ventured into what is called the Old City where, except for electricity and running water, life—with its narrow streets, dark alleyways, teeming crowds, and vendors in the bazaars—seemed little changed from biblical days. As he made his way across an open intersection, he was shocked by a figure coming toward him. She was tiny, thin, and frail, covered from head to ankles in a dirty black robe. Only her hands, eyes, and bare feet were showing, but it was still obvious from her creased and leathery skin that she was old—or perhaps her hard life had aged her beyond her years.

As my friend stopped and watched her coming, he had only one thought: "This is the poorest person I have ever seen."

Leaning forward, her eyes on the ground, her robe clutched tightly, and her bare feet barely touching the stone street as she moved silently past him, my friend noticed that she was walking fast, as if she were ashamed to be seen in public.

As the man watched her disappear into the crowd behind him, he immediately felt conflicted. There he stood with fashionable, more-than-adequate clothes, shoes on his feet, an expensive camera slung over one shoulder, a travel bag full of personal-care items slung over the other, and money in his pocket. And he had just allowed the poorest, most pitiful person he had ever seen to go by as if she were a piece of video footage on the evening news. But he was not in America watching a news story about poverty in the Middle East. This poor woman had walked by so close to him that he could have reached out and touched her. But he hadn't—and she was gone.

So he prayed: "Lord, if You will let me see that woman again, I will help her. Please let my path cross hers again before I leave this place."

He finished his trek through the Old City and made his way back toward his hotel. His eyes scanned the crowds for the wisp of a woman he had seen earlier—and there she was! He startled her when he motioned to her to stop, and her eyes met his. He didn't know any Hebrew or Arabic and didn't think she would know any English, so he simply held out his hand and said, "Jesus." She took the money he offered her and began nodding and making murmuring sounds that were muffled by her robe. Her eyes were smiling at the corners as she again pulled her thin garment tightly around her and, on leathery soles as thick as those of his shoes, disappeared again into her limited world.

COMPASSION IS ABOUT THE MOMENT

Would my friend ever see this woman again? No. Would he have any way of knowing whether the money he gave her was used for a good purpose? No. Did any of that matter to him at that moment? No. Should it have mattered? No!

What mattered to him at that moment was that he, a well-fed, healthy, blessed-by-God person, had just come in contact with a desperately poor woman who looked as if she were starving. She had what appeared to be abundant needs, and he had the ability to meet at least a few of those needs for the next few days. So he did what mattered at the moment: he had compassion on someone God had brought across his path. . . .

In a sermon I heard seminary professor Haddon Robinson preach on Jesus' Good Samaritan story (Luke 10:25–37), he answered the lawyer's question "And who is my neighbor?" this way: "Your neighbor is anyone who has a need, whose need you are able to meet."

In order to see that need, however, we have to view the world through compassion-colored glasses. As Jesus told the story, He said it was compassion that caused the Samaritan to stop and help the man who lay injured by the side of the road: "But a certain Samaritan, as he journeyed, came where he was. And when he saw him, he had compassion" (verse 33).

So compassion is about the moment. Yes, there are longer-term expressions of compassion we can and should be involved in. But in this set of readings I want to focus on those times in our lives when God intends for us to be the healer . . . the helper . . . the holder . . . the hero in the life of another person, those times when God expects our arms to be outstretched and extending comfort and care to a friend or a stranger. . . .

William Blake was an English poet and painter who had a hard-to-pinpoint relationship with God. While his theology might have been suspect at points, his understanding of man's responsibility to be the compassionate hand of God was not:

> Why stand we here trembling around
> Calling on God for help, and not ourselves, in whom God dwells,
> Stretching a hand to save the falling man?[1]

This verse reminds me of a story I heard about a Christian leader who was invited to speak to a large gathering of women in an affluent church. Before he spoke, the woman leading the meeting learned of an urgent financial need that one of the church's missionaries was facing. She asked if the speaker would lead the group in prayer and ask God to supply the need. He walked to the podium and shocked the group when he said he would not lead the group in the requested prayer; he would do something else instead. He would contribute all the money he had in his pockets to meet the need if all the rest of the women in the group would do the same. If, when that money was collected and counted, funds were still lacking, he would be happy to lead in prayer for God to supply the remainder.

You can no doubt guess what happened. When the money was collected, there was more than enough to meet the missionary's emergency need.

Compassion is about the moment! It is about using what I have at hand—money, talent, encouragement, or a shoulder to cry on—to meet another person's need.

COMPASSION IS ABOUT TEARS FROM HEAVEN

Science tells us there are three kinds of tears. *Basal* tears flow continually into our eyes to lubricate the eyeball and flush away debris, and *reflex* tears flow as a response to either pain or contact with an irritant (like when we're chopping an onion!). It is the third kind of tears—*emotional* tears—that only we humans have.[2] And that is because only we humans are created in the image of God (Genesis 1:26–27). Only human beings can look upon the plight of another and shed tears of compassion; only humans can be brought to tears by the tears of another person.

When Jesus arrived at the grave of His friend Lazarus, He wept (John 11:35). His tears vividly illustrate the meaning of compassion: to suffer (*passion*) with (*com*). Jesus' tears reflected both His own sadness prompted by the loss of His friend and His sharing in the suffering and grief felt by Lazarus's loved ones. God Himself was willing to mingle His tears with those of His earthly friends, and we are called to do the same.

It is clear from Scripture that God expects His children to bring the tears of heaven to earth through the exercise of compassion toward others. The compassion Jesus demonstrated (Matthew 15:32; 20:34; Mark 1:41; 6:34; Luke 7:13) is to be extended through those of us who believe in Him:

- "Be of one mind, having compassion for one another" (1 Peter 3:8).
- "Be kind and compassionate to one another" (Ephesians 4:32 NIV).
- "Be patient, bearing with one another in love" (Ephesians 4:2 NIV)
- "Weep with those who weep" (Romans 12:15).
- "Bear one another's burdens" (Galatians 6:2).

It was the colonial Quaker William Penn who said, "Though our Savior's Passion is over, His compassion is not."[3] And the way the world will know the compassion of Christ is by seeing and experiencing the comforting arms of His followers.

signs of Life

Life Sign: Compassion is my passion.

Life Verse: *Be kind to one another, tenderhearted, forgiving one another, even as God in Christ forgave you.*

—Ephesians 4:32

Life in Action: What can I do to be more conscious of the people around me who have needs I can help meet? What lifestyle changes do I need to make in order to have the time to care for the hurting people God has cross my path?

Pietà: "I Care"

*Jesus expects you to be a channel of His compassion
to those who need Him today.*

One of the most moving photographs taken at Ground Zero in
New York City on September 11, 2001, has come to be known
as the *American Pietà*. In the photo, four firemen and a police-
man are carrying the body of Father Mychal Judge, chaplain of the Fire
Department of New York and the first recorded victim of the 9/11 ter-
rorist attack in New York City.

The picture is called *American Pietà* because of the way Father Judge's
lifeless body is draped over the chair his rescuers used to transport him out
of the rubble. It is a stark reminder of Michelangelo's *Pietà* in St. Peter's
Basilica in Rome. It's easy to see how the *American Pietà* took its name
from Michelangelo's work. In his sculpture, Mary, the mother of Jesus,
sits cradling the lifeless body of her Son, who lies draped across her lap.[1]

In the grand period of Renaissance art, many pietàs were carved,
but Michelangelo's is the most famous, completed in AD 1500 when the
young prodigy was only twenty-two years old. These sculptures of Mary
grieving over her crucified Son got their name from the Italian word

for compassion: *pietà*. *Pietà* can also be translated into English as *mercy, pity,* and *piety,* all of which are conveyed when one gazes upon Michelangelo's remarkable sculpture.

In practical terms, we express pietà to another person when we say, "I care" by acting with compassion. When looking at the tender expression on the face of Mary in Michelangelo's *Pietà,* we see what human compassion looks like.

Unfortunately, it's easy to feign an expression of pietà or compassion. Like actors in a Greek drama, guests at a masquerade ball, or revelers at Mardi Gras, we can all too easily don a mask of compassion and have our insincerity go unnoticed in today's world where superficiality often reigns. Even as Christians—as people who are blessed by the true and tender compassion of God—we are tempted to *appear* compassionate when our heart is facing another direction altogether.

Let me contrast the Pietà Mask with true compassion by telling you the story of two very different types of men. The first one wore the Pietà Mask all his life.

THE PIETÀ MASK

Look up the word *Casanova* in your dictionary, and you'll find that it refers to "a man who is amorously and gallantly attentive to women, a promiscuous man, a philanderer" (*American Heritage Dictionary*). And that definition accurately summarizes the life of one Giovanni Jacopo Casanova de Seingalt, the son of an actor and actress in the 1800s.

It might be easier to list the roles in life Casanova *didn't* play than the roles he *did.* At various times in his seventy years, Casanova was a lawyer, seminary student, novitiate in the Catholic church, violinist, practitioner of cabalistic magic, Freemason, writer, prison escapee, state lottery manager, bond trader, entrepreneur, knight in the Papal Order of the Holy Spur, persona non grata in several countries and cities, publisher, and librarian.

Lest you think Casanova the proverbial Renaissance man who is to be lauded for his skills in all the liberal arts, think again. His colorful life was the result of his chameleonlike propensity to redefine himself in order to endear himself (more accurately, *ingratiate* himself) to those who could sponsor him financially, especially wealthy women and church and government officials. Europe was his stage as he moved from one love affair to another.[2]

While appearing to be sincere, compassionate, loving, and committed, Casanova was, in reality, a man wearing a Pietà Mask. His compassion was nothing but a front for a self-indulgent lifestyle.

PIETÀ PERSONIFIED

On the other hand, some people wear no mask at all. We encounter such a man in the Bible, the focus of a story Jesus told. Two of the three main characters in this story are wearing the Pietà Mask; the other one is an unexpected pietà.

The story, found in Luke 10:30–37, is about a man traveling from Jerusalem to Jericho when thieves beat him, robbed him, and left him naked and "half dead" by the side of the road. Soon someone came along who might be expected to treat the traveler with compassion: this Jewish priest was probably on his way to serve in the temple in Jerusalem. Sadly, he wore the face of compassion—a Pietà Mask, a face not animated by a heart of true compassion—and he looked the other way as he passed by the injured traveler.

The next person to come by—a Levite—could also have been expected to help. These descendants of Levi, set apart in Israel to serve God alone, should have been more compassionate than anyone: "The Levites shall be Mine," the Lord had said (Numbers 3:12). But when the Levite came upon the dying traveler, he "looked, and passed by on the other side" (Luke 10:32). Many who knew this Levite probably saw him as a compassionate man. In reality, what they were seeing was his Pietà Mask.

Finally, the last person one would expect to have compassion on a

Jewish traveler came along. Looking at his face, a native of the area might have detected the Samaritan features and known not to expect him to extend compassion to any Jew. There was no love—or compassion—lost between Jews and Samaritans. And this truth made the message of Jesus' story quite striking, for it was the Samaritan who saved the Jewish traveler's life. This compassionate Samaritan wore no mask. Instead, he was pietà personified—the compassionate neighbor that Jesus calls all of us to be.

THE COMPASSIONATE CHRIST

In no one, however, has compassion ever been manifested so purely and deeply as in Jesus Christ. It is because of Christ's loving compassion, demonstrated in His life until His last breath, that He has even been revered by leaders and members of other religions throughout history. No one has ever accused Jesus of wearing a mask—of being self-serving, duplicitous, hypocritical, or two-faced. He is the eternal template for the marriage of a compassionate heart with compassionate hands. With Jesus, the true compassion you see is the true compassion you get.

Think of all the people for whom Christ felt *and* acted with compassion:

- The spiritually lost (Matthew 9:36): Jesus was brokenhearted over the lost sheep in the house of Israel.

- The sick (Mark 1:41): He healed innumerable individuals of their physical afflictions, releasing them into a new life.

- The needy (Matthew 15:32): Jesus was compassionate toward the hungry, the weary, the grief-stricken; toward all who lacked life's basic necessities.

- Widows and mothers (Luke 7:13): Jesus felt the grief of a widow whose only son had died, and He gave her back the one she had lost.

THE COMPASSIONATE CHRISTIAN

The world has a right to expect the followers of Christ to be like their Master. For that reason, Peter admonished us to "[have] compassion for one another; love as brothers, be tenderhearted, be courteous" (1 Peter 3:8). That doesn't mean we are to merely act or look compassionate—we are to *be* compassionate. From the core of our heart and flowing through our hands, we are to be like the compassionate Christ.

You may not be able to heal the sick or feed the hungry the way Jesus did. But that's okay; He doesn't expect you to. He simply expects you to be a channel of His compassion to those who need Him today, and you can't do that by just wearing a mask. You can only be a channel of Jesus' compassion if you have a heart of true compassion that comes with having Him live in your heart. When Jesus fills your heart, you'll have no need for the Pietà Mask you've been trying to keep in place.

So if you have been wearing a Pietà Mask—if you've been living behind a veneer of compassion instead of living out the real thing—why not take off that mask today?

signs of Life

Life Sign: I care . . . regardless.

Life Verse: *Finally, all of you be of one mind, having compassion for one another; love as brothers, be tenderhearted, be courteous.*
—1 Peter 3:8

Life in Action: What fears keep me from reaching out to people who need a touch of compassion? What can I do to overcome these fears and be a courageous Good Samaritan?

Our Basic Identity

Christians are known by our love.
That's our basic identity.

L ook down at your shirt for a moment. Is there a little emblem on the pocket? Or perhaps you have a certain swoosh on your tennis shoes or distinctive rivets on your jeans. If you're drinking coffee while reading this chapter, is there a green circle on the cup? If you're sitting at the kitchen table, is Tony the Tiger nearby? . . .

These are examples of "branding"—a marketing strategy by which companies give their products distinctive identities. A brand is a collection of images and ideas that symbolize a particular product or company. What comes to mind, for instance, when you think of a set of golden arches, a little Apple with a bite missing, or, if you're a football fan, a big blue/gray star with white trim?

Companies are no longer interested in creating a product; they want to establish a brand—a distinctive, instantly recognizable identity that strikes positive chords in the consumer and that can be extended to new products. Branding tries to sell a feeling as much as a product, and companies spend millions of dollars on establishing just the right symbol, slogan, color scheme, and package design for branding a product, an author, a company, or a concept.

What about a brand called YOU?

What's distinctive about you? What feeling do others have when they think of you? What do your appearance, attitudes, and activities communicate to others? What makes you different from the rest?

Long before Starbucks, Nike, or Apple Computer, Jesus Christ understood the importance of branding, and He designed a particular "look" for all His disciples. He wanted to give them a definite identity, which He explained in John 13:34–35: "A new commandment I give to you, that you love one another; as I have loved you, that you also love one another. By this all will know that you are My disciples, if you have love for one another."

Jesus' love is a brand more powerful than any ever concocted by Madison Avenue, and this Christlike love is so important that without it, nothing else in our lives rings true. . . .

Consider the story Dr. Harry Ironside told about a missionary in China who was translating the New Testament into the Chinese language. He was assisted by an eminent Chinese scholar, a Confucianist who had never before been exposed to Christianity. Week after week and month after month they sat side by side working through the biblical text.

When the project was nearly completed, the missionary told his friend, "You have been of great help to me. I could never have gotten along without you. Now I want to ask you a question. As we have gone together through the New Testament, hasn't the beauty of Christianity touched you? Wouldn't you like to become a Christian?"

The Confucianist replied, "Yes, Christianity does appeal to me. I think it presents the most wonderful system of ethics I have ever known.

I believe that if I ever saw a Christian, I might become more interested in becoming one myself."

"But," exclaimed the missionary, "I am a Christian!"

"You?" the scholar replied. "You, a Christian? I hope you will not take offense, but I must tell you that I have observed you and listened to you from the beginning. If I understand the New Testament, a Christian is one who follows Jesus; and Jesus said, 'By this all will know that you are My disciples, if you have love for one another.'

"You cannot be a Christian, for I have listened to you as you have talked about others in an unkind way. I have observed, too, that whereas your New Testament says that God will supply all your needs, you do not trust Him. You worry about this and about that; and if your check is a day late, you become dreadfully concerned. No, you cannot be a Christian. But I think that if I ever see one, I should like to be one."

Pierced to the heart, the missionary broke down, sobbed out a confession, and asked God for forgiveness. He asked for the scholar's forgiveness as well. This man was so broken that the Confucianist later remarked, "Well, perhaps I have seen a Christian after all."[1] . . .

Christians aren't known to the world because we all dress the same, comb our hair alike, or vote identically. We are known by our love. That's our basic identity.

Recalling the words he had heard our Lord speak (John 13), the apostle John restated them in his first epistle: "We know that we have passed from death to life, because we love the brethren. . . . By this we know love, because He laid down His life for us. And we also ought to lay down our lives for the brethren" (1 John 3:14, 16).

Does this statement mean if someone fires a gun at another person, we should step in front of the bullet? Well, yes, but that doesn't happen very often—thank goodness! John explained in the next verse that he was thinking of our daily obligation as Christians to deny ourselves in order to meet one another's needs: "Whoever has this world's goods, and sees his brother in need, and shuts up his heart from him, how does the love of God abide in him? My little children, let us not love in word or in tongue, but in deed and in truth" (verses 17–18). . . .

🙢

During the Vietnam War, two men were shot down over North Vietnam in separate incidents that occurred at about the same time. One was Porter Halyburton, a Southern white boy who was something of a racist. The other was Fred Cherry, the first black officer captured by the North Vietnamese.

The two men were thrown into the same cell amid the squalor of the infamous Hanoi Hilton, and it didn't look like Fred Cherry would survive. He had been seriously injured, and Porter soon discovered that he had to care for Fred in very personal ways, peeling off the clothes that were glued to his skin by pus, cleaning out his festering and decaying flesh, helping him get onto the waste bucket, washing and bathing him, and giving him his own food and clothes. When Fred appeared to be near death, burning with fever, Porter hovered over him day and night, tending his loathsome wounds and exhorting him to hold on.

At one point, Fred hadn't been able to wash his hair in months, and when he ran his hand through his thick Afro, he pulled out a glob of oil and smeared it on the ground. Instantly an army of ants appeared from various cracks in the cell walls and began climbing up Fred's body to get to his hair. The two men tried to swat them off, but it was like a plague; there seemed to be millions of them. Porter finally persuaded a guard to let him take Fred to the shower room.

Arriving there, they found the room repulsive. It was cold, dark, and dirty. The floor was covered with snails, and they stood in a quarter inch of slime. Fred couldn't move his arm because of his injury, so Porter helped him undress and positioned him under the cold water. Then, rubbing soap in his hands, Porter began washing Fred's hair. At first nothing much happened, but finally the dirt, oil, and grease turned into a paste and began to ooze off his scalp and down his body.

"You won't believe this," Porter said. "I'm going to have to wash your hair again." He washed the man's hair again and again and again until finally he broke through the grease and grime.

After the men were finally liberated, Fred Cherry said that he would not have survived without Porter Halyburton. But Porter said the reverse is also true. Caring for Fred gave him a sense of mission and purpose, it enabled him to forget his own problems and serve someone else, and it taught him to love a brother in need. And that, Porter says, is why he survived the Hanoi Hilton.[2]

To lay down our lives for someone doesn't always mean that we're literally going to die for them, although that's exactly what Christ did for us. Laying down our lives means we die to ourselves—to our own wishes, desires, plans—and live to meet the needs of others in Christ's name. As followers of Christ, how can we do anything less?

After all, that kind of love is our identity. It's the core of our Christlikeness. As Zechariah 3:2 says, each of us is a "*brand* plucked from the fire" (emphasis added). And the world will know we are Christians by our love.

SiGNS of Life

Life Sign: Others will know I am a Christian by my love.

Life Verse: *My little children, let us not love in word or in tongue, but in deed and in truth.*

—1 John 3:18

Life in Action: What characteristics of Jesus' love do I fail to demonstrate? What can I do to incorporate those characteristics in my life?

A Portrait in Crimson

When we set up the easel of our soul in front of Calvary,
we learn to imitate the perfect
love of the Master.

Who would expect a cemetery to be one of Southern California's top tourist attractions? In 1917, Dr. Hubert Eaton wanted to change the way Americans think of death, so he developed Forest Lawn in Glendale, the nation's first "memorial park" and a combination of beauty, art, landscaping, chapels, museums, splashing fountains, swans, sculptures, and, of course, room for a quarter-million graves.

Over a million people now visit the park's six hundred acres each year. After all, at Forest Lawn you can stand within six feet of such superstars as Clark Gable, Jimmy Stewart, Humphrey Bogart, Walt Disney, Red Skelton, George Burns, and Gracie Allen. Visitors can also view exact replicas of Michelangelo's greatest works, including *David, Moses,* and the *Pietà.* Leonardo da Vinci's *The Last Supper* is recreated in stained glass. Forest Lawn is even a popular spot for weddings.

Among the highlights at Forest Lawn are two of the world's largest paintings, *The Crucifixion* and *The Resurrection*, both by Polish artist Jan Styka.

The Crucifixion, the larger of the two paintings, is breathtakingly immense, measuring 195 feet long by 45 feet high. It is arguably the world's largest and most dramatic painting on canvas. It was shipped to America for the 1904 St. Louis World's Fair, but it was impounded over tax issues. Since there was no pavilion large enough to display it, the painting was stored in warehouses for many years before a special chapel with an enlarged hall was built for it at Forest Lawn.[1]

Perhaps the artist's greatest message is that the Crucifixion is larger than life, larger than death, and larger than our ability to fully comprehend it. The Crucifixion reveals a love so vast, deep, wide, and long that our mind can't fathom it. God's love is greater far than tongue or pen— or the stroke of an artist's brush—can ever tell.

By gazing at this immense masterpiece that testifies to God's love— Styka's painting of the Crucifixion—we can learn something about our two greatest duties in life: loving God and loving one another. Let me explain, but first I'll ask a question. Have you ever visited a museum and watched amateur artists set up their easels in front of the canvases in order to imitate the masters? In the same way, when we set up the easel of the soul at the foot of Calvary, we learn to imitate the perfect love of the Master. There, as Jesus' broken body hangs on the old rugged cross, we see something about the purposeful, selfless, unconditional, and sacrificial nature of God's love.

PURPOSEFUL LOVE

God's love is not some vaporous feeling that ebbs and flows with unpredictable undercurrents and uncertain tides. God's love is a divine attribute that is as strong as steel, as solid as granite, and as deliberate as a marching army. Its laser light locates needs and prompts in our heart and mind ways to meet them. Jesus said,

"Greater love has no one than this, than to lay down one's life for his friends" (John 15:13). . . .

Recently in Charleston, West Virginia, Mike Overton was driving across a bridge to get a haircut. Seeing a woman throw her leg over the guard railing, he slammed on his brakes, jumped out of his car, and managed to hold on to her. She was crying, and her steady refrain was that no one loved her. Ironically, while he was holding her, the woman's cell phone rang twice: one call was from her daughter and the other from her husband, both of whom were worried about her. Yet in her depression and grief, the woman felt utterly alone.[2]

God's love reaches out and grabs us at Calvary—and there is enough grace at Calvary to cover every single person who has ever lived, is living now, or will ever live. Jesus died for everyone.

Puritan writer Richard Baxter used to say, "If God had said there was mercy for Richard Baxter, I am so vile a sinner that I would have thought He meant some other Richard Baxter. When He said 'whosoever' (in John 3:16), I know that includes me, the worst of all the Richard Baxters there ever was."[3]

Now, since Jesus loved us with such a deliberate, purposeful love, shouldn't we love with that same kind of love? In terms of loving others with Jesus' love, His example means noticing, discovering, and meeting people's needs. In terms of loving God, Jesus' example means obeying Him. Jesus said, "If you love Me, keep My commandments. . . . If anyone loves Me, he will keep My word. . . . He who does not love Me does not keep My words" (John 14:15, 23, 24).

What sin, if any, are you tolerating in your life? What unconfessed habit has its hold on you? Are you harboring bitterness toward someone for whom Christ died? Learn to paint over people's sins with the forgiving brush of Calvary. Obey Jesus fully and serve others purposefully.

SELFLESS LOVE

In addition to being purposeful, Christ's love is selfless, and that's in sharp contrast to mere human love.

As we look around today, we see human love failing again and again. In fact, its rate of failure is becoming astronomical. Marriages are falling apart. Children are growing up without parents. The love of Christ is overshadowed by cheap lust, which is nothing but selfish greed barely hidden under a thin coat of silver paint. But when God's love fills our hearts, we begin loving with divine dimensions of love. We become more and more concerned about others—and less and less worried about our own needs.

Christians indwelt by God's Spirit are more able to act and react as Christ did when He walked the earth. In our humanness, we can't be kind to those who are unkind to us. But when we have God's love in us, He loves people through us. If we love a person in spite of his wrong spirit or her sharp tongue, we've begun to enter into Jesus' love. When we love our spouse even when he or she has been unkind . . . when we love our children even when they have been rebellious . . . when we love our friends even when they let us down . . . we show that we are learning the brushstrokes of God's love.

UNCONDITIONAL LOVE

Besides loving us purposefully and selflessly, God loves us without strings. A. W. Tozer once prayed this way:

> If nothing in us can win Thy love, nothing in the universe can prevent Thee from loving us. Thy love is uncaused and undeserved. Thou art thyself the reason for the love wherewith we are loved. Help us to believe in the intensity, the eternity of the love that has found us. Then love will cast out fear; and our troubled hearts will be at peace.[4]

I don't know if this has ever crossed your mind, but I remember when I first began to understand the Gospel for myself. I grew up with God's truth, but when I was a teenager I wrestled with certain aspects of it. I remember struggling to comprehend how one person could die for every other single person in history. That's a pretty hard concept to grasp, isn't it?

Then I realized that *the world*—as in "God so loved the world"— was a collective term that simply means me and all the other me's. I thought of the thief at Calvary. While Jesus was hanging on the cross for the sins of the whole world, He turned to one single me hanging on an adjacent cross and forgave that person's sins, saying, "Today you will be with Me in Paradise" (Luke 23:43). It was as if God were saying to all of us, "I love the whole world, but I love each one as if he or she were the only one to love."

Do you love the world? your family? your church? Those are collective terms that mean you love the individuals themselves. Love— Christlike and unconditional love—is a personal, intimate thing. It's a crimson portrait that touches even the loneliest heart.

SACRIFICIAL LOVE

Finally, as we imitate the brushstrokes of Jesus' love, we see its sacrificial color.

When my wife Donna and I were in London, we visited St. Paul's Cathedral. I'll never forget a life-sized marble statue of Jesus Christ. It was actually an ugly and disturbing image—a sculpture of Christ writhing in anguish. Beneath it were the words "This is how God loved the world." We can never fully probe the costliness of His love toward us, can we?

How, then, are we supposed to love as He loved? First, we can receive the love of the Master Artist into our hearts. We can also let His Spirit work His transforming artistry in our hearts. We can learn to paint our world with the rich colors of Jesus' compassion. His Spirit can shape the scenes of life with touches of His purposeful, selfless, unconditional, and sacrificial love. If you want to make a mark on this world with Jesus' brush of love, set your easel on the slopes of Calvary. There you'll see "love so amazing, so divine, [love that] demands my soul, my life, my all" (Isaac Watts).

signs of Life

Life Sign: My love for others is not conditional on their meeting my standards.

Life Verse: *Greater love has no one than this, than to lay down one's life for his friends.*

—John 15:13

Life in Action: What can I do to express my appreciation of God's sacrificial and unconditional love?

Graced and Gracious

We need to freely dispense the same grace God showed us.

Christiana Tsai was one of twenty siblings born to a Chinese ruling family during the Manchu dynasty. She enjoyed a good education, personal servants, and an isolated life, almost never venturing outside the walls of her family's palace. But Christiana's father, despite his Buddhist convictions, wanted Christiana to attend a Christian school run by missionaries from America. "Just be sure you don't eat Christianity!" he said, meaning he didn't want his daughter converting to the foreign religion.

At boarding school, Christiana heard the Gospel and was drawn to Jesus Christ, as was her classmate, Miss Wu. Her conversion so shocked Miss Wu's family that a relative was dispatched to bring her home. On the boat ride home, he gave her a rope and a knife. "You have disgraced your family by eating the Christian religion," he told her, warning that if she did not renounce her faith, she would have "to choose between this rope to hang yourself, this knife to stab yourself, or this canal to drown yourself."

Christiana also bore the wrath of her family, who savagely tore her

Bible and hymnbook into pieces and threw them in her face. She was kept as a prisoner. "But," Christiana later wrote, "I did not argue; I only prayed for wisdom, and God gave me grace."

One day a brother said to her, "Tell me about Christianity and why you became a Christian." When Christiana told him, he replied, "That was a remarkable experience. And I have noticed that, in spite of the way we treat you now, you seem much happier than you used to be. I think I would like to believe too."

In the course of time, fifty-five relatives received Jesus, including the brother who had torn up her Bible and hymnbook. Christiana Tsai found the secret of conveying to others the grace she herself had received: her gracious spirit drew her family to Christ.[1]

Unfortunately, not every Grace Receiver is a Grace Giver. Case in point. Have you ever talked to a young person who works Sundays at some popular restaurant? Almost universally, they claim that the "church crowd" is the most difficult and demanding group they serve—and they leave the smallest tips.

Why do we so frequently fail to dispense the same grace God has shown us? Why do we, who have received God's unmerited favor, fail to extend unmerited favor to those He allows to enter our life? Sometimes we're disgusted by the actions of unbelievers, and, instead of overflowing with grace, we get riled up with righteous indignation (which isn't always inappropriate). Other times we're afraid of being taken advantage of, so we don't extend grace. Sometimes we just aren't sure how and when to extend grace. And then, of course, sometimes we're just out of sorts. . . .

As you read this, you may be thinking to yourself, *I need more patience! I need to be kinder and more gracious!* Perhaps you're thinking, *I need to forgive my friend for hurting my feelings. I need to forgive my co-worker for the wound she inflicted.*

A bitter spirit is like a spoonful of acid in your stomach that slowly eats away at your vital organs. The Bible warns us to not "fall short of the grace of God; lest any root of bitterness springing up cause trouble, and by this many become defiled" (Hebrews 12:15). So, I ask, "How can we become a Grace Giver to others?"

STUDY JESUS

The most important thing is to study Jesus and learn from His example. This is the underlying theme of the book of 1 Peter, which repeatedly tells us to respond to persecution and personal attack as Jesus did—with grace, with dignity, and with quiet forgiveness. "For to this you were called," wrote Peter, "because Christ also suffered for us, leaving us an example, that you should follow His steps: 'Who committed no sin, nor was deceit found in His mouth'; who, when He was reviled, did not revile in return; when He suffered, He did not threaten, but committed Himself to Him who judges righteously" (1 Peter 2:21–23).

If your attitude is critical and demanding, I encourage you to read through 1 Peter—it's only five chapters—and study what Peter says about Jesus. Find some verses to post on your refrigerator and on the tablets of your memory. How different, for example, would your attitude be if you memorized and then seriously tried to live according to 1 Peter 3:8–9?

> All of you be of one mind, having compassion for one another; love as brothers, be tenderhearted, be courteous; not returning evil for evil or reviling for reviling, but on the contrary blessing, knowing that you were called to this, that you may inherit a blessing.

It's hard to remold a piece of clay that's been hardened, and sometimes we feel that our personalities and attitudes are already "set," that we're "just the way we are." But the Christian is always moldable, under construction, and capable of becoming more like Christ. You can become a conveyer of His grace to others as you keep your eyes on Him, study His life, and commit yourself to becoming more and more like Him. . . .

Deliberately Forgive

We also do a better job being a channel of God's grace when we—like Christ—deliberately forgive those who have sinned against us.

By God's grace, hymn writer Fanny Crosby was able not only to forgive the doctor who ruined her vision, but she was also able to thank God for her blindness. She wrote this little prayer: "I am praying, Blessed Savior, to be more and more like Thee. I am praying that Thy Spirit like a dove may rest on me."[2]

And her blessed Savior—and ours—once told a story of a servant who owed an enormous sum of money to his master. It was impossible for him to pay it, so the master graciously forgave the debt. But the debtor, freed from his obligation, found a man who owed him a small sum and threw him into debtor's prison for failing to repay the loan. When the master heard of it, he summoned his servant and said, "You wicked servant! I forgave you all that debt because you begged me. Should you not also have had compassion on your fellow servant, just as I had pity on you?" The master threw his servant to the torturers.

Then Jesus spoke these stark words: "So My heavenly Father also will do to you if each of you, from his heart, does not forgive his brother his trespasses" (Matthew 18:35). . . .

❧

Psychologists are discovering how the act of forgiving others actually improves mental and even physical health. In one recently published study, participants attended a six-hour workshop explaining how holding a grudge can cause psychological and physical damage; they were also taught techniques for forgiving others. The majority of those people who chose to forgive reported significant improvement in their relationships as well as in their physical and emotional health.[3]

How relevant is the Bible's advice!

PRACTICE EMPATHY

An effective tool for forgiving others is empathy, and empathy comes when we pause long enough to look at others through the lens of their own experience. . . .

❦

Writer F. W. Boreham once lost patience with a difficult man named Crittingden, who had spoken many critical words. Boreham wrote a flaming letter designed to rebuke the complainer. He walked to the mailbox to post the letter. Since it was a lovely night for a walk, he passed the mailbox without dropping the letter in, thinking he'd mail it on the way back. Further on he met a friend who said, "Poor old Crittingden is dead."

Boreham was shocked. "Is he, indeed? When did this happen?"

"Oh, he died suddenly early this afternoon. It's really for the best, you know. He's had a hard time. You know all about it, I suppose?"

"No, I don't."

"Oh, I thought everybody knew. He only had two children, a son and a daughter. The son was killed soon after his wife died, and the daughter lost her mind and is in the asylum. Poor old Crittingden never got over it. It soured him."

Boreham returned to his fireside that night, humbled and ashamed. He tore the letter into small fragments and burned them one by one. And as he knelt before the blaze, he prayed that, in days to come, he might find grace to deal gently and lovingly with difficult people.[4] . . .

❦

Thomas à Kempis once wrote, "Know all and you will pardon all."[5]

We should be more patient, more gracious, and more cheerful with others. We should smile more and complain less. We should build up rather than tear down, and we should forgive others even as we ourselves have received the grace of God's forgiveness. When we fully understand the amazing goodness of God's grace, we become Grace Givers—and that's just what the world is looking for.

So let's make up our minds to "be kind to one another, tender-hearted, forgiving one another, even as God in Christ forgave [us]" (Ephesians 4:32).

signs of Life

Life Sign: I am a channel of God's grace to others.

Life Verse: *Let your speech always be with grace, seasoned with salt, that you may know how you ought to answer each one.*
—Colossians 4:6

Life in Action: What can I do so that I will be able to deal more gently and lovingly with the difficult people in my life?

Afterword

As we conclude our forty-day journey, I want to tell you about the way we at our church here in El Cajon, California, have tried to apply these Signs of Life lessons. Our effort was the subject of the article "Church Gives School 'Extreme Makeover,'" written by Meredith Day for The Baptist Press. *Here, with her permission, is that story.*

Cindy Wilcken warned the congregation at Shadow Mountain Community Church that she might cry as she addressed them on Sunday evening, April 15. Her audience laughed when she told them that her third-grade students at Logan Elementary School know to expect a few tears from her whenever she tells them stories about her family and other people who are dear to her. And as she spoke to Shadow Mountain, Wilcken cried a few tears of gratitude on behalf of those students whose lives she says have been impacted by a single day of service.

Three weeks earlier, on the morning of Saturday, March 24, more than 500 volunteers from Shadow Mountain arrived at Logan Elementary. They came ready to paint, clean, landscape, hang banners, plant a vegetable garden, build soccer goals, and tackle any other project that needed to be done. The day was an opportunity to put into action the church's Signs of Life campaign, a six-week series of teaching focused on living like Jesus, with dusty shoes, worn-out knees, rolled-up sleeves, open hands, and outstretched arms.

Several months ago, the church, led by Pastor David Jeremiah, approached the San Diego Unified School District with the idea of an "extreme makeover" for a local school. Shadow Mountain is located in

El Cajon, in the eastern part of San Diego County, but the church was interested in reaching out to a different part of the city. . . .

Logan Elementary, located in an impoverished neighborhood near downtown San Diego, impressed church leaders with a commitment to excellence and to its students. In the weeks leading up to the makeover, the congregation heard from school leaders, including Shadow Mountain member and Logan Elementary counselor Danielle Stilwell, who referred to the school as a "security blanket" for its students. By reaching out to the school through the makeover, Stilwell said, Shadow Mountain had a great opportunity to enhance that security blanket.

Working with different business people within the church, Shadow Mountain gathered the materials needed for the makeover. New signs and pennants, concrete, office furniture, paint, turf—all were donated or offered at a deep discount. And when the call for volunteers went out, there were too many responses and not enough space at Logan. But the hundreds of volunteers who offered help after the cap was set still had an opportunity to serve. After the majority of the makeover work was done in the morning, 2,000 people, including volunteers and the Logan community, joined for a celebration in a neighborhood park. The event offered food, live music, and a thank-you from San Diego Mayor Jerry Sanders, who complimented the effort by the church and the community to work together. Boxes of food and personal care items also were distributed through partnering ministry Feed the Children.

The makeover and celebration were about exhibiting "signs of life," living in such a way that the church is focused outwardly. In the days leading up to the project and during the event, Shadow Mountain's media ministry team collected video footage to create a documentary that the church hopes will help other churches that want to reach into their communities. In the documentary, [Pastor David] Jeremiah explains how the Logan Elementary outreach is meant to help reverse a trend that separates churches from the people who surround them.

"This is what the church is all about," Jeremiah said. "For so long, we've thought the church was what happened when we all got together in a building on Sunday, but this is the way the church is supposed to function."

At the close of the documentary, after several minutes of footage of painting and cleaning and serving, new faces come into view. They are smiling, laughing, excited faces. The students of Logan Elementary probably had no idea what their school would look like after the makeover, but Shadow Mountain's cameras caught their reaction when they returned after the weekend. Principal Antonio Villar says the impact made on his students isn't something that can be measured:

"They will remember that Monday morning for the rest of their lives."

Meredith Day, "Church gives school 'extreme makeover.'" *Baptist Press,* posted 4/20/07.

Forty Signs of Life

My words and actions evidence Christ's indwelling.
My faith is expressed through works.
I am a source of light in a dark world.
Every moment of my life is a *living moment* with God.
I am conscious of influencing those around me.
Those who witness my life see Jesus.
The imprint of my Christian life will remain for eternity.
I am willing to get my feet dusty in the streets of my community.
My walk supports my Christian talk.
Opportunities to share Christ are divine appointments.
The most important thing I can say is "Jesus loves you."
The needs of others are as important as my own.
I am a walking, living advertisement for the Lord.
Every day I create incriminating evidence to prove that I am a follower of Christ.
Hearing the Lord's direction begins with prayer.
I am open and listening for God's direction.
Unconditional surrender to God brings me spiritual victory.
My love for God is greater than my affection for anything in this desirable but deadly world.
My life is not plagued by worry because I am held tightly in God's hands.
I am willing to be pliable in the hands of God.
I participate in personal ministry that impacts my community.
The world sees the heart of God through the work of my hands.

The major theme of my life is love.

My behavior reflects the teachings of Jesus.

Those who come in contact with me leave encouraged.

I courageously walk through the open doors God puts before me.

My life makes waves in the hearts of those around me.

Humility is the hallmark of my service.

I look for ways to generously give to others.

I give to others because God has given richly to me.

Nothing stands in my way of following Jesus.

God is free to use any area of my life to do His will.

I am a faithful steward of all God has given me.

I take time each day to mine God's Word.

There is always more I can do for God's kingdom.

Compassion is my passion.

I care . . . regardless.

Others will know I am a Christian by my love.

My love for others is not conditional on their meeting my standards.

I am a channel of God's grace to others.

Appendix:
The Poor

Scripture contains more than 150 verses that refer directly to the poor. Some are God's promises to the poor, other verses are promises God makes to those who care for the poor, and still others are His warnings for those who mistreat the poor.

PROVIDENCE OF THE LORD

The LORD makes poor and makes rich;
He brings low and lifts up. (1 Samuel 2: 7)

Yet He is not partial to princes,
Nor does He regard the rich more than the poor;
for they are all the work of His hands. (Job 34:19)

The rich and the poor have this in common,
The LORD is the maker of them all. (Proverbs 22:2)

The poor man and the oppressor have this in common:
The LORD gives light to the eyes of both. (Proverbs 29:13)

For you know the grace of our Lord Jesus Christ, that though He was rich, yet for your sakes He became poor, that you through His poverty might become rich. (2 Corinthians 8:9)

PREVALENCE OF THE POOR

For the poor will never cease from the land; therefore I command you, saying, "You shall open your hand wide to your brother, to your poor and your needy, in your land." (Deuteronomy 15:11)

For you have the poor with you always, but Me you do not have always.
(Matthew 26:11)

*For you have the poor with you always, and whenever you wish you may
do them good; but Me you do not have always.* (Mark 14:7)

For the poor you have with you always, but Me you do not have always.
(John 12:8)

PROMISES IN THE OLD TESTAMENT

OBEDIENT GIVING

*And the Levite, because he has no portion nor inheritance with you, and
the stranger and the fatherless and the widow who are within your gates,
may come and eat and be satisfied, **that the LORD your God may bless
you in all the work of your hand which you do.*** (Deuteronomy 14:29)

COMPASSIONATE GIVING

*At the end of every seven years you shall grant a release of debts. And this is
the form of the release: Every creditor who has lent anything to his neighbor
shall release it; he shall not require it of his neighbor or his brother, because
it is called the LORD's release. Of a foreigner you may require it; but your
hand shall release what is owed by your brother, except when there may be
no poor among you; **for the LORD will greatly bless you in the land
which the LORD your God is giving you to possess as an inheritance.***
(Deuteronomy 15:1–6)

GENEROUS GIVING

*If there is among you a poor man of your brethren, within any of the gates
in your land which the LORD your God is giving you, you shall not harden
your heart nor shut your hand from your poor brother, but you shall open
your hand wide to him and willingly lend him sufficient for his need,
whatever he needs. Beware lest there be a wicked thought in your heart,
saying, "The seventh year, the year of release, is at hand," and your eye be*

evil against your poor brother and you give him nothing, and he cry out to the LORD *against you, and it become sin among you. You shall surely give to him, and your heart should not be grieved when you give to him, because **for this thing the** LORD **your God will bless you in all your works and in all to which you put your hand.** For the poor will never cease from the land; therefore I command you, saying, "You shall open your hand wide to your brother, to your poor and your needy, in your land."* (Deuteronomy 15:7–11)

RIGHTEOUS GIVING

And if the man is poor, you shall not keep his pledge overnight. You shall in any case return the pledge to him again when the sun goes down, that he may sleep in his own garment and bless you; and it shall be righteousness to you before the LORD *your God.* (Deuteronomy 24:12–13)

UNSELFISH LIVING

*When you reap your harvest in your field, and forget a sheaf in the field, you shall not go back to get it; it shall be for the stranger, the fatherless, and the widow, **that the** LORD **your God may bless you in all the work of your hands.*** (Deuteronomy 24:19)

Blessed is he who considers the poor;
The LORD *will deliver him in time of trouble.*
The LORD *will preserve him and keep him alive,*
And he will be blessed on the earth;
The LORD *will strengthen him on his bed of illness.* (Psalm 41:1–2b, 3)

You will sustain him on his sickbed.
A good man deals graciously and lends;
He will guide his affairs with discretion.
Surely he will never be shaken;
The righteous will be in everlasting remembrance.
He will not be afraid of evil tidings;
His heart is steadfast, trusting in the LORD.

His heart is established;
He will not be afraid,
Until he sees his desire upon his enemies.
He has dispersed abroad,
He has given to the poor;
His righteousness endures forever;
His horn will be exalted with honor. (Psalm 112:5–9)

He who despises his neighbor sins;
But he who has mercy on the poor, happy is he. (Proverbs 14:21)

He who has pity on the poor lends to the LORD,
And He will pay back what he has given. (Proverbs 19:17)

He who has a generous eye will be blessed,
For he gives of his bread to the poor. (Proverbs 22:9)

He who gives to the poor will not lack,
But he who hides his eyes will have many curses. (Proverbs 28:27)

The king who judges the poor with truth,
His throne will be established forever. (Proverbs 29:14)

Is this not the fast that I have chosen:
To loose the bonds of wickedness,
To undo the heavy burdens,
To let the oppressed go free,
And that you break every yoke?
Is it not to share your bread with the hungry,
And that you bring to your house the poor who are cast out;
When you see the naked, that you cover him,
And not hide yourself from your own flesh?
Then your light shall break forth like the morning,
Your healing shall spring forth speedily,
And your righteousness shall go before you;
The glory of the LORD shall be your rear guard.
Then you shall call, and the LORD will answer;
You shall cry, and He will say, "Here I am." (Isaiah 58:6–9)

If you extend your soul to the hungry
And satisfy the afflicted soul,
Then your light shall dawn in the darkness,
And your darkness shall be as the noonday.
The LORD *will guide you continually,*
And satisfy your soul in drought,
And strengthen your bones;
You shall be like a watered garden,
And like a spring of water, whose waters do not fail.
Those from among you
Shall build the old waste places;
You shall raise up the foundations of many generations;
And you shall be called the Repairer of the Breach,
The Restorer of Streets to Dwell In. (Isaiah 58:10–12)

Therefore, O king, let my advice be acceptable to you; break off your sins by being righteous, and your iniquities by showing mercy to the poor. Perhaps there may be a lengthening of your prosperity. (Daniel 4:27)

PENALTIES FOR MISTREATMENT

For he has oppressed and forsaken the poor,
He has violently seized a house which he did not build.
Because he knows no quietness in his heart,
He will not save anything he desires.
Nothing is left for him to eat;
Therefore his well-being will not last. (Job 20:19–21)

Whoever shuts his ears to the cry of the poor will also cry himself and not be heard. (Proverbs 21:13)

He who oppresses the poor to increase his riches,
And he who gives to the rich, will surely come to poverty. (Proverbs 22:16)

Do not rob the poor because he is poor,
Nor oppress the afflicted at the gate.

For the L<small>ORD</small> *will plead their cause,*
And plunder the soul of those who plunder them. (Proverbs 22: 22–23)

The L<small>ORD</small> *will enter into judgment with the elders of His people and His princes: "For you have eaten up the vineyard; the plunder of the poor is in your houses."* (Isaiah 3:14)

Woe to those who decree unrighteous decrees,
Who write misfortune,
Which they have prescribed
To rob the needy of justice,
And to take what is right from the poor of My people,
That widows may be their prey,
And that they may rob the fatherless.
What will you do in the day of punishment,
And in the desolation which shall come from afar?
To whom will you flee for help?
And where will you leave your glory? (Isaiah 10:1–3)

Thus says the L<small>ORD</small>:
"For three transgressions of Israel, and for four,
I will not turn away its punishment,
Because they sell the righteous for silver,
And the poor for a pair of sandals." (Amos 2:6)

Therefore, because you tread down the poor
And take grain taxes from him,
Though you have built houses of hewn stone,
Yet you shall not dwell in them;
You have planted pleasant vineyards,
But you shall not drink wine from them. (Amos 5:11)

Hear this, you who swallow up the needy,
And make the poor of the land fail,
Saying:
"When will the New Moon be past,
That we may sell grain?
And the Sabbath,

That we may trade wheat?
Making the ephah small and the shekel large,
Falsifying the balances by deceit,
That we may buy the poor for silver,
And the needy for a pair of sandals—
Even sell the bad wheat?"
The LORD *has sworn by the pride of Jacob:*
"Surely I will never forget any of their works.
Shall the land not tremble for this,
And everyone mourn who dwells in it?" (Amos 8:4–8a)

"Do not oppress the widow or the fatherless,
The alien or the poor.
Let none of you plan evil in his heart
Against his brother."'
But they refused to heed, shrugged their shoulders, and stopped their ears so
that they could not hear. . . . Therefore it happened, that just as He
proclaimed and they would not hear, so they called out and I would not
listen," says the LORD *of hosts.* (Zechariah 7:10–11,13)

PROMISES FOR THE POOR

The LORD *makes poor and makes rich;*
He brings low and lifts up.
He raises the poor from the dust
And lifts the beggar from the ash heap,
To set them among princes
And make them inherit the throne of glory. (1 Samuel 2:7–8a)

So that they caused the cry of the poor to come to Him;
For He hears the cry of the afflicted. (Job 34:28)

He delivers the poor in their affliction,
And opens their ears in oppression. (Job 36:15)

For the needy shall not always be forgotten;
The expectation of the poor shall not perish forever. (Psalm 9:18)

"For the oppression of the poor, for the sighing of the needy,
Now I will arise," says the LORD;
"I will set him in the safety for which he yearns." (Psalm 12:5)

You shame the counsel of the poor,
But the LORD is his refuge. (Psalm 14:6)

The poor shall eat and be satisfied;
Those who seek Him will praise the LORD.
Let your heart live forever! (Psalm 22:26)

All my bones shall say,
"LORD, who is like You,
Delivering the poor from him who is too strong for him,
Yes, the poor and the needy from him who plunders him?" (Psalm 35:10)

I have been young, and now am old;
Yet I have not seen the righteous forsaken,
Nor his descendants begging bread.
He is ever merciful, and lends;
And his descendants are blessed. (Psalm 37:25–26)

But I am poor and needy;
Yet the LORD thinks upon me.
You are my help and my deliverer;
Do not delay, O my God. (Psalm 40:17)

You, O God, provided from Your goodness for the poor. (Psalm 68:10)

For the LORD hears the poor,
And does not despise His prisoners. (Psalm 69:33)

But I am poor and needy;
Make haste to me, O God!
You are my help and my deliverer;
O LORD, do not delay. (Psalm 70:5)

He will bring justice to the poor of the people;
He will save the children of the needy,
And will break in pieces the oppressor. (Psalm 72:4)

For He will deliver the needy when he cries,
The poor also, and him who has no helper
He will spare the poor and needy,
And will save the souls of the needy. (Psalm 72:12–13)

Yet He sets the poor on high, far from affliction,
And makes their families like a flock. (Psalm 107:41)

For He shall stand at the right hand of the poor,
To save him from those who condemn him. (Psalm 109:31)

He raises the poor out of the dust,
And lifts the needy out of the ash heap. (Psalm 113:7)

I will abundantly bless her provision;
I will satisfy her poor with bread. (Psalm 132:15)

I know that the LORD will maintain
The cause of the afflicted,
And justice for the poor. (Psalm 140:12)

But with righteousness He shall judge the poor,
And decide with equity for the meek of the earth;
He shall strike the earth with the rod of His mouth,
And with the breath of His lips He shall slay the wicked. (Isaiah 11:4)

What will they answer the messengers of the nation?
That the LORD has founded Zion,
And the poor of His people shall take refuge in it. (Isaiah 14:32)

For You have been a strength to the poor,
A strength to the needy in his distress,
A refuge from the storm,
A shade from the heat;
For the blast of the terrible ones is as a storm against the wall. (Isaiah 25:4)

The poor and needy seek water, but there is none,
And their tongues fail for thirst,
I, the LORD, will hear them;
I, the God of Israel, will not forsake them. (Isaiah 41:17)

Sing to the LORD! Praise the LORD!
For He has delivered the life of the poor
From the hand of evildoers. (Jeremiah 20:13)

PARTIALITY FORBIDDEN

You shall not show partiality to a poor man in his dispute. (Exodus 23:3)

You shall not pervert the judgment of your poor in his dispute. (Exodus 23:6)

The rich shall not give more and the poor shall not give less than half a shekel, when you give an offering to the LORD, to make atonement for yourselves. (Exodus 30:15)

But if he is poor and cannot afford it, then he shall take one male lamb as a trespass offering to be waved, to make atonement for him, one-tenth of an ephah of fine flour mixed with oil as a grain offering, a log of oil, and two turtledoves or two young pigeons, such as he is able to afford: one shall be a sin offering and the other a burnt offering. (Leviticus 14:21–22)

You shall do no injustice in judgment. You shall not be partial to the poor, nor honor the person of the mighty. In righteousness you shall judge your neighbor. (Leviticus 19:15)

PROVISION FOR PHYSICAL NEEDS

But the seventh year you shall let it rest and lie fallow, that the poor of your people may eat; and what they leave, the beasts of the field may eat. In like manner you shall do with your vineyard and your olive grove. (Exodus 23:11)

And you shall not glean your vineyard, nor shall you gather every grape of your vineyard; you shall leave them for the poor and the stranger: I am the LORD your God. (Leviticus 19:10)

When you reap the harvest of your land, you shall not wholly reap the corners of your field when you reap, nor shall you gather any gleaning from your harvest. You shall leave them for the poor and for the stranger: I am the LORD your God. (Leviticus 23:22)

If one of your brethren becomes poor, and has sold some of his possession, and if his redeeming relative comes to redeem it, then he may redeem what his brother sold. (Leviticus 25:25)

If one of your brethren becomes poor, and falls into poverty among you, then you shall help him, like a stranger or a sojourner, that he may live with you. Take no usury or interest from him; but fear your God, that your brother may live with you. You shall not lend him your money for usury, nor lend him your food at a profit. I am the LORD your God, who brought you out of the land of Egypt, to give you the land of Canaan and to be your God. (Leviticus 25:35–38)

For they are My servants, whom I brought out of the land of Egypt; they shall not be sold as slaves. (Leviticus 25:42)

THE PERILS OF MISTREATING THE POOR

The wicked in his pride persecutes the poor;
Let them be caught in the plots which they have devised. (Psalm 10:2)

Let the iniquity of his fathers be remembered before the LORD,
And let not the sin of his mother be blotted out.
Let them be continually before the LORD,
That He may cut off the memory of them from the earth;
Because he did not remember to show mercy,
But persecuted the poor and needy man,
That he might even slay the broken in heart. (Psalm 109:14–16)

He who oppresses the poor reproaches his Maker,
But he who honors Him has mercy on the needy. (Proverbs 14:31)

He who mocks the poor reproaches his Maker;
He who is glad at calamity will not go unpunished. (Proverbs 17:5)

Whoever shuts his ears to the cry of the poor
Will also cry himself and not be heard. (Proverbs 21:13)

He who oppresses the poor to increase his riches,
And he who gives to the rich, will surely come to poverty. (Proverbs 22:16)

One who increases his possessions by usury and extortion
Gathers it for him who will pity the poor. (Proverbs 28:8)

He who gives to the poor will not lack,
But he who hides his eyes will have many curses. (Proverbs 28:27)

The LORD will enter into judgment
With the elders of His people
And His princes:
"For you have eaten up the vineyard;
The plunder of the poor is in your houses.
What do you mean by crushing My people
And grinding the faces of the poor?"
Says the Lord GOD of hosts. (Isaiah 3:14–15)

Look, this was the iniquity of your sister Sodom: She and her daughter had
pride, fullness of food, and abundance of idleness; neither did she
strengthen the hand of the poor and needy. (Ezekiel 16:49)

If he has oppressed the poor and needy,
Robbed by violence,
Not restored the pledge,
Lifted his eyes to the idols,
Or committed abomination;
If he has exacted usury
Or taken increase—
Shall he then live?
He shall not live!
If he has done any of these abominations,
He shall surely die;
His blood shall be upon him. (Ezekiel 18:12–13)

PRINCIPLES IN THE NEW TESTAMENT

Blessed are *the poor in spirit,*
    For theirs is the kingdom of heaven. (Matthew 5:3)

*The blind see and the lame walk; the lepers are cleansed and the deaf hear;
the dead are raised up and the poor have the gospel preached to them.*
(Matthew 11:5)

*Jesus said to him, "If you want to be perfect, go, sell what you have and
give to the poor, and you will have treasure in heaven; and come, follow
Me."* (Matthew 19:21)

*Then Jesus, looking at him, loved him, and said to him, "One thing you
lack: Go your way, sell whatever you have and give to the poor, and you
will have treasure in heaven; and come, take up the cross, and follow Me."*
(Mark 10:21)

*Then one poor widow came and threw in two mites, which make a quad-
rans. So He called His disciples to Himself and said to them, "Assuredly, I
say to you that this poor widow has put in more than all those who have
given to the treasury."* (Mark 12:42–43)

The Spirit of the LORD *is upon Me,
Because He has anointed Me to preach the gospel to the poor;
He has sent Me to heal the brokenhearted,
To preach deliverance to the captives
And recovery of sight to the blind,
To set at liberty those who are oppressed . . .* (Luke 4:18)

*Then He lifted up His eyes toward His disciples, and said:
"Blessed are you poor,
For yours is the kingdom of God."* (Luke 6:20)

*Give, and it will be given to you: good measure, pressed down, shaken
together, and running over will be put into your bosom. For with the same
measure that you use, it will be measured back to you.* (Luke 6:38)

*Jesus answered and said to them, "Go and tell John the things you have
seen and heard: that the blind see, the lame walk, the lepers are cleansed,
the deaf hear, the dead are raised, the poor have the gospel preached to
them."* (Luke 7:22)

Sell what you have and give alms; provide yourselves money bags which do not grow old, a treasure in the heavens that does not fail, where no thief approaches nor moth destroys. (Luke 12:33)

But when you give a feast, invite the poor, the maimed, the lame, the blind. And you will be blessed, because they cannot repay you; for you shall be repaid at the resurrection of the just. (Luke 14:13–14)

So that servant came and reported these things to his master. Then the master of the house, being angry, said to his servant, "Go out quickly into the streets and lanes of the city, and bring in here the poor and the maimed and the lame and the blind." (Luke 14:21)

So when Jesus heard these things, He said to him, "You still lack one thing. Sell all that you have and distribute to the poor, and you will have treasure in heaven; and come, follow Me." (Luke 18:22)

Yes, you yourselves know that these hands have provided for my necessities, and for those who were with me. I have shown you in every way, by laboring like this, that you must support the weak. And remember the words of the Lord Jesus, that He said, "It is more blessed to give than to receive." (Acts 20:34–35)

For it pleased those from Macedonia and Achaia to make a certain contribution for the poor among the saints who are in Jerusalem. (Romans 15:26)

Now may He who supplies seed to the sower, and bread for food, supply and multiply the seed you have sown and increase the fruits of your righteousness, while you are enriched in everything for all liberality, which causes thanksgiving through us to God. (2 Corinthians 9:10–11)

Notes

Introduction

1. http://www.stlawrenceattur.com/thesaint.html.
2. Isaac Leib Peretz and Ruth R. Wisse, *Isaac Leib Peretz Reader* (New Haven: Yale University Press, 2002), 178.

Day 2

1. "Tumble from Tightrope Injures Performer," *The New York Times,* April 7, 2004.
2. Alvin J. Schmidt, *How Christianity Changed the World* (Grand Rapids, MI: Zondervan, 2004), 130.
3. Charles Allen, *You Are Never Alone* (Old Tappan: Revell, 1978), 143-144.
4. Manfred George Gutzke, *Plain Talk on James* (Grand Rapids, MI: Zondervan, 1969), 81.

Day 3

1. Ace Collins, *Stories Behind the Great Traditions of Christmas* (Grand Rapids: Zondervan, 2003), 199-120.
2. http://www.pastorjeff.com/QuotesJ.html, accessed June 11, 2007.
3. *Voices of the Faithful: Inspiring Stories of Courage from Christians Serving Around the World,* comp. Kim P. Davis with Beth Moore (Brentwood, TN: Integrity, 2005), 164.

Day 4

1. http://www.ecommercetimes.com/story/44502.html.

Day 5

1. Newt Gingrich, *Rediscovering God in America: Reflections on the Role of Faith in Our Nation's History* (Nashville, TN: Thomas Nelson, 2006), 74.

2. R. Kent Hughes, *Acts: The Church Afire,* Preaching the Word Series (Wheaton, IL: Crossway, 1996), 16.

3. R. Kent Hughes, *The Sermon on the Mount: The Message of the Kingdom,* Preaching the Word Series (Wheaton, IL: Crossway, 2001), 80.

Day 6

1. "Courtroom Artist Looks Back at Some Famous Trials and Drawings", CNN.com transcripts 3/31/00. http://transcripts.cnn.com/TRANSCRIPTS/0003/31/wt.09.html

2. Jay Kesler, *Ten Mistakes Parents Make with Teenagers: And How to Avoid Them* (Brentwood, TN: Wolgemuth and Hyatt, 1988), 29-30.

3. Edgar Guest, quoted in Patrick M. Morley and David Delk, *The Dad in the Mirror: How to See Your Heart for God Reflected in Your Children* (Grand Rapids, MI: Zondervan, 2003), 128.

4. William Mitchell Ramsay, *Second Corinthians* (Louisville, KY: Westminster John Knox Press, 2004), 21-22.

5. Phillip W. Keller, *A Layman Looks at the Lord's Prayer* (Minneapolis: World Wide Publications, 1976), 66-67.

6. Keller, *A Layman Looks at the Lord's Prayer,* 66–67.

7. Annie Johnson Flint in *The Speaker's Treasury of 400 Quotable Poems,* comp. Croft M. Pentz (Grand Rapids, MI: Zondervan, 1963), 24.

Day 7

1. Colin Wilson and Damon Wilson, *Written in Blood: A History of Forensic Detection* (New York: Carroll & Graff Publishers, 2003), 130-132.

2. Eugene Myers Harrison, "John Geddie: Messenger of the Love of Christ in Eastern Melanesia," http://www.wholesomewords. org/missions/biogeddie.html.
3. http://www.donelson.org/pocket/pp-980809.html.
4. Allen C. Emery, *A Turtle on a Fencepost* (Minneapolis: World Wide Publications, 1979), 27, 29.
5. http://www.sermonillustrations.com/a-z/p/prayer.htm, accessed June 18, 2007.
6. David Roach, "Dentist commits life to Christ after 24-year spiritual journey," *Baptist Press,* September 8, 2003.
7. *Augsburg Sermons 3: Gospels: Series C.3* (Minneapolis: Augsburg Fortress, 1994), 218.
8. Words and music by Jon Mohr; Birdwing Music (a division of the Sparrow Corp./Jonathan Mark Music (admin. by Gaither Copyright Management) (ASCAP), 1987.

Day 8
1. Josiah Strong, *The New Era: or, The Coming Kingdom* (Charlotte, NC: Baker & Taylor, 1898), 351.
2. Janet Benge and Geoff Benge, *William Booth: Soup, Soap, and Salvation* (Seattle, WA: YWAM, 2002), 165.
3. Edward Harvey McKinley, *Marching to Glory: The History of the Salvation Army in the US, 1880-1980* (New York: Harper & Row, 1980), 53.
4. http://www.salvationarmydanecounty.org/links/.
5. McKinley, *Marching to Glory,* 45.
6. http://www.salvationarmydanecounty.org/links/.
7. Roy Hattersley, "Faith does breed charity," *The Guardian,* 9/12/05. http://www.guardian.co.uk/comment./story.

Day 9
1. Carolly Erickson, *To the Scaffold: The Life of Marie Antoinette* (New York: St. Martin's Griffin, 2004), 14.
2. A. W. Tozer, *The Knowledge of the Holy: The Attributes of God:*

Their Meaning in the Christian Life (New York: Harper & Row, 1961), 78.

3. William Revell Moody, *The Life of Dwight L. Moody* (Old Tappan: Revell, 1900), 42.

4. http://www.Dukemednews.duke.edu/news/article, accessed January 12, 2004.

Day 10

1. http://thespeakersgroup.com/speaker_243.html.

Day 11

1. Wilbur M. Smith, *Before I Forget* (Chicago: Moody, 1971), 8–9.

2. Kenneth S. Wuest, *Acts through Ephesians: Wuest's Expanded Translation of the New Testament*, vol. 2 (Grand Rapids: Eerdmans, 1958), on *Libronix Digital Library Version 2*, Logos Research Systems, Inc., 2003.

3. Lorne C. Sanny, *The Art of Personal Witnessing* (Chicago: Moody, 1957), 23.

4. *The Gideon* (Nashville, TN: Gideons International), January 2007.

Day 13

1. Seth Livingstone, "Plenty Goes into Designing NASCAR Paint Jobs," in *USA Today,* May 3, 2006, http://www.usatoday.com/sports/motor/nascar/2006-05-03-sw-paint-cover_x.htm, accessed June 13, 2007.

2. http://mns.foxsports.com/nascar/story/3489526, accessed July 23, 2007.

3. Lewis Drummond and Betty Drummond, *Women of Awakenings: The Historic Contribution of Women to Revival Movements* (Grand Rapids, MN: Kregel, 1997), 215-216.

4. Sam James, *Servant on the Edge of History: Risking All for the Gospel in War-Ravaged Vietnam* (Garland, TX: Hannibal, 2005), 24.

5. Bob Latford, *Built for Speed: The Ultimate Guide to Stock Car Racetracks* (Philadelphia: Running Press, 2002), 52, 74, 64.
6. Arthur T. Pierson, *The Heart of the Gospel: Sermons on the Life-Changing Power of the Good News* (Grand Rapids, MI: Kregel, 1996), 229.

Day 14

1. http://www.pubmedcentral.nih.gov/articlerender.fcgi?artid= 228486, accessed on July 17, 2007.
2. Richard Saferstein, *Criminalistics: An Introduction to Forensic Science,* 6th ed. (Englewood, NJ: Prentice Hall, 1997), 36.
3. Paul Leland Kirk, *Crime Investigation* (New York: Wiley & Son, 1974), 2.
4. http://72.14.253.104/search?q=cache:qHNRPZyLy6UJ:info. ci.ftlaud.fl.us/Focus/03augsep.pdf+Tom+Hill+Ft.+Lauderdale +%22physical+evidence%22&hl=en&ct=clnk&cd=3&gl=us &lr=lang_en.

Day 15

1. Stephen Van Dulken, *Inventing the 19th Century: 100 Inventions That Shaped the Vistorian Age from Aspirin to the Zeppelin* (New York: New York University, 2001), 36.
2. William Cowper, "Exhortation to Prayer," *The Poetical Works* (London: Macmillan, 1889), 32.
3. Catherine Marshall, *Adventures in Prayer* (Old Tappan, NJ: Spire Books, 1975), 30-31.
4. Elmer L. Towns, "Praying in Tune," *Pray!,* January/February 2003, 17.
5. Rosalind Goforth, *How I Know God Answers Prayer* (Grand Rapids, MI: Zondervan, 1921), 16.
6. David Martyn Lloyd-Jones, *Studies in the Sermon on the Mount, vol. 2* (London: Inter-Varsity Fellowship, 1962), 45.
7. Charles H. Spurgeon, "Comfort for Those Whose Prayers Are

Feeble," *Sword and the Trowel* 5/1872. http://www.spurgeon.org/s_and_t/feeble.htm

8. John N. Hamblin, *Fire in the Pulpit* (Murfreesboro, TN: Sword of the Lord, n.d.), 82.

Day 16

1. Robert J. Morgan, "Praying of the Wrong Frequency," March 16, 2003, http://www.donelson.org/pocket/pp-030316.html.

2. James Stalker, *Imago Christi: The Example of Jesus Christ* (Cincinnati: Cranston & Curts, 1894), 131.

3. Oswald Sanders, *The Incomparable Christ* (Chicago: Moody, 1952), 135-136.

4. Christian History Institute, http://chi.gospelcom.net/DAILYF/2002/06/daily-06-11-2002.shtml.

5. William Walford, "Sweet Hour of Prayer," 1845, http://www.hymnsite.com/lyrics/umh496.sht.

Day 17

1. *The Last of the Mohicans,* directed by Michael Mann, Morgan Creek Productions, 1992.

Day 18

1. http://quote.robertgenn.com/auth_search.php?name=Andy%20Warhol, accessed June 13, 2007.

2. http://landscapingabout.com/library/bl_goldenrod.thm.

3. Billy Graham, *How to Be Born Again* (Waco: Word, 1977), 77-78.

Day 19

1. Eugene Peterson, *The Message* (Colorado Springs: NavPress, 2002).

2. Donald Grey Barnhouse, *Let Me Illustrate* (Tarrytown, NY: Fleming H. Revell, 1994), 253-254.

3. Rosalind Goforth, *How I Know God Answers Prayer* (Grand Rapids, MI: Zondervan, 1921), 50-52.

4. Joseph Parker, *A Preacher's Life: An Autobiography and an Album* (London: Hodder & Stoughton, n.d.), 99.

Day 20

1. Anne Graham Lotz, *Why?: Trusting God When You Don't Understand* (Nashville, TN: W Publishing, 2004), 22.
2. Robert J. Morgan, *Then Sings My Soul* (Nashville, TN: Thomas Nelson, 2006), 519.
3. Adelaide Pollard, "Have Thine Own Way," 1906, http://www.hymnsite.com/lyrics/umh382.sht.

Day 21

1. Philip Yancey, *Prayer: Does It Make Any Difference?* (Grand Rapids, MI: Zondervan, 2006), 120.
2. Victor Hugo, *Les Miserables* (New York: Signet Classic, 1987), 932.
3. *Science Desk Reference American Scientific* (New York: Wiley, 1999), 180.
4. Harald Ellingsen, *Homiletic Studies in the Gospels,* vol. 3 (Grand Rapids, MI: Baker, 1950), 209.
5. Adapted from John Phillips, *Exploring the Gospel of John,* John Phillips Commentary Series (Grand Rapids, MI: Kregel, 1989), 271.

Day 22

1. Deirdre M. Maloney, *American Catholic Lay Groups and Transatlantic Social Reform in the Progressive Era* (Chapel Hill, NC: University of North Carolina Press, 2002), 182.
2. "Gallaudet's Silent Treatment" 10/3/1852. http://chi.gospelcom.net/DAILYF/2001/10/daily-10-03-2001.shtml.
3. John Burke, *No Perfect People Allowed* (Grand Rapids, MI: Zondervan, 2005), 193.
4. http://www.nhlink.net/plainpress/html/stories/2007-06/parentsafetypatrol.htm.
5. Kay Adkins, "More than a clinic: Churches team up for unique outreach." http://www.baptistpress.org/bpnews.asp?id=260066. Accessed July 23, 2007.

6. Rebecca Santana, Associated Press, "Soldiers in Iraq Need More Silly String," December 7, 2006.
7. Franklin Graham, *Bob Pierce: This One Thing I Do* (Dallas: Word, 1983), 180.

Day 23

1. Helmut T. Lehmann, ed., *Luther's Works,* vol. 54, (Minneapolis, MN: Augsburg Fortress, 1967), 292.

Day 24

1. Wayne Petherick, *Criminal Profiling: How It Got Started and How It Is Used* @ crimelibrary.com/criminal_mind/profiling.
2. Petherick, *Criminal Profiling* @ crimelibrary.com/criminal_mind/profiling.
3. http://www.fbi.gov/hq/td/academy/bsu/bsu.htm.

Day 25

1. Wayne Rice, *Hot Illustrations for Youth Talks: 100 Attention-Getting Stories, Parables and Anecdotes* (Grand Rapids, MI: Zondervan, 1993), 151.
2. *You've Got Mail,* directed by Nora Ephron, Warner Bros. Pictures, 1998.

Day 26

1. Pat Williams, *The Paradox of Power* (New York: Warner Faith, 2004), 12-13.
2. Roy B. Zuck, *Speaker's Quote Book: Over 4,500 Illustrations and Quotes for All Occasions* (Grand Rapids, MI: Kregel, 1997), 275.

Day 27

1. James Burke, *Connections* TV documentary series, Episode 1, "The Trigger Effect," BBC, 1978.
2. Adapted from a sermon by Dr. James Allan Francis in *The Real Jesus and Other Sermons* (Valley Forge, PA: Judson Press, 1926), 123.

Day 28

1. Jim McGuiggan, *Jesus, Hero of Thy Soul: Impressions Left by the Savior's Touch* (West Monroe, LA: Howard Publishing, 1998), 97–98.

2. Henry Drummond, *The Greatest Thing in the World* (Kila, MT: Kessinger Publishing, 1998), 27.

Day 29

1. Robert S. Boynton, review of *By the Sword*, by Richard Cohen, *New York Times Book Review,* March 2, 2003, http://www.robert-boynton.com/ articleDisplay.php?article_id=82.

2. "The Devil's Bait," *Our Daily Bread*, Radio Bible Class, February 8, 2003.

3. Roy B. Zuck, *Speaker's Quote Book: Over 4,500 Illustrations and Quotes for All Occasions* (Grand Rapids, MI: Zondervan, 1997), 275.

Day 30

1. http://www.bbc.co.uk/dna/h2g2/A798159.

Day 31

1. http://www.ctlibrary.com/ct/1997/july14/7t814b.html, accessed July 17, 2007.

2. Elisabeth Elliot, *Through Gates of Splendor* (Lincoln, NE: Back to the Bible, 1986), 172.

Day 33

1. http://www.hasbro.com/monopoly/default.cfm?page=history, accessed on June 18, 2007.

2. http://www.hasbro.com/monopoly/defautl.cfm?page=history.

3. Quoted in Mihaly Csikszentmihalyi, "If We Are So Rich, Why Aren't We Happy?" in *American Psychologist,* October 1999. http://sparta. rice.edu/~erinm/Mihaly.html, accessed July 17, 2007.

4. http://www.hutchcraft.com/awwy/awwy2001/oct2001/awwy3842.htm.

Day 34

1. Mareva Brown, "Prospectors Still Prowl the Hills in Gold Fever's Grip," *The Sacramento Bee,* January 18, 1998, http://www. cal-goldrush.com/part4/04modern.html accessed on October 24, 2006.
2. Malcom J. Rohrbough, *Days of Gold: The California Gold Rush and the American Nation* (Berkley, CA: University of California, 1995), 20.
3. Mary Wilder Tileston, *Prayers Ancient and Modern* (New York: Doubleday & McClure, 1897), January 31, at http://books.google. com.
4. Tileston, *Prayers Ancient and Modern,* September 9.
5. Johnson Oatman, Jr., "Higher Ground," 1898, http://www. cyberhymnal.org/htm/h/i/highergr.htm.
6. Roy B. Zuck, *The Speaker's Quote Book: Over 4,500 Illustrations and Quotations for All Occasions* (Grand Rapids, MI: Zondervan, 1997), 380.
7. Geoffrey Bull, *When Iron Gates Yield* (Chicago: Moody, 1958), 200.

Day 35

1. Barbara Bush, *Barbara Bush: A Memoir* (New York: Scribner, 1994), 332.
2. Ezeamalu Kingsley, "As we grow older," http://poemhunter. com/ezeamalu-kingsley/.
3. V. Raymond Edman, *The Disciplines of Life* (Minneapolis, MN: World Wide Publishers, 1982), 141.
4. Dennis J. De Haan, "Life's Seasons" in *Our Daily Bread,* March 17, 2004, www.rbc.org.
5. Lewis Drummond and Betty Drummond, *Women of Awakenings: The Historic Contribution of Women to Revival Movements* (Grand Rapids, MN: Kregel, 1997), 293.
6. http://www.floridabaptistwitness.com/4194.article, accessed June 18, 2007.

7. Richard Watson, *The Life of Rev. John Wesley: Founder of the Methodist Societies* (Cincinnati, OH: Swormstedt & Poe, 1857), 270, 339 at http://books.google.com/books.
8. Franklin Graham, *Bob Pierce: This One Thing I Do* (Dallas: Word, 1983), 77.
9. Howard Culbertson, "History of Nazarene world evangelism outreach," Southern Nazarene University, http://home.snu.edu/~HCULBERT/nazhist.htm.
10. Warren W. Wiersbe, *Be Myself: Memoirs of a Bridge Builder* (Wheaton: Victor, 1994), 323.
11. Wiersbe, *Be Myself,* 324.
12. *Schindler's List,* directed by Steven Spielberg, Amblin Entertainment, 1993.

Day 36

1. William Blake, "Jerusalem," in *Blake: Complete Writings,* ed. Geoffrey Keynes, (New York: Oxford University Press, 1972), 672.
2. Tom Lutz, *Crying: The Natural and Cultural History of Tears* (New York: W. W. Norton, 2002), 67.
3. Mason Locke Weems, *The Life of William Penn: The Settler of Pennsylvania* (N.p: Applegate & Sons, 1859), 32.

Day 37

1. *Saint of 9/11: The True Story of Father Mychal Judge,* directed by Glenn Holsten, DVD Documentary, Equality Forum, 2006.
2. http://www.1911encyclopedia.org/Giovanni_Jacopo_Casanova_de_Seingalt.

Day 38

1. Robert J. Morgan, "Legacy of Flowers, Legacy of Faith," http://www.donelson.org/pocket/pp-061231.html, 12/31/06.
2. James S. Hirsch, *Two Souls Indivisible: The Friendship That Saved Two POWs in Vietnam* (Boston: Houghton Mifflin, 2004), passim.

Day 39

1. http://en.wikipedia.org/wiki/Forest_Lawn_Memorial_ Park_(Glendale), accessed June 18, 2007.
2. "Woman Tries to Jump Off Bridge," *The Sunday Gazette,* October 10, 2004, B7, at http://library.cnpapers.com.
3. Ira David Sankey, *My Life and the Story of the Gospel Hymns* (Philadelphia: Sunday School Times, 1907), 345.
4. A. W. Tozer, *The Knowledge of the Holy: The Attributes of God: Their Meaning in the Christian Life* (New York: Harper & Row, 1961), 104.

Day 40

1. Christiana Tsai, as told to Ellen L. Drummond, *Queen of the Dark Chamber* (Paradise, PA: Ambassadors for Christ, 1986), 69–74.
2. Fanny Crosby, "Hear and Answer Prayer," in *Songs of Redemption* by Joshua Gill and others (Boston, MA: Christian Witness, 1899), 41.
3. Kathleen Lavey, "Learning to Forgive: Benefits Are Spiritual, Mental, and Physical Well-Being," *The Lansing State Journal,* November 6, 2005, at http://www.lsj.com/apps/pbcs.dll/article? AID=/20051106/LIFE04/511060315/1079/life, accessed on November 19, 2005.
4. Robert J. Morgan, *Nelson's Complete Book of Stories, Illustrations and Quotes* (Nashville: Thomas Nelson, 2000), 255-256.
5. http://www.tentmaker.org/Quotes/forgivenessquotes.htm, accessed on June 11, 2007.

How to Get the Most
from Signs of Life

This book consists of forty daily readings divided into six chapters: "Signs of Life," "Dusty Shoes," "Worn-Out Knees," "Rolled-Up Sleeves," "Open Hands," and "Outstretched Arms." I strongly urge you to read only one selection each day so that you will have time to process the information and reflect on what God is calling you to do in response to it. You may be tempted to read ahead, but *Signs of Life* will be a far richer experience if you let each day's truth impact your life for a twenty-four hour period before you proceed to the next.

Too often we do not grasp the full meaning of a book because we rush through the content without taking time to live with a truth that has been revealed. The life-changing application of God's truths takes reflection and action. Only then can we successfully incorporate them into our lives. So, again, I urge you to be patient and to focus on one selection a day for forty days. If you do, you'll finish this study with a more complete understanding of the five Signs of Life.

I also encourage you to interact with the material in this book. Read with a pen and a highlighter in hand. As you read along, underline text that speaks to you. In the margins, note what you're learning and feeling. Highlight Scripture that speaks powerfully to you. These study methods will not only help you learn as you read, but they will enable you to go back later when you want to review a particular topic or a Scripture passage that was especially significant for you.

SIGNS ALONG THE WAY

As you take this forty-day journey, how will you know that you are mastering the *life signs* in this book? By taking time and making the effort to do the "Signs of Life" activities along the way.

A section called "Signs of Life" comes at the end of each daily reading and is designed to help you apply the message of the reading. These steps are simple and help make it easier to live out God's truth.

- **Life Sign**—As you incorporate each Life Sign into your daily activities, it will identify you as a follower of Christ. Reflect on the specific call to action throughout your day. I suggest that you write the day's Life Sign on your calendar, in your journal, or on a Post-it Note to remind you of the day's focus.

- **Life Verse**—Specially selected Bible verses correlate with the truths found in each day's reading. To better retain the Life Verse, commit it to memory. Write the verse out in your journal or on a note pad. Recite the verse out loud and use 3x5 cards as easy reference tools that you can carry with you wherever you go.

  Many people decide to find a Life Signs partner to whom they can recite the daily Life Verse and who will encourage them to live out the day's Life Sign. This kind of daily accountability—whether by e-mail, phone, or face to face—will encourage you both to learn the day's Life Verse and to live out the Life Sign as well.

- **Life in Action**—Signs of Life need to be evident in our lives. It is not enough for us to simply know biblical truths; we must actively live them out. As James put it, we must be doers of the Word, not just hearers (1:22).

  So, in the Life in Action sections, you will be asked simple questions that focus on a particular area of your Christian walk. Take a moment to write out your answers either in the space provided on the Signs of Life page or in your journal or notebook.

  Take a further action step by discussing your answers with your

Life Signs partner. That accountability will improve the odds that you'll actually take the actions steps you want to take.

LIFE SIGNS PARTNERSHIPS

Another great way to get the most out of this study and to stay motivated throughout the entire forty-day *Signs of Life* journey is to partner with others. A Life Signs Partnership is a covenant you make with another person or persons. This partnership is a threefold pledge:

1. **Accountability**—I will be faithful and regularly ask my partner how his/her *Signs of Life* journey is progressing.

2. **Dependability**—I will be reliable and attend each appointed Life Signs Partners Bible study.

3. **Responsibility**—I will actively pray for and encourage my partner to fulfill the commitments he/she makes to God as a result of this study.

Now consider which will work better for you—a One-to-One Partnership or a Small-Group Bible Study Partnership.

A One-to-One Life Signs Partner

The following steps will help you successfully build a strong partnership with a Life Signs partner:

- Ask God to direct you to the right partner.

- Look for someone you know to be reliable and with whom you feel spiritually compatible when choosing a partner.

- Find a partner whose schedule is similar to yours.

- Once you have chosen a partner, pray together and make a commitment to God and to each other to faithfully fulfill the threefold pledge of a Life Signs Partner.

- Decide together how you will structure your partnership (phone calls, e-mail, or face-to-face meetings).

- Next, decide how often you will communicate during the forty days. Perhaps you will communicate daily with a brief e-mail or phone call, and maybe you'll schedule occasional face-to-face meetings over lunch or coffee.

- Schedule at least two or three face-to-face meetings during the course of the forty days. I would suggest one at the beginning; the second, during week three; and the final meeting, at the end of the forty days so that each of you can summarize what God has done in you through *Signs of Life.*

A Small-Group Bible Study Partnership

Another great way to assimilate the information found in this book is to organize and participate in a small-group Bible study. Small-group Bible studies are caring support groups dedicated to the spiritual growth of each of its members. *Signs of Life* is perfect for a six-week group Bible study.

You certainly can journey through *Signs of Life* on your own, but why not broaden the scope of your learning and enrich the forty days by involving others in your study? God gives each of us special insights into His Word and unique experiences in the Christian walk. A Signs of Life Partner or Small Group can make the journey much more enjoyable and profoundly life changing.

READY TO BEGIN

If every Christian showed the five signs of a life transformed by Jesus Christ, we could change our world. After all, people are watching to catch a glimpse of the Savior in us. They are straining to see His hands through our actions, hear His voice in our speech, feel His love through our kind acts, and know His grace through our embrace.

So I encourage you to decide right now to commit to reading *Signs of Life* for the next forty days. After all, getting a little dust on your shoes is the first step in reaching the world for Christ!

DAVID JEREMIAH WANTS TO HELP YOU LIVE AN AUTHENTIC CHRISTIAN LIFE!

here are four ways to further your study of Signs of Life

LIFE
STEP **1** *2* *3* *4*

ACCESS ADDITIONAL *SIGNS OF LIFE* MATERIALS ABSOLUTELY FREE!

Log on to www.SignsofLife.org where you can obtain additional *Signs of Life* resources.

These online materials include:

- Signs of Life Scripture Guide
- Additional articles by Dr. Jeremiah
- Practical ideas on how you and your church can demonstrate Signs of Life in your community
- Trailer of the Logan Elementary Extreme School Makeover video
- Meaningful ways your congregation can be a Signs of Life church
- *Signs of Life* reference materials & bookstore

LIFE
STEP   1   2   3   4

FULLY PARTICIPATE WITH THIS BOOK

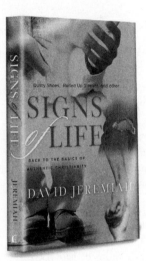

Read:

This book is conveniently organized into a 40-day reading plan that will help you systematically read through *Signs of Life*. Follow the structured reading plan, or read at your own pace.

Focus:

Each daily reading is followed by a Life Sign that encapsulates the main subject of that day's material. These Life Signs were created to help you focus on a single practice to incorporate into your daily life.

Claim:

You will notice a Scripture to go with each day's reading. Take the time to look up the verses in your Bible, underline them, and write the correlating Life Sign in the margins. As you read your Bible, these notations will be a constant reminder of how to live an authentic Christian life.

Apply:

Read the special personal application pages and commit to taking the Life in Action steps suggested. Use the book margins to answer the questions or record your thoughts in a notebook or journal. When you incorporate Signs of Life into your daily life, you will discover how much more completely you will live a relevant, yielded, authentic, generous, and compassionate life for God.

LIFE
STEP   1   2   **3**   4

TAKING *SIGNS OF LIFE* A STEP FARTHER

Signs of Life Audio Message Album

These 12 audio messages will lead you to a fuller
understanding of the marks that identify you as a
Christian—signs that will advertise your faith and
personal imprints on the world that can impact souls
for eternity.

SLFALCD

Signs of Life Study Guide

This 128-page study resource correlates with the *Signs
of Life* audio messages. Each lesson provides an outline,
overview, application, and study questions.

The lessons in this study guide are suitable for personal
or group studies.

SLFSG

Signs of Life DVD Messages

Live presentations of Dr. Jeremiah delivering the six
signature *Signs of Life* messages are in this special DVD
collection. Messages included: Signs of Life, Dusty Shoes
– Living a Relevant Life, Worn-Out Knees – Living a
Yielded Life, Rolled-Up Sleeves – Living an Authentic
Life, Open Hands – Living a Generous Life, and
Outstretched Arms – Living a Compassionate Life.

SLFALDV

Order these fine Signs of Life *products at*
www.SignsOfLife.org or www.DavidJeremiah.org.

LIFE
STEP   1   2   3   4

STAY CONNECTED

Take advantage of two great ways to let Dr. David Jeremiah give you spiritual direction every day! Both are absolutely FREE!

Turning Points MAGAZINE & DEVOTIONAL

Receive Dr. David Jeremiah's monthly magazine,
Turning Points each month:

- Monthly Study Focus
- 48 Pages of Life-Changing Reading
- Relevant Articles
- Special Features
- Humor Section
- Family Section
- Daily Devotional Readings for Each Day of the Month
- Bible Study Resource Offers
- Live Event Schedule
- Radio & Television Information

AND ASK FOR . . .

Your daily Turning Point E-Devotional

Start your day off right! Find words of inspiration and spiritual motivation waiting for you on your computer every morning! You can receive a daily e-devotion communication from David Jeremiah that will strengthen your walk with God and encourage you to live an authentic Christian Life.

Stay connected! Sign up for these two free services by visiting us online at www.DavidJeremiah.org or www.SignsOfLife.org. Click on DEVOTIONALS to sign up for your monthly copy of Turning Points *and your Daily Turning Point.*

THE
SIGNS OF LIFE
NEW TESTAMENT

This unique New Testament is designed to help you explore five Signs of Life: Dusty Shoes, Worn-Out Knees, Rolled-Up Sleeves, Open Hands, and Outstretched Arms. Jesus himself displayed evidence of a heart filled with real love and a desire to help others. Jesus knew how to pray, serve, work, give, and comfort people. And the more you let His example guide you, the more serious you will become about impacting your world.

That's the idea behind this *Signs of Life New Testament*. You'll find the straight Word of God along with some basics on how to increase your scope of influence in the lives of the unbelieving people who need Jesus most. As you read through this New Testament, you will find color-coded passages that easily connect with each Sign of Life as well as a 40-day Life in Action Interactive Plan that will help you track your growth and progress through each Sign.

Also included in the *Signs of Life New Testament:*

- Guide for Christian Workers
- Romans Road – Plan of Salvation
- "What God Says About . . ." Topical Reference Guide
- "30 Days with Jesus" Bible Reading
- Signs of Life Introductions
- Correlations with Dr. Jeremiah's book *Signs of Life*

This New Testament, in paperback edition, is perfect to take everywhere you go. User friendly and practical!

The Signs of Life New Testament *can only be ordered at www.SignsOfLife.org or www.DavidJeremiah.org.*

OTHER BOOKS
BY DR. DAVID JEREMIAH

Captured by Grace

By following the dramatic story of the "Amazing Grace" hymnwriter John Newton and the apostle Paul's own encounter with the God of grace, David Jeremiah helps readers understand the freeing power of permanent forgiveness and mercy.

CBGHBK

Life Wide Open

In this energizing book, Dr. David Jeremiah opens our eyes to how we can live a life that exudes an attitude of hope and enthusiasm . . . a life of passion . . . a LIFE WIDE OPEN! *Life Wide Open* offers a vision, both spiritual and practical, of what our life can be when we allow the power of passion to permeate our souls.

LWOHBK

Escape the Coming Night

Dr. Jeremiah offers a fresh, biblically sound explanation of the signs, symbols, prophecies, and omens of the end times. *Escape the Coming Night* is a penetrating look at the prophetic time machine that is in the book of Revelation and a vivid reminder of how, in the face of coming darkness, we should live today.

REVBK

The Handwriting on the Wall

In this bestseller, Dr. Jeremiah gives you a look into the book of Daniel and how an understanding of prophecy can open the pathway to dynamic living. *The Handwriting on the Wall* delivers a story full of dramatic history, prophetic insights, and hope for today's Christians.

HOWBK

My Heart's Desire

How would you answer a pollster who appeared at your church asking for a definition of worship? Is it really a sin to worship without sacrifice? When you finish studying *My Heart's Desire*, you'll have not just an answer, but the biblical answer to that all-important question.

MHDBK

Searching for Heaven on Earth

Join Dr. Jeremiah as he traces Solomon's path through the futility of:
- The search for wisdom and knowledge
- Wild living and the pursuit of pleasure
- Burying oneself in work
- Acquiring as much wealth as possible.

Dr. Jeremiah takes readers on a discovery to find out what really matters in life, the secret to enjoying "heaven on earth."

SFHHBK

When Your World Falls Apart

When Your World Falls Apart recounts Dr. Jeremiah's battle against cancer and the real-life stories of others who have struggled with tragedy. Highlighting ten Psalms of encouragement, each chapter is a beacon of light in those moments when life seems hopeless.

WFABK

Slaying the Giants in Your Life

Loneliness. Discouragement. Worry. Anger. Procrastination. Doubt. Fear. Guilt. Temptation. Resentment. Failure. Jealousy. Have these giants infiltrated your life? Do you need the tools to slay these daunting foes? With practical appeal and personal warmth, Dr. Jeremiah's book, *Slaying the Giants in Your Life* will become your very own giant-slaying manual.

STGBK

Turning Points & Sanctuary

Two 365-day devotionals by Dr. Jeremiah that will equip you to live with God's perspective. These topically arranged devotionals enable you to relate biblical truths to the reality of everyday living—every day of the year. Perfect for yourself or your next gift giving occasion, *Turning Points* and *Sanctuary* are beautifully packaged with a padded cover, original artwork throughout, and a ribbon page marker.

TPDHBK
SANHBK

These resources from Dr. David Jeremiah can be ordered at www.DavidJeremiah.org

NOW AVAILABLE FROM DAVID JEREMIAH'S MAXIMUM CHURCH

SIGNS OF LIFE
CHURCH-WIDE CAMPAIGN

A 40-day journey to get your church living the authentic Christian life!
by David Jeremiah

Lead your church to become one of Christlike influence in your community as you take the five Life Signs discussed in this book and apply them to the lives of your congregation.

Here are just some of the elements contained in Dr. Jeremiah's *Signs of Life Church Campaign Kit:*

- Campaign Director's Notebook
- Ready-to-Preach Sermon Notes from Dr. David Jeremiah
- Sermon PowerPoint Graphics
- Audio Messages on CD & MP3
- Drama Scripts & DVD Presentations
- Small Group Leader's Guide
- Small Group Participant Workbook
- Email Devotions (40 days)
- Ready-to-Send Pastor Communication Emails
- Adult, Youth, and Children's Sunday School Curriculum
- Logan Elementary Extreme Makeover DVD
- Signs of Life Graphic Design Library
  - And more

PLUS . . . special discounted pricing for churches on all *SIGNS OF LIFE* books.

**Put LIFE back into your church! GROW your congregation!
IMPACT your community like never before!
Make a DIFFERENCE for eternity!**

For more information or to order the Signs of Life Church
Campaign, visit us at www.MaximumChurch.com

Downloadable Samples Available online!